THE KRAYS

Colin Fry was born in Hillingdon, Middlesex, an identical twin like Ron and Reg Kray. He worked in the film and music industries, appearing in the Oscar-award-winning film *Patton*, before turning to writing. His other books include *The Kray Files* and *The Krays: The Final Countdown*, and he wrote *Doing the Business* in collaboration with Charlie Kray.

THE KRAYS:
A VIOLENT BUSINESS

THE DEFINITIVE INSIDE STORY OF BRITAIN'S MOST NOTORIOUS BROTHERS IN CRIME

COLIN FRY

MAINSTREAM
PUBLISHING

EDINBURGH AND LONDON

First published in Great Britain in 2010 by
MAINSTREAM PUBLISHING COMPANY
(EDINBURGH) LTD
7 Albany Street
Edinburgh EH1 3UG

ISBN 9781845967741

A catalogue record for this book is available
from the British Library

Printed in Great Britain by
Clays Ltd, St Ives plc

1 3 5 7 9 10 8 6 4 2

In memory of my twin brother, Rod

CONTENTS

ACKNOWLEDGEMENTS

George Burns once said I have written six books. Now that's not bad for a guy who has only read two! If you don't know who George Burns is or was, then check him out on the Internet or elsewhere, and if you don't then shame on you. Having the chance of writing a book is something that doesn't happen too often to too many people. I have been fortunate in that respect, since this is my fourth offering and it is once again all down to the patience of Bill Campbell at Mainstream Publishing in Edinburgh. The fact that I have only read a few books in my lifetime is neither here nor there.

My wife Eva has, as usual, kept me supplied with coffee and sustenance during the small hours, and my children, Alexander and Christian, have always been on hand to bring me back down to earth. Now, that is something that they really are good at, and anyone with children will know what I mean.

I would like to thank Rod, my twin brother, for reading through my chapter on twins some time ago. I know it was a pain, but his efforts were much appreciated. Likewise, my mother has always encouraged me with my work. My brother and my mother are now no longer with us, but their memory lingers on, just as my memories of the Krays have not faded through the years. With so much in the press and on television almost every day, it is not easy to escape my past in any way.

Friends, too, have been supportive of my new profession. Lalit Bagai in Denmark and Charles Rosenblatt in Florida in the USA have always given me the best pragmatic advice based on their long years in business. Thanks to you both.

Newspapers have always been an invaluable source of

information, although not exactly reliable for investigative endeavours, and the Internet is proving itself a tremendous source of all kinds and types of useful knowledge. These two sources in particular, coupled with my own intimate knowledge of the Krays, have helped me greatly in the early stages of my investigations. Sifting through the inaccurate and sometimes misleading stories becomes simply a habit, but then this is the stuff of legends and make believe plays its part in creating the imagery of the celebrity.

But we must not forget the academics who gave this book a new interpretation on the Krays. Some time ago, I contacted Professor Chris Jenks at Goldsmiths College in London, where he is head of the sociology department. He has written a paper entitled 'The Kray Fascination', and I have regularly referred to this work within my own text. Also, Tim Trimble, who previously lectured in psychology at King Alfred's College, Winchester, was invaluable in the psychological analysis of the background material. Without their guiding framework, this investigative work would have been almost impossible. Other academics include Dr Dick Hobbs, previously of Durham University, now at LSE, with whom I share a book title, *Doing the Business*, and Audrey Sandbank, a family psychiatrist with TAMBA, the twins society. Thanks for the help; it was outstanding and led me in all directions, enabling me to build up the big picture that I was aiming at.

Thank you all for helping to ensure that *The Krays: A Violent Business* is a well-balanced and in-depth analysis of the Krays.

PREFACE

I first met Charlie Kray back in the early 1980s, when I was in England working in the record business. One evening, in a public house somewhere in London, I made acquaintance with this jovial character who was telling stories of the old days and entertaining the girls with tales from far and wide, including the USA and Canada, Spain and Germany, Switzerland and Nigeria.

But what really got my interest was when he said he had twin brothers. Being a twin myself, I was naturally interested. 'What do they do?' I asked. 'Where do they live?' The reply was a little shocking. He told me that his twin brothers were both in jail for murder, but that he thought they would be out soon.

After I wiped the gin and tonic from my tie and shirt, I continued with my questioning. 'But you are in the music business, aren't you?'

He smiled as he answered. 'Yes,' he told me. 'I used to manage a band called Stray, but nowadays I run the bodyguard business set up by my brothers. We look after a lot of celebrities and rock stars, even Americans.'

I was intrigued. But how could I approach the subject of his twin brothers without getting a punch on the jaw? So I bit the bullet and asked the obvious question. 'Just who are you and who are your brothers?'

Charlie looked me in the eye and smiled. 'You don't know who I am, do you?' he asked.

'Sorry,' I said. 'I don't live in England any more, so I don't read the newspapers or see television. I just found your stories interesting.'

Charlie smiled again and breathed a sigh of relief. 'Well, I'm

Charlie Kray,' he said at last. 'And my brothers are Ronnie and Reggie.' He looked at me again. 'You still don't know who I am, do you?'

The look on my face must have said it all. I didn't know who he was or who his brothers were, so I waited. Charlie then relaxed, and we had a good chat about his brothers. This was the first time I had ever heard of the Krays. But after that evening I knew a lot more.

We kept in touch and met up regularly in London during the mid and late 1980s, and I helped him out with a few business deals that he was negotiating. Everything was fine, and then he asked me if I would like to get involved in a new book to be written about his life and that of his brothers. There had been a film made about his brothers, and accordingly there was a terrific demand for a book written by someone in the family.

I first got involved in the film *The Krays* when Charlie asked me to help deal with the liquidators, Cork Gully, when the film's distributor, Parkfield, got into serious financial trouble. Charlie was afraid that he and his brothers wouldn't get paid, and Charlie needed the money. I knew he had already sold off his royalties to the film, and I was keen to help in any way I could. It was, after all, possibly the only way I could get the money back that I had lent him through the years. I knew that I was only one among many, but I gave him the benefit of the doubt and loaned him the money – after all, he was 'Champagne Charlie' and a genuinely likeable villain.

So I took a break from writing our book about Charlie, the twins and their dealings with the American Mafia and had a few meetings with Cork Gully at their London offices. They were very helpful and polite and all appeared to be going well, although there was a huge amount of paperwork to go through with regards to the actual procedures that Charlie Kray had secured for the payment of their royalties. There was no hue and cry at the time about murderers receiving dirty money for the sale of their story; no one appeared to mind. So I just got on with the task of trying to secure the Krays their payout.

While I was investigating their business dealings with Parkfield, I spent a day with their old pal Joe Pyle at his office at Pinewood

Film Studios. I used to live nearby in the village of Iver, so for me it was like coming home. Joe made me very welcome and together we checked out the contract that Charlie had negotiated for the film. After some time we settled on an approach, all legal and above board, although Joe did suggest that there was another way – the Kray way.

Joe enjoyed being at Pinewood, with his office just across the road from the James Bond set, but shortly afterwards he was sent to prison for cocaine smuggling. So his association with the film business was short-lived.

Charlie and his brothers finally got their money, so the Krays were happy. But it was not so happy for those, including myself, who had invested time and money in Charlie. By the time that Charlie had got his hands on the cash, well over £100,000, it was all gone again. It turned out he had sold his royalties over and over again, so all I got for my troubles was a little something to cover some of my costs. Ultimately, though, I was happy to get something back.

A few months ago I was asked if I would like to write another Kray book by Bill Campbell of Mainstream Publishing, who had previously published some of my work. As I had already written three books, I wondered at first if there was really room for a fourth but then I agreed and told him, 'This time I will include everything that I wasn't allowed to write previously.'

How many times have I heard the words, 'I don't think we should mention that, some of the people involved are still alive!' I heard it when talking with Charlie in his home, I heard it when visiting Reg in prison and I heard it when I met Ron in Broadmoor.

So why write another Kray book?

After the release of *Our Story* by Ron and Reg, Ron was offered a lucrative new book deal. The deal was done and the money paid, but Reg insisted that his name be kept out of the book because he didn't want his homosexuality coming to light. Ron eventually decided that it was all just too difficult; he couldn't write about his twin brother who was so secretive about his life, he couldn't write about certain activities that Reg thought were too sensitive, and he couldn't talk about the other killings.

Reg believed that any mention of other murders would keep him in jail forever, and he couldn't understand why his brother would even contemplate doing that to him.

Admitting to new murders could also have caused serious problems for elder brother Charlie, who was commonly known among the members of the Firm as the 'undertaker'.

And there was the story of Ron's relationship with Peter Sutcliffe, otherwise known as the 'Yorkshire Ripper'. One particular incident between the two men hastened the downfall and eventual death of Ron Kray. Reg didn't want the truth coming out about that and could not believe that Ron would shame the Kray name by making the story public.

Ron ran the Kray Firm with his twin brother Reg, aided by elder brother Charlie. They are the best known of the UK's home-grown gangsters, rivalling Jack the Ripper for the number one spot in the annals of UK criminal history. This book tells you everything they didn't want you to know and, in some cases, what no one dared to ask.

For Lords and Ladies, gentlemen and celebrities, villains and plain hangers-on theirs was a fatal attraction. The gloves are now off with all three Kray brothers dead and buried and NO holds are barred. Let the truth be told at last.

INTRODUCTION: THE EARLY YEARS

For as long as anyone can remember, there have always been gangs in and around the East End of London. It was here that immigrants first made their home in the city, and it was here that the different communities tried to defend their cultures, their languages and their rights as they saw them.

Around the turn of the twentieth century, the area had a huge working-class population, and it was overcrowded and dirty. People were poor and lived in filthy conditions. Boozing, fights and prostitution were everyday events, and there were numerous brothels. In fact, crime was rife, with rape, assault and robbery endemic. There was rubbish and excrement everywhere, and some of the excrement was actually used locally in the tanning houses around the docks. Compared with the West End of London, it was another world. With poor street lighting, it was always a dark night for villains, reminiscent of a scene out of a Dickens novel or one of the stories of Sir Arthur Conan Doyle, with Sherlock Holmes just about to solve a crime.

The area was heavily industrialised, with factories of all kinds offering piteously low wages. There were glue factories, slaughterhouses, soap plants and coal bunkers located just to the north of the docks, which were themselves thriving at that time. There were breweries from which the stench of hops and yeast wafted on the breeze and spread throughout the East End.

It was not by coincidence that the factories were located here. They were placed to the east of the West End of London because the rich people of that area didn't want the smells and the riff-raff that came with them. The wind was predominantly from the west, so the rich could spit in the wind and see it carried to the East

End, only to land on some poor immigrant who couldn't afford to complain about it. The only smell they wanted in the West End was the smell of money.

It was, quite naturally, here that the first real London gangs appeared. There were the Odessian and the Bessarabian gangs, who worked their trade around the Whitechapel area made famous, or should that be infamous, by Jack the Ripper. They preyed on Russian immigrants in the area. People also had many other gangs to fear, such as the Blind Beggar Gang, who worked out of the pub later made famous by Ron Kray in 1966 as the place he shot and killed George Cornell. There were also the Titanics, the Hoxton Mob and the Vendetta Mob, but these were all just collections of pickpockets, small-time thieves and the like, who gave themselves a collective name just to gain some respect in the East End.

Before the First World War, the gangs were predominantly made up of members from the same ethnic groups or nationalities – the Jewish gangs, the Italian gangs, the Maltese gangs and so on. All gangs had a limited sphere of operation, a small territory to defend, and were only concerned with defending what they already called their own. There was no ambition, no intent or desire to take over a larger territory and definitely no grand plan in their schemes.

That all changed after the war, with groups of so-called 'families' emerging, made up of different races and different ethnic cultures, and their main concern was money.

The first major crime syndicate was the Sabini Brothers. They had brought their ideas from Sicily, from where they originated, but they had married into various other groups, especially the Irish, and this blend of Italian and Irish thinking had evolved into the biggest gang of its time. Their home turf was an area of London called Clerkenwell. The Sabinis were around for more than 20 years, often importing criminals from the 'old country' to carry out crimes in London and especially to help protect them from their main rivals, known as the Elephant and Castle Mob.

Crime was only one of the things that kept them together, however. They were also held together by class, culture, location and family. Most of their fights were territorial conflicts that took on a violent nature right from the beginning. It was all about family business and protecting their rights, both old and new. In reality, they had taken their attitude towards crime directly from their own past and adopted the old warlord structure from the country of their birth, Sicily.

Their main opponents were other rival gangs from around the Hackney area of East London. They were always trying to muscle in on the Sabinis' money-lending operations, which were very successful, but the best business to be had was at the racetrack, where they protected illegal bookies.

Charles 'Darby' Sabini and his gang worked Epsom and Brighton racecourses in the main, going further afield when the opportunity arose and the money was right. All bookies at that time ran stalls out in the open, and they usually held a lot of cash during a meeting. When 'Mad' Frankie Fraser, a future enforcer in the Richardson gang, was ten years old, he worked for the Sabinis at Epsom as a bucket boy. His task was to wash the chalk from the bookies' boards that showed the odds on the horses. It was as good a start in life as any, and he got a taste for it. The bookies were always in need of protection and the Sabinis obliged with weapons and their fists. Their main weapon was the cut-throat razor, and the Sabinis were very skilled at using this particular piece of armoury.

Because of their activity at the racecourses, where most bookies were Jewish, the Sabini gang took on Jewish gang members to control the business, and they were very good at it. In fact, their business continued to flourish up until the Second World War, when life as people knew it changed for ever. It was said at the time that the Sabinis would even bribe the police to keep other gangs away from their business, but we will never know for sure.

The Sabinis had the power and they had the money, but then they ran out of steam and a power vacuum developed. They were eventually replaced by another family, known as the Whites, who came from Islington in North London.

Like the Sabinis, this was another family who didn't appear to want to get involved outside of their own particular territory; in fact, it was left to their successors, Jack Spot and Billy Hill, to try their hand at gaining a foothold on crime throughout the city, and especially the West End.

Initially Jack Spot, real name Jack Comer, worked with Billy Hill to take over crime in London. They even called themselves the 'Kings of the Underworld', a title they had earned as they controlled most of the crime in London at that time. For some reason, however, they fell out, and Jack Spot had his face slashed one evening in Soho, in the West End.

Spot needed someone to help him restore the balance of power in gangland, so he hired the Kray twins to protect him and his reputation. For some time there was stalemate, but one night in May 1956 Spot was attacked, on the orders of Hill, outside his flat in Bayswater by 'Mad' Frankie Fraser and a lad known as Alf Warren. That was it for Jack Spot, who retired and bought an antiques shop. Billy Hill also took early retirement and moved to the Costa del Sol in the south of Spain.

Reginald Kray was born on 24 October 1933 at eight o'clock in the morning. Some ten minutes later, he was followed by his identical twin Ronald.

Their parents, Charlie and Violet, were overjoyed at having twins. They already had another son, Charles junior, born on 9 July 1926, seven years before the twins, and the young Charlie didn't know what to make of the new arrivals. 'They can see right through me,' he told his pals. Gradually, he began to feel isolated, as everything Violet did was centred on her twins. Things had changed for the young Charlie, and he knew it.

There had been another baby born previously to Charlie and Violet. The girl, born in 1929, had been called Violet, like her mother, and she was a joy to behold but died when only a baby. This was common in those days, with diphtheria, pneumonia and tuberculosis rife throughout the country.

Early on, the family lived in Stene Street in Hoxton, but in 1939 they moved to Vallance Road, Bethnal Green. This was still the East End and it was still overcrowded. It was a small terraced house with no bathroom, although there was a toilet located in the back yard. Maybe there were even a couple of cats.

At that time the area was a ghetto, pure and simple. There were brothels, gambling houses, seedy pubs and billiard halls. Everyone drank, and all the men boxed in one way or another. After all, with the high unemployment in the area there was not much else they could do.

Ron and Reg were only five years old when their father, old man Charlie Kray, deserted from the British army. At the start of the Second World War, in 1939, he had been conscripted into the Armed Forces, but he was more intent on serving himself than his country; even his family came off second best.

Charlie Kray senior had been an able fighter, like all the Krays before him. Their pedigree went back to the bare-knuckle fighting days; they were proud and let everyone know it. But he wasn't interested in his country, only in his own well-being. And that meant staying a free man and not stuck in some army barracks in the back of beyond or, even worse, facing German troops in Europe. All he wanted to do was to travel the south of the country in search of anything from clothes to gold and silver to sell on at a profit. He worked throughout the south, even travelling as far afield as South Wales. He was often away, and he liked it like that.

When he did come home, the twins were roped in to help keep their father out of the clutches of the local constabulary and away from the front line. On one occasion, the twins hid their father under the dining table when the house was searched by the police. When one elderly policeman glanced at the table, Ron said nonchalantly, 'You don't expect to find him there, do you?' They continued to search the house but didn't look under the table. Another time the twins hid him in a cupboard, again with great success.

For six long years, during a crucial period in the twins' development, Charlie senior was on the run and generally not at home at Vallance Road. Their mother, Violet, and Aunt Rose who lived nearby took on all the parental responsibilities, and they cherished and nurtured the twins into adolescence. It was this mother–son relationship that was to dominate their lives and the only one who could influence Ron and Reg was Violet. They idolised her and always took her side in an argument against their father, no matter who was right and who was wrong. They would protect their father, all right, but not at the cost of causing their mother any harm. She wanted them to take care of their father, and so they did, not because of any affection they may have had for him – not in any way. It was simply because of a promise to their mother.

From the very early days, she would call the twins 'special'. Violet also considered herself to be special, since no one else in the neighbourhood had twins. People would stop her in the street and gaze in amazement, and friends would come around to the house to ask if they could take the twins for a ride in the pram. This was glamour in the eyes of Violet Kray; it made her feel different, just like her two lovely sons.

When the twins were three years old, they fell ill with diphtheria and were separated and kept at different hospitals. Violet saw them both every day, and after three months Reg was able to come home to Vallance Road. Ron was still ill, however, and doctors were not predicting much of a chance of survival. Violet took matters into her own hands and brought Ronnie home, saying, 'I know my boys best. He misses his brother.' She was right – after all, a mother knows best – and soon they were both out playing in the street, happy and contented.

Their brother Charlie had witnessed the care and attention devoted to the twins by his mother. He was now in second place, with the twins firmly positioned on top of the heap. Exactly how this made him feel is not well recorded, but I bet he hated it. His mother treated them like royalty, pandering to their every wish, while Charlie had to take on part-time work outside school hours and help his mother with the chores around the house.

In 1940, the Kray family was evacuated to Hadleigh, a little village in Suffolk. Young Charlie loved it there and so did little Ronnie and Reggie. Unfortunately, Violet missed her friends and family from around Vallance Road, so, after a year in the country, the Krays moved back to London and the old neighbourhood. The children hated being back, away from the green fields and tranquillity of Suffolk, but home they were and home they had to stay.

Their father was still on the run and watching him having to hide from the police must have had an effect on the young twins.

It undoubtedly contributed to their hatred of authority of any kind and, almost from day one, the police had been their sworn enemy. Why should the twins talk to them? Why should they trust them? Why should they believe them? This antipathy toward the police became a kind of code. They made up their own rules and punished anyone who dared break them. This ideology of sorts was to stay with them all their lives. It influenced their way of being, their actions and their thoughts; indeed, it even culminated in them killing people. Killing, to the Krays, was the ultimate punishment for not playing the game according to their rules.

'We'll take care of ourselves and we'll put no trust in the law,' was the order of the day; Ron and Reg lived by that code and, eventually, they would both die by it.

Being wary of the 'Old Bill' was a way of life in the East End. Everyone knew a rogue or two, even an out-and-out villain who could get hard-to-come-by goods at a fraction of the usual price. This was a normal occurrence in this socially deprived area of London, where the working classes did not have the spending power of their West End counterparts. Buying something out of the back door or from the boot of a car was an almost everyday event. This had always been the case in the East End and became even more so after the Second World War, when the twins were growing up in Bethnal Green. It was a time of opportunities for them, and they quickly developed their independence in the blitzed ruins of society.

The twins were always keen to fight. If they couldn't find someone to have a fight with, then they would fight each other. They were not cheerful children, not by any means. In fact, they were serious most of the time, with the one continually trying to outsmart the other. They had their own way of sharing things, but it often came to a fight to determine who would get his way. In general, it was Ron who came out on top. He would urge his brother on, only to knock him down. Even at this early age, Ron knew how to control Reg, and, remember, Ron was the younger of the twins.

Even when their parents argued, Ron and Reg wanted to join in, always taking their mother's side in any row. They didn't know their father very well, even after the war, since he was still a wanted deserter. With all the years of buying and selling all over the south of England and Wales before the war and trying to escape the police after the war, old man Charlie Kray really didn't know his sons.

Young Charlie was a teenager now and, with his dad still on the run from the army, he took on the role of man of the house and the responsibilities that his father would normally have pursued. He was very interested in boxing and taught the twins to box, later advising them to turn professional and make a living from the sport. He encouraged them to fight, even fighting on the same bill with them later at the Royal Albert Hall. He did all an elder brother should. But he could not entirely replace the father that the twins so desperately needed.

At the age of 14, he took a job at Lloyd's in the City, working as a messenger. It was a full-time job, and it took young Charlie and his bike all over London. At nights, he would still box, using makeshift punchbags and other gym equipment that he had scrounged, but then he contracted rheumatic fever and everything was put on hold for a while. As soon as he was fully recovered, he joined the Naval Cadets, where he could train properly. Charlie was serious about boxing and getting fit, and it showed in everything he did, even in his cycling around London. He certainly wouldn't let a little thing like rheumatic fever stop him.

Soon afterwards he joined the Royal Navy, and then all his training really paid off. He regularly boxed for the navy at welterweight and won many a championship, taking his trophies home to Vallance Road. Ronnie and Reggie could just stare at the trophies, sitting up high on the mantelpiece. To the twins, they were the stuff that dreams were made of. But Charlie started to get migraine attacks and soon he was back home for good, receiving an honourable discharge from the navy on the grounds of being unfit for duty.

Without any true guidance from their father, and with Charlie junior being away, the twins made up their own rules and their mother encouraged them; after all, they were special.

Whether or not their father, old man Charlie, would have made any difference to their lives at this time is debatable, but there are good psychological grounds for saying that families without a prominent father figure have more problems with their male offspring than those with a so-called normal two-parent family. This does not mean that single parents always have problems with their children, but it does mean that the chances for trouble are increased. That, unfortunately, is just a way of life, and it can be verified statistically.

So, to summarise, the twins had no father figure. They lived in an environment where going to the police for help was frowned upon. They were constantly hiding their father from the police, and they were continually running foul of the law because they lived by their own rules and not by the law of the land. This was a recipe for disaster.

When the twins were eight years old, school began again in the East End of London, but the twins didn't take to the education system very well. They were always fighting on the old bomb sites with one gang or another and soon had their own bunch of followers. The Krays always led from the front; they never followed. Of the two, it was Reg who did better at school, but Ron got his own back as soon as school was over. They soon became known as the 'Terrible Twins'.

Reg liked to have his pals around him, but Ron was a loner, often preferring to take his Alsatian dog, Freda, for walks among the bomb sites, hoping to find something he could use or sell. But both of the twins loved to listen to the radio, and their favourites of the day were *Dick Barton* and *Just William*.

By the time they were nine, the twins knew how to handle the law. Their street, Vallance Road, was called 'Deserters' Corner', and the Lees (Violet was a Lee) were everywhere. There was Aunt Rose, Aunt May, Grandfather Lee, Grandmother Lee and many more all dotted along and around Vallance Road, and the twins used to go from one house to another through the open doors or through the back yards. When the police came to call and their father was away, the twins would tell them that their parents were divorced and that their father didn't live there any more. Aunt May's husband was also on the run, so too were many friends of the family. Grassing to the Old Bill was a real no-no.

When their father did make it back home for a weekend, he often took them over to see old fighter friends across the river, pals who made a living as pickpockets and small-time crooks. He filled their ears with tales of conflict and of violence, completely different to the bedtime stories they had from their mother and Aunt Rose. The twins lived in a paradoxical world: full of love on the one hand and full of hate on the other.

Reg would always remember one particular day when he was eight and playing with a pal called Tommy in Bethnal Green. They were messing around, not doing anything in particular, just walking around chatting and laughing. Tommy suddenly nudged Reg and pointed out a bread van parked by the kerb with the driver further up the street delivering bread. Just for fun, Tommy and Reg jumped up in the van and played at driving cars. Tommy then saw that the keys were in the vehicle, and he took a chance and turned the key. What happened next was to remain with Reg all his life.

As he turned the ignition, the van lurched backwards. Unknown to the boys, it had been left in reverse gear. They heard a cry and a crunching sound, so they sprang from the van and went to the rear to see what had happened. A young boy lay dying in the street, knocked down by the van as it reversed.

For many weeks afterwards, Reg expected to hear the police knocking on the door, but no one came. There was an inquest and a verdict of accidental death was pronounced, but Reg and his pal Tommy were never questioned. From then on, Reg Kray knew that violence and death would be a way of life.

Every year there was a fair in Victoria Park. The twins would go with Grandfather Lee, with their dad Charlie scowling in the background, as he was still a wanted man. They loved the fights, with blood and sweat pouring off the fighters. The most interesting part of the boxing was when one or more of the local lads got into the ring to fight one of the main boxers who had been hired to fight all comers. The twins watched and waited. Soon it was their turn.

'Who'll be the next?' asked the ringmaster, as one poor soul was carried from the ring. 'There's a fiver in it.' He looked around the marquee; no one was taking him up on the challenge.

'I'll do it,' said Ron, only 11 years old but ready for the big time. The ringmaster looked at him and started to laugh. He couldn't see who he could fight as he was so much lighter than the 'professionals'. The crowd began to laugh, and it all got too much for brother Reg.

'I'll fight him,' said Reg, getting into the ring. The crowd were ready, and the twins didn't let anyone down. They bruised each other, gave each other bloodied eyes and noses and generally tore one another to pieces. Eventually the ringmaster had to call a halt and call it a draw. Ron would have kept on fighting, but the crowd had had their money's worth, and he reluctantly decided to call it a day.

Their father had seen it all and was pleased with his boys as they were living up to the fighting Kray and Lee names. Their family history was full of prizefighters, drunkards and small-time rogues; Charlie was happy to see that the twins had inherited something that he could be proud of.

Violet, on the other hand, was fuming when she heard about the fight, and she made Ronnie and Reggie promise not to fight each other ever again. They promised their mother and from then on they would always fight on the same side, often against authority in general, but more often than not against the police in particular.

Their first real piece of trouble came when they were 12 years old. There had been skirmishes with the law before but they were now put on probation when found guilty of firing an airgun in a public place; even at this age they were both interested in guns. But probation meant nothing to them, and they carried on as usual with their gang fights, which became more and more intense. They would both use shards of glass or knives or chains, anything they could find to use as a weapon, and they would never stop when they had their opponents down. This was just the way it was. Get them down and keep them down was the order of the day.

At 16, they bruised and bloodied a young lad from another gang, using chains and bars. But there were witnesses who saw the wicked deed, and the police became involved. At the magistrates' court they were remanded in custody accused of grievous bodily harm and sent to the Old Bailey for trial. However, the witnesses were soon scared off with promises of beatings and other sordid threats, so the police were unable to convict them. Even the lad they had beaten was encouraged not to give evidence; it just wasn't done in the East End of London since it broke one of their oldest codes. 'You don't grass,' he was told, so he didn't. And the Krays got away with it.

At the trial, the judge remarked, 'Don't go around thinking you are the Sabini Brothers!' When Ron and Reg Kray got to meet 'Darby' Sabini some years later they had a good laugh recalling this outburst. They didn't think they were the Sabini Brothers; they knew that they were much, much better than the Sabinis could ever have been.

Only a short while later, they were in trouble again. The twins were hanging around Bethnal Green Road on a busy Saturday afternoon chatting to some pals when a young policeman, PC Baynton, approached and told them to move on. He didn't just tell them, he decided to shove one of them, hitting him in the stomach. And that someone was young Ronnie Kray. Just why he acted in that way when they were only out for a stroll can only be a matter for speculation. But Ronnie took offence to being shoved, especially in front of his friends, and punched the officer in the face. That was it. He was carted down the station, leaving Reg wondering what had happened.

Charlie junior rushed down to the police station as soon as he heard about the incident, and what he saw didn't please him at all. Ronnie's face was in a real mess, bruised and bloodied all over. 'What the hell's going on?' Charlie screamed at the officers near the cell. The officers were still sniggering and taunting Ronnie, but Charlie soon put an end to that by telling them that he would get a lawyer if they didn't stop. They did. Charlie then told them that he was taking Ronnie to see a doctor, and the two of them walked out of the police station with no one trying to stop them.

Reg wasn't a happy young man. He felt that he had let his brother down, so he searched all afternoon for PC Baynton. When he found him, he punched him in the face, just like his brother Ron had. He then casually went home and waited for the law to catch up with him. When they eventually came for him, Charlie told the police not to do what they had done to Ronnie or the Kray family would sue for damages. Reg went quietly, and that evening he sat in the same cell that Ron had occupied earlier in the day, but no one came near him.

The only thing that saved them at the trial was their good reverend, Father Hetherington, who said that it was all out of character for the twins, who had helped him in the past on numerous occasions. Despite the magistrate praising PC Baynton for his courage in such a cowardly attack, he put them on parole and the twins once again walked free. This was to become a bit of a habit throughout their lives, although they didn't beat the courts every time. They did what they wanted to do and in the main they got away with it.

Very soon, the twins were involved in hijacking lorry loads of cigarettes and furniture; they began dealing in stolen goods and were diversifying into all kinds of criminal activity. The more they got away with it the more they wanted to do, and so it escalated until the killings of Cornell and McVitie. The seeds were now sown.

YOUR COUNTRY NEEDS YOU: PRIVATES ON PARADE

That was a funny time when Ron and I were in the guardhouse. We both went to see the officer on this particular day and we were cuffed together. There was a Captain sitting there who was reading some papers, or was making out to, and Ron saw a cup of coffee. So he leaned over and picked it up and drank it in front of the escort. The Captain went mad. He said, 'Take him out, take him out!' Ron looked at him and then gave it to him straight. 'You greedy bastard,' he said. 'I only wanted a cup of coffee!'

Reg Kray

In February 1952, the postman delivered two important letters to 178 Vallance Road in Bethnal Green. They were addressed to Ron and Reg Kray and the twins looked at them for a while before opening them. When they did open the letters, they looked at each other and said nothing. There wasn't really much to say. Violet reached over to see what it was all about and then she gasped. Her little boys had just received their call-up papers; they were wanted in the army.

In the early part of March, Ron and Reg put on their best identical suits and took the bus to the Tower of London, where they were to be enlisted into the Royal Fusiliers. They had little difficulty finding the place since it was the same regiment that their father had deserted from all those years earlier. He had often told them the story of his great escape.

A corporal took control and they were soon outfitted with their uniforms and various bits and pieces. After a light meal they were ready, with a bunch of other raw recruits, to be shown the ropes, and the corporal spelt it all out, by the numbers. The twins weren't used to being told what to do and certainly not how to do it. The barracks were bare and tasteless, typical army grey. They didn't like it.

The twins listened patiently for a while, but the corporal was beginning to get on their nerves. Without saying a word and without motioning to each other in any way, they slowly walked towards the door.

'And where do you think you two are going?' asked the corporal, not used to anyone walking out on him. After all, these men were now in the British army.

The twins stopped and turned round. They looked at each other, but said nothing.

'Well, where are you off to?' he asked again, not believing his eyes. He looked first at one and then at the other. Was it Ron or Reg, or Reg or Ron? He couldn't tell the difference.

'We don't like it here,' said Ron. He could have said 'fuck the army' but he chose his words carefully. 'We're off home to our mum,' he added as they both turned again to face the door.

At that moment the corporal grabbed at the twins. He obviously didn't like anyone walking out on him, especially two at a time, but he had overreacted and the answer from the twins came swiftly.

Suddenly the corporal was on the floor, knocked out cold. Just who had hit him was anyone's guess but there were plenty of witnesses in the barracks. The twins had won the argument, so they went home to mum for tea, just as they said they would.

Later the following morning they were picked up by the police at Vallance Road and taken back to the Tower. They caused no bother and went quietly. Once there they were delivered to the Military Police and thrown into the guardroom, so they could spend the rest of the day in deep meditation. But the Krays were prepared. They knew what they were doing, all right. They may have been only 18 years old but they were smart, streetwise and not to be messed with.

The following day they were brought before the Commanding Officer, along with other prisoners. The CO had a real problem to solve that day. His normal reaction would be to sling any man who had committed such an act out of the army, but he didn't know which one had punched the corporal and he couldn't risk court-martialling the wrong man. The other new recruits in the barracks couldn't say which one had knocked the corporal down – they looked identical – so the CO was in a quandary.

'So which one of you attacked the corporal?' asked the CO. 'Was it you?' he asked, looking first at Reg and then at Ron.

'It wasn't me, sir,' said Reg, standing nose to nose with his CO.

'It wasn't me, sir,' said Ron, as the CO moved over to stare him in the eyes. Now, staring into Ron's eyes was a big mistake, since Ron could see through most any man.

'It must have been one of you, so who did it?' screamed the CO. He was getting a little fed up with the charade. But he was beginning to feel defeated; the enemy was using tactics beyond his capability.

'Did what, sir?' said Ron, still keeping his cool. He knew he had gone far enough.

The CO had only one option left. That was to send both men to the guardhouse for seven days, with only a blanket for company and bread and water to survive on.

This incident came to mark a turning point in the career of the twins. They had always been top dogs in Bethnal Green, but this was the British army; if they could beat them then what, at 18 years old, couldn't they achieve?

With them in the guardroom was another lad from the East End, by the name of Dickie Morgan. Morgan had spent time in borstal and knew the system well; he also knew how to use it. The twins talked with Dickie Morgan about what they would do outside, where they would go, what they would get up to in the way of villainy. The strange and dismal setting of the guardhouse made cellmates of them all. A bond developed that brought them closer together.

After seven days in the guardhouse, Ron and Reg, with Dickie Morgan in tow, were on the run again. They left the barracks and headed towards the London docks where Morgan had friends among the petty crooks and villains of the area. They were introduced to booze, cigarettes and wild times, which was a bit of an eye-opener for the twins. They had never experienced anything like this before, but they were learning fast and Dickie Morgan was a good teacher. One day they took a trip to Southend in a pal's car, just for the fun of it. While there they found time to send the CO at the Tower barracks a postcard. It simply said: 'Having a great time, from your pals Ron and Reg Kray and Dickie Morgan.'

The next few months were spent in and out of the guardhouse at the Tower of London. They would be captured, then escape. Then captured, then escape. This routine was the order of the day right up until November, when they decided that it was time for a change.

They were enjoying their period of freedom sure enough, but they were also getting a little bored. They knew that they couldn't exist like this forever; indeed they didn't want to live like this at all, so something had to give. One day when the twins were in a café on the Mile End Road, they approached a policeman, PC Fisher, who had arrested them earlier in the summer and gave themselves up. This was indeed a strange thing to do, since they knew what would happen to them. And to turn themselves in to a policeman – it was both the first and the last time they would do such a thing.

This resulted in a one-month prison sentence in Wormwood Scrubs, the first time the twins were imprisoned in a real jail. The peculiar thing about their time in the army was that the authorities saw fit to keep the twins together, even sending them to the same prison. It was as though they thought Reg was a calming influence on Ron, but the truth was it was Ron who had full control over his twin brother and this meant chaos wherever they went.

After prison there were more escapes and further re-captures, until finally, in the spring of 1953, the army gave up on the Kray twins. They were sent down to an army prison in Canterbury, Kent, along with their old pal Dickie Morgan, and summarily court-martialled on 11 June. Their sentence was to be a nine-month stretch in the Military Prison in Shepton Mallet, Somerset.

Once in Somerset, they continued to play their mind games

with authority. They were completely uncontrollable and even Charlie was asked to come down to talk to them; maybe he could calm them down. But it didn't help. Their mother Violet came to see them too, but that didn't help either. They had decided that their rules were more important than any army regulations and they would beat them at all costs.

But the twins learned a lot from the army, about the control and manipulation of people and about organisation, something that they would put to good use when they established their gang, known as the Firm. Ron even took on the mantle of 'The Colonel', not because he respected the army or any authority, but because in his mind he had beaten them at their own game. He deserved the title and he would use it. During their sentence they also met all the best (or worst) young offenders in the entire country, all gathered in one place where they could all learn from each other.

By the early part of the next year, 1954, the twins were free men, dishonourably discharged from the army. They didn't care about the disgrace, since they were back in Bethnal Green and in their eyes, kings of their manor. In its own way, the army had made real men of the Kray twins.

2

A TRADITION OF GANG WARFARE

A feller was going to shoot Ron and Ron found this particular feller in the Green Dragon and he says to the feller, 'I hear you're going to shoot me.' Ron gave the feller a gun that he had in his pocket. Of course the feller backed off and didn't fancy shooting Ron. So Ron took the gun back off him and smacked him round the bleedin' face with it.

Another time again, a feller was going to shoot me. I found out about this so I slipped someone in to sell him a gun. What I did was, I got it fixed in such a way that if ever he used it on me, or anyone, then it would blow back and blow his fuckin' hand off!

Reg Kray

If you want a taste of what it was like back in the bygone, war-torn days of London, then I suggest you take a magical mystery tour past Tower Bridge, heading east along the Whitechapel Road, through that area haunted (as if forever) by Jack the Ripper, and out along the Mile End Road to the district known simply as the East End.

It is like a time warp, a virtual reality *Mad Men* experience, for any other dweller of suburban London or for any inter-galactic tourist trying to find a wormhole leading home. It is a strange new (out of the old) world, waiting for discovery by anyone who dares enter into its dwindling domain and for those thirsting for the ultimate time-travel experience.

This is still an area of tradition, where many cling to a culture almost unrecognisable and incomprehensible to any other area of that great metropolis known as London; a place where family ties and old-fashioned values still hide among the modern-day exterior of post-war megaliths. But what are these values, these social aspects of daily life, still cherished and worshipped by many East Enders, young and old alike?

It is time to go back to the days of the East End after the Second World War, a time of those great aristocrats of crime Billy Hill and Jack Spot and to the scene of criminal innovation (often derived from the USA) that arose out of the ashes of the Blitz. This is a period of lawlessness as in the early days of the Wild West of America. This was the era of the gang wars.

Just why and how did the Krays, like so many other gangs, emerge from the ashes of the Second World War? And how did the Krays come to dominate the '50s and '60s, which saw an explosion of criminal underworld activity and a developing society full of opportunities for those who were willing and able to impose themselves through violence, intimidation and fear of retribution?

The pre-war community of the East End of London was a very closely knit collection of multiple ethnic groupings. Almost all immigrant groups were there: from the Jewish community through to the Italian; from the Maltese to the Irish; from Asian to Romany. All were represented in the ancient fabric of the East End and within its mainly working-class communities.

'London, like many large conurbations, expanded initially in relation to function and density but divided latterly in terms of largely social and cultural factors,' say Professor Chris Jenks and Justin J. Lorentzen of Goldsmiths College, London, who wrote an academic paper entitled 'The Kray Fascination'. The East End, we are told, was a disease-ridden den of iniquity, where deprivation and poverty were the order of the day and criminal and political dissidence the norm. Or so it was up until the end of the Second World War, when most of the area lay in ruins and there was no option other than to build it up all over again.

Crime was a known phenomenon, but people left their doors unlocked since there was little or no fear of being robbed.

Neighbour supported neighbour and, when there were problems, everyone wanted to help; they were supportive to the extreme.

But the war changed all of that. Violence crept in, weaving its bloody trail through the winding streets of both east and west of the City of London. There was a blossoming of protection rackets, drinking and gambling clubs and prostitution. The war was a great time for the villains. They ran the black markets and used the Blitz as cover for their ram-raiding and theft from the West End stores, where they would masquerade as Air Raid Precaution wardens, police or ambulance crews in order to go unnoticed. 'For the West End to know the East at all was to apprehend the threat and intimidation, the exotic and even the bizarre,' says Chris Jenks, reflecting on this urban 'great divide'.

Everything was rationed, but people had insatiable desires that led to almost everyone buying something through connections or off the back of a truck. Get it at all costs was the name of the game, and people didn't mind how they got it. They turned a blind eye to theft and to crime in general. Everyone managed their own lives the best they could. This was the start of the egoistic era of the '50s and '60s. The desire of things and the acquisition thereof became the order of the day. Eggs, meat, clothing, fuel coupons: they were all highly marketable products in the hands of the crooks. The material world was born.

The criminal has always looked after himself first and everyone else last. And so it was with the war. Hitler and Oswald Mosley were seen as guiding lights; Hitler killed and maimed, and succeeded. So the gangsters of the East End began turning the screws. They became more violent, more sadistic and more aggressive.

The crooks and criminals would go to any length to get out of the call-up. No trick was barred. Indeed, if you didn't escape the clutches of the military, then you were not a member of the 'club'. All the best villains got out of military service in one way or another. One such small-time gangster by the name of Frankie Fraser actually caused such a rumpus at his medical that he was certified insane and sent to an asylum. So it was these people, the tricksters and the petty villains, who came to rule the East End of London during the Second World War.

Even the West End was full of deserters and Soho attracted them in their droves. There was money to be made and punters to rob. Business was good, and the villains and rogues of the East came West in search of an easy target.

The cultural inheritance of the East End of London 'does not conform to either proletarian or bourgeois cultural stereotypes,' says Dr Dick Hobbs, author of a book on East End culture, *Doing the Business*, and referring to the attitude of the East End villain. This is in both a materialistic and an ideological way, since the Krays, for example, came from both Jewish and Romany stock, but 'showed a response to poverty and hardship which was at once protective, itinerant and entrepreneurial'. Being a rogue in Bethnal Green was not just accepted, it was welcomed.

The war, however, was a watershed in the history of crime. The fires of the Blitz shielded the villains, who coolly went about their business. They were busy with their robberies and easy money dealings, and there were few police officers around to hinder them as they were all kept busy by the air raids. There was a large amount of freedom and they exploited it as much as they could.

The villain, previously only tolerated by the East Enders, became a true friend who could provide the good things in life. He became an acceptable part of everyday life. The rogues didn't exist any more; only the villains survived.

By the early '50s, the world of the East End had changed. London was in the grips of a violent mindset, of men who would stop at nothing to get what they wanted.

Billy Hill and Jack Spot, real name Comer, had run the underworld successfully for more than ten years, with their base in the West End of London. Hill was a thief with a passion for organisation, whereas Spot was the minder who arranged the heavy stuff. They were the very best and everyone knew it: from the Krays to the Richardsons and throughout the entire city of London. These men were the uncrowned kings of crime.

By 1955, however, things were changing, and the team of Hill and Spot had a falling out. They disbanded the old guard and formed new allies. Jack Spot turned to the Krays.

Spot introduced Ron and Reg to real money at the Epsom Races in April 1955. Organised crime has always seen an easy racket in supplying protection to bookmakers. If the bookmakers didn't pay then they would be roughed up, so they ended up paying people like the Krays for protection. Violence was now the tool of the gangster and knives and guns became the tools of the trade.

Jack Spot was not a young man and he had been badly cut around the face just a short time before by 'Mad' Frankie Fraser, who had joined Billy Hill's gang, so getting the Krays on his side was a bit of a coup for him. The twins were keen to learn and took time off from The Regal billiard hall that they were managing to size up the opposition. They were fast becoming good businessmen themselves and were quick to spot an opportunity. They could smell the money.

Billy Hill was not generally a man of violence and would sooner make a deal and share the profits rather than risk a war – it just wasn't good for business, but he could see that the whole underworld scene was hotting up, and violence was now the key.

Previously gang met gang in minor skirmishes, only using knives or fists. They would arrange for a meet on one of London's eternal bomb sites, where rubble still littered the streets and back alleys. But these were not important events; they only showed which gangs were the dominant ones. The big business was making money, not war.

Robberies were executed with bloody efficiency. The stakes were high and crimes of violence commonplace. The crooks wanted the good life, no matter what, and these callous people committed the most violent of crimes in the knowledge that, once caught, they would face harsh treatment in prison. Sentences were long, the cat-o'-nine-tails was still around, and the birch was available for serious offenders. In this dark world of the criminal, brutality bred brutality, and there was no one better than Ron and Reg when it came to out-and-out violence.

This was the time for Spot and Hill to beat a hasty retreat. In the summer of 1956 Billy Hill retired to his villa in southern Spain and Jack Spot took over a furniture business in the West End. They got out while the going was good and before the killings started. It is a pity that the Richardsons and the Krays couldn't have done the same.

For the bosses of the underworld, it was a very busy time. They began stockpiling weapons of all kinds in readiness for the war that was sure to come. In the end, however, it was only a war of words, not of deeds. All the prominent gangs were ultimately each responsible for their own downfall, and the bosses never met each other in a gangland brawl, as was expected. Just who was the biggest and the best was never decided, as the clash of the titans never took place.

In the early part of 1960, one of the Nash brothers was involved in a car accident. The other man involved was Selwyn Cooney, who ran a spieler (gambling den) in Whitechapel, an area frequented by known villains. Unfortunately for Cooney, the other guy came off worse. And when the other guy is a Nash then you can expect trouble.

At around midnight on 8 February, Jimmy Nash, the leader of the gang and one of the most respected villains in London, arrived at the back door of Cooney's club with two other men. Inside were Cooney and his moll, Fay Sadler; they weren't expecting trouble, but that is just what they got.

Jimmy Nash was a powerful man and, at 28 years old, was thought by many to be destined to remain a top underworld figure for many years to come. He and his six brothers had a string of gambling clubs and were involved in theft and other corrupt activities and he was a very popular figure throughout London. There was no need for Jimmy Nash to be at Cooney's, but he took it personally, and retribution was on his mind.

When Nash stepped into the spieler brandishing a gun, Billy Ambrose stepped in between Nash and Cooney. Ambrose was only a customer, so he really should have known better. Nash shot him, although it wasn't fatal. Then Nash turned to Cooney and shot him at point-blank range. Cooney died instantly with a bullet in the brain.

When the police arrived at the club, they found carnage. There were three witnesses, including Fay Sadler, and they were all willing to talk.

The trial, however, had to be staged twice because of threats and attempted intimidation of the jury. But in the end, Jimmy Nash was sent to prison for five years for killing Cooney. Many at the time thought he would be hanged.

The Nash family gave up most of their business enterprises in Islington, North London after Jimmy's sentence. They slowly and quietly disappeared. The last I heard of them, they were all living peacefully on the Costa del Sol in Spain, but that really is another story.

The most powerful of all the gangs and the richest by far was that belonging to Charlie and Eddie Richardson. Charlie Richardson was a shrewd businessman and after the war he had entered the field of surplus stocks and scrap metal, but he also ran a wholesale chemist's business, which shows the versatility of the man. The Richardsons, from Lambeth in South London, spent many years building up a respectable business empire, but there was an evil side to their nature and they had a sideline in debt collecting, blackmail and extortion. It was this over-indulgence in violence that was eventually to be their downfall.

Charlie Richardson had contacts everywhere. He even had corrupt policemen on his payroll from Scotland Yard itself. A phone call from Charlie and cases were dropped. Even when it came to government contacts he had friends in high places. Corruption was a key player in their game. It was the '50s and '60s, a time of good living, and everyone wanted more of the same. An office in prestigious Park Lane was a natural consequence of his success, and the gold mine that he owned in South Africa was a constant reminder to other gangs like the Krays that here were real adventurers; they would go anywhere and do anything for the dosh.

As a part of the debt-collecting set-up, in 1962 Charlie Richardson hired 'Mad' Frankie Fraser, a real thug who was hungry for trouble. Fraser was feared by all. He was the best at his game, and had even sliced up Jack Spot, the old gangland leader. Fraser, in turn, was afraid of no man.

The hiring of Fraser was a big mistake, since it forced everyone and everything up a gear. The pace got hotter, the events more violent and serious, and there was always trouble in the air. Exactly why Charlie Richardson hired Fraser is also a bit of a mystery, since he had good working relationships throughout London and had secured recognisable boundaries for his business operations. The threat, however, was to come from another madman, Ronnie Kray, but this was in a way set up by Fraser himself.

With his Scotland Yard pals behind him keeping the gang out of trouble, Charlie Richardson set about a period of expansion. Many gangs were involved in long-firm frauds. The idea of a long firm is to build up debts, only to fold the company overnight and get away with the money. The Richardsons were good at it. The long-firm frauds continued, but Charlie wanted more income from them. Debts of £25,000 became normal at this time, so profits were naturally good.

The Krays were also involved in long-firm frauds. Leslie Payne, their business manager, had set up a whole string of them throughout the East End. Again, money was good, so the Krays continued to build up their empire on the back of dishonest and devious dealings.

However, the Richardsons had grander ideas: they wanted to be the underworld bosses and the Krays had no place in their business strategy. A meeting was called, with the Richardsons and the Krays putting across their own particular point of view and trying to establish some kind of territorial domain for each gang. The Richardsons didn't see how the Krays could fit into their plans, and the meeting broke up with everyone expecting out-and-out war.

'Clear off, we don't need you!' was Charlie Richardson's closing remark to Ron and Reg.

The Krays went home and brought out the arsenal. Once again, it was not needed, much to Ron's disappointment.

Billy Haywood was a thief and, together with his pal Billy Gardner, ran a spieler in Lewisham. It gave them a good living and gangsters were not allowed. Thieves, however, were allowed into the place, and many came to talk and chat and to plan deals. Thieves kept to themselves – they didn't like the gangsters, who wanted to take everything away from them.

Eddie Richardson, together with 'Mad' Frankie Fraser, visited the club and asked for protection money. Haywood and Gardner weren't interested. Eddie Richardson and the much-feared Fraser left empty handed.

Fraser had a reputation to live up to, or to live down to if you like it better that way. So he phoned Haywood to invite him and Gardner to a meeting at Mr Smiths, a gambling club in Catford. Haywood had already been warned, so he and Gardner and a group of pals turned up at the club, heavily armed. Fraser, with Eddie Richardson and a dozen or so members of the gang were already there. They, too, were heavily armed.

The shooting had to start sooner or later, but it happened sooner than anyone had imagined. Eddie Richardson said only a few words and that was it. Shots were fired everywhere. All the gang members dived for cover, and there were blood and guts all over the floor of the club.

Dickie Hart, a member of the Kray gang but who was by chance out with the Lewisham gang that night, fired at will. He wasn't very accurate but he did manage to hit one of the Richardson gang. Fraser saw the incident and managed to shoot and kill Hart, but not before Hart had managed to shoot Fraser in the leg.

When the police arrived all they had to do was to go around and pick up the bodies. There was no resistance, and even Fraser went peacefully. The scene at the back of the club, from where the police took away the bodies, resembled a bloodbath. The police found weapons everywhere. There were guns, iron bars, knives; anything and everything that could be used to kill or maim.

Incredibly, only one man was killed: Dickie Hart. 'Mad' Frankie Fraser stood trial for the killing of Hart, but he was found not guilty. He and Eddie Richardson, however, were convicted of causing grievous bodily harm and given five-year sentences.

For Haywood and Gardner the trouble was not finished. Over the next few years everyone who had taken their side in the battle was killed. Only Haywood and Gardner themselves were left unscathed. Whether or not this was retribution on the part of Charlie Richardson has never been proved, but the thought remained ever present in the minds of Billy Haywood and Billy Gardner.

Charlie Richardson kept the business going with new recruits, and he continued to collect money on behalf of his clients. One of his debtors was a man called Jimmy Taggart, who actually told the police of his treatment. Knowing that the Richardsons had spies everywhere he gave a statement, but only agreed to sign it when he knew Charlie Richardson was safely behind bars.

Taggart's statement was staggering. It revealed all about the Richardson gang's use of electric shocks, pliers to pull out fingernails and to cut off fingers, drugs and suchlike. It was serious torture according to anyone's standards, and it all took place at a yard in Rotherhithe, just south of the River Thames. There was even doctor's evidence to back up the statement, since Taggart had to have medical treatment after his torture at a flat in North London.

Charlie Richardson was pulled in and Jimmy Taggart signed his statement. It was all over bar the shouting for Charlie Richardson. Only five months after his brother's arrest he received twenty-five years in jail for his part in the crimes, for violence and demanding money with menace. It was only now that the police realised that there was a connection between the long-firm frauds and the beatings at Rotherhithe. That connection was Charlie Richardson.

But it wasn't only this that caused Scotland Yard to pursue Charlie Richardson. Other evidence was coming in from other sources, far away in South Africa, of Richardson's dealings there and his involvement in a murder.

A man by the name of Thomas Waldeck had been murdered by two men, Harry Prince and Johnny Bradbury. Bradbury was an old pal of Charlie Richardson's who had escaped to South Africa in 1964 because he thought he was going to be targeted by the Krays. Harry Prince was the hired assassin, but he needed help from Bradbury to locate his man. The man in question was Waldeck, a man who had committed a most heinous crime: he had borrowed money from Charlie Richardson and hadn't paid it back.

Prince vanished and left Bradbury to stand trial alone. Bradbury was eventually found guilty and sentenced to hang in 1966. In return for a pardon he informed on Richardson to Scotland Yard, who sent police officers down to South Africa to question him. Bradbury spent 11 years in jail, but the game was over for the Richardsons.

Eddie Richardson and Frankie Fraser were tried again and given 15 years each for their involvement, and Charlie Richardson's 25-year sentence reflected his involvement in the South African affair.

The Richardsons had become just another London gang who had apparently committed suicide, and Fraser was the man with the shooter.

Sir Frederick Lawton, who tried the Richardsons and Fraser, called it 'The Torture Case' since he had never heard of anything as horrible as the evidence presented in court. Charlie Richardson kept complaining to the bitter end. 'I only want my money,' he would continually remark, as if he had done nothing wrong, but he and the others were, for once, found guilty and his pals at the Yard couldn't help him.

The police method of investigation for the Richardsons was to mark a significant change in tactics that had repercussions in later cases, including against the Krays. The fact that these criminals were locked up, without bail, while police investigations could take place was a change in normal procedure, and gave witnesses the chance of telling the truth without the fear of reprisals.

The end of the Richardsons meant that the Krays were left alone to take over the West End of London, with a little help from their pals in the US Mafia.

The start of the Krays' empire was The Regal, an old, dilapidated billiards hall. They were only 21 when they bought it, and they had to borrow the money from elder brother Charlie, but it was a start. They bought new tables and Ron supplied the smoky atmosphere, just like in the American movies. From then on, the rise up the underworld ladder was relentless – local crooks would come to The Regal to trade goods or to hide weapons. This was when Ron Kray started taking an interest in knives and guns.

Helping Jack Spot at Epsom was the next step on the ladder to the top. They started going to The Vienna Rooms, off Edgware Road, where they could listen to their heroes, Billy Hill and Jack Spot, telling all, or almost all, about the 'good old days'.

What really made everyone sit up and take notice of the Krays, however, was when a Maltese gang tried to get protection money from them one night. The Maltese were usually into prostitution and not known as fearless mobsters, but the events that night set the record straight about the Krays.

When the leader of the Maltese gang asked for the money Ron stared him in the face. It went terribly quiet in The Regal, as this kind of situation was unheard of and no one knew what would happen – except Ron and Reg, of course.

'Protection from what?' asked Ron, as he drew a cutlass.

Reg pulled out a knife and the twins lashed into the Maltese gang, who fled in terror whilst the twins only built up a light sweat.

'They've not got a lot of bottle, these Continentals, especially when the knives come out,' Reg was heard to remark about the battle.

This showed everyone in the place that these two youngsters were here to stay. They would defend what was theirs with their lives; and the lives of anyone else who got in their way.

There were other fights, such as that with the dockers who again wanted protection money from the Krays. Now, anyone would have thought that they would have learned from what happened to the Maltese gang, but no!

The dockers, all from Poplar in East London, invited the twins to meet them in a pub on the Mile End Road. The twins were busy that evening at The Regal, but everyone knew that they had been called out by the dockers. Again, everyone waited to see and hear what would happen. At the end of the evening, late in the autumn of 1954, Ron and Reg put down their teacups, put on their jackets and walked slowly but deliberately out of The Regal.

It was only a short walk down to the Mile End Road and the dockers were waiting for them in the private bar, drinking light ale. They looked up when the twins entered the bar and grinned at the two youngsters. Now, that was not a good idea.

'Here you are, sonny,' said one of the dockers. 'You are just about old enough for a shandy.'

That was it. This was downright disrespectful. Ron, once again fearless in battle, laid into the dockers with his bare fists. Reg joined in and before long they had beaten the big men to pulp. Reg had to pull Ron off one of the dockers; Ron couldn't stop hitting him and could easily have killed him with his constant punches.

It was all over as quickly as it had started, and Ron and Reg smartened themselves up and walked out into the brisk night air. The job was done; the record set straight. On the way back to The Regal they discussed plans for getting into the protection racket themselves.

Protection became the Krays' biggest business. They had all kinds of traders and tradespeople on their lists. If they wanted cars, then they would just go and take one. If they wanted food, then they would send someone over to collect some. If they wanted booze, then they would go out and drink all night and let the establishment pay for it. They paid for nothing, and everyone paid them for it.

Clubs, too, became big business, especially after the 1961 Gaming Act, and by the time the twins were eventually taken into custody they had shares in more than 30 clubs, dotted all over the country. The Double R was the next club they owned after The Regal, and then came a few others leading up to The Kentucky. But pride of place was Esmeralda's Barn, located just off Wilton Place, in the heart of Knightsbridge. It was one of the best casinos in London and the guests were all from *Who's Who*. The Krays had climbed right to the top of the heap, but they soon found out that it was quicker tumbling down than climbing up.

The twins were bonded by both rivalry and devotion and they had quickly built up a reputation. It was in the mid-1950s that they started building their gang, the Firm.

Headquarters was at 178 Vallance Road, where they and their mother had lived since the twins returned home from the country and where they stayed during the war. Old man Charlie joined them when he could, since he was still officially a deserter. This simple two-up, two-down terraced house was their fortress, and they called it Fort Vallance.

The Firm was a loose conglomeration of, in the main, small-time gangsters. Ron, who called himself 'The Colonel', was the boss, together with his brother Reg. But in any disagreement between the twins it was generally Ron who came out best. Charlie junior was only involved as and when needed; he played no role in the protection rackets but was deeply involved in the organisation of the clubs. He, too, was good at his job; that is, when Ron allowed him to do it. It was this that was the real problem within the gang. Whereas Jimmy Nash and Charlie Richardson were the natural bosses of their respective gangs, the twins could never decide between themselves who really was the leader. It was always a joint decision, even if one of them disagreed, and Charlie was never asked for an opinion.

Over a few years, the shape of the Firm fell into place. Apart from Ron and Reg there was their cousin Ronnie Hart, pals such as Albert Donoghue, Ian Barrie, Pat Connolly, 'Big' Tommy Brown, Connie Whitehead, Dave Simmonds, Sammy Lederman, Nobby Clarke, Ronnie Bender, John Barry and 'Scotch Jack' Dickson, and then there were the Lambrianou brothers, Tony and Chris. It was a well-established and well-known gang in and around the East End.

Members of the gang used the Kray name to sell themselves and to make some money. Tony and Chris Lambrianou are typical of this type of gang member. They would travel the country playing for high stakes using the reputation of Reg and Ron Kray. The deal was not complicated: if they made some money from one or other crooked deal, then the twins would receive a share. It was that simple. The twins never asked what they were doing, just how much was coming to them from the profits of the Lambrianou rackets. Most of these deals were connected to protection, but they were not limited to anything in particular. Tony and Chris Lambrianou could do whatever they pleased, as long as the twins were paid.

Other members of the Firm also collected the protection money and shared out the pensions. They had two different kinds of list: the big names for the big payouts and the so-called 'tipping list' for the smaller incomes. They would collect from the big names on the first list in ready cash, but collection from the smaller operators could be in goods, such as crates of booze or cartons of cigarettes.

As for the clubs owned by the Krays, it was usually someone trusted who ran the establishment. They didn't trust many outside of the family, so there were many relations by the name of Kray employed in the business, but generally brother Charlie was not on the board. Only in the case of the Double R did he figure as a boss, but as soon as Ron got out of jail Charlie was told to take a back seat, as usual.

Ron and Reg did not favour their elder brother Charlie being involved in their business dealings. Maybe they thought that Charlie was too clever, or maybe they simply did not trust him.

As gangs go, the Firm was not a real success, apart from supplying the Krays with protection money, that is. They did far better with clubs and casinos like Esmeralda's Barn and with their Mafia deals, such as sharing profits from the Colony Club, which was operated by Hollywood actor George Raft.

The long-firm frauds also worked well, but when the twins decided to get rid of Leslie Payne they lost the only business partner who could handle the intricacies of such deals. When Payne decided to get out of his own accord, it forced the twins to try to get rid of him, permanently. The man chosen for the job was Jack 'The Hat' McVitie. We'll see what happened with that later on in the book.

Scotland Yard just didn't know how to handle the Krays. When George Cornell was shot and killed in The Blind Beggar, as we shall see later on, rumours quickly found their way to the Yard where Assistant Commissioner Brodie was waiting for a break. He had already appointed Chief Superintendent Tommy Butler to the case, Butler having been successful with the Great Train Robbery case in 1963.

Brodie thought that Butler needed help and enlisted the services of Leonard 'Nipper' Read, who had previously worked with Butler on the train robbery. Read had, however, some years earlier, caused a bit of bother in police circles when his photograph appeared in the national press, where he was pictured drinking in the company of none other than the Krays themselves. 'Nipper' was cleared of improper behaviour and taken off the Kray case, but not before he was promoted. Leonard 'Nipper' Read was therefore no stranger to the Krays.

Memos from Chief Superintendent Tommy Butler described his anguish in dealing with the Krays. He knew as early as 1960 that things were getting out of hand and he wrote a few words on the Krays. These are just a few of his comments, made over a short period of time in the early '60s:

'During the past three years the Kray twins have welded themselves into a formidable criminal association.'

'At present this is directed towards club owners, café proprietors, billiard hall owners, publicans and motor car dealers operating in the East End of London.'

'They have organised their protection technique and the keystones of their confederacy are violence and intimidation.'

'That they will spread their operations to other districts in due course may be taken for granted.'

'Their reputation is already such that persons threatened almost frantically deny visitations by anyone connected with the Kray twins.'

'Not one victim can be persuaded to give evidence against anyone connected with their organisation.'

'They are content to remain in the background, emerging only to convince any particularly difficult client of the force of their demands.'

'For this reason their arrest will only be achieved by unorthodox police methods, or by good fortune.'

And then he added, just for luck, the following:

'The fact that Ron Kray is certainly mentally unstable (to put it at its very least) is of immense importance to the others and adds considerably to the victim's urge to comply with demands made upon him and to his atrocious memory when questioned by police.'

So he knew Ron and Reg Kray really well! What were others doing all this time? I, for one, cannot believe that he was the only policeman in London who knew this, so why wasn't something done about them much sooner? And he wasn't the only one to know how dangerous the Krays were. Another police officer made the following remarks:

'Coercion of the main witness was an astute move on the part of the Kray advisers. From the outset I concluded that this witness was the stronger of the two main ones for the prosecution.'

The case collapsed when the main witness changed his story, probably influenced by the Krays.

And still another said: 'Witnesses have been duffed up by the Krays.'

But it wasn't just their own thoughts that were put down on paper. People, no one knows who, wrote to the police about the Krays. One letter, received just after the Cornell killing, said the following:

'It is pretty evident that these men are not doing these things without some assistance from the police. Why is this being allowed to continue? They are getting money from all sorts of operations. They have been known to have machine guns and shotguns in hordes. What exactly is going on when it is common knowledge and the police are powerless to do anything about it? It will not stop at this one murder.'

Another letter said: 'There are two families here in the East End, namely the Nashes and the Kray brothers, that have been having a glorious time on the proceeds of violence and crime. So I think that it is about time that you stepped in and have this thing stopped.'

And still another, in August 1966, said: 'The Kray brothers are too clever and tricky for you. Certain big people are terrified of these two, like everyone in underworld London.' This letter was signed simply: 'By one who knows'.

An uneasy stalemate developed between the police and the Krays, and this was only broken when, once again, 'Nipper' was re-assigned to the Kray case. It appears that Scotland Yard just couldn't make up their minds about the Krays and about the involvement of Read, who would eventually prove to be their greatest asset.

In the autumn of 1967, Read was back in the picture as a Detective Superintendent, assigned to the Murder Squad at Scotland Yard. The new Commissioner of the Metropolitan Police, Sir John Waldron, was concerned about the publicity surrounding the Richardson case and about the constant and embarrassing way the Krays flaunted themselves in public, so he immediately put Read in charge of getting the Krays, once and for all.

It was 'Nipper' Read who started contacting old pals of the Krays looking for evidence, but all he managed to get was a 200-page statement from Leslie Payne, Ron's ex-business manager and the man who had been targeted for killing, on the orders of the Krays, by Jack 'The Hat' McVitie. This statement was not completely reliable because of Payne's own involvement, but it gave Read some good ideas on who to talk to and how to proceed. He had also learned from the Richardson case, where the rats deserted the sinking ship only after the Richardsons were safely behind bars, so, when he took his great gamble in May of 1968, he was fully prepared.

As with the Richardson enquiry, the police breakthrough came by accident when a moment of madness changed history. Ron could not stop himself from killing George Cornell and that was to be his downfall. Ron's constant provocation of his own twin brother was also the final nail in Reg's coffin and this, too, was brought on by Ron's chronic paranoid schizophrenic tendencies.

Read won the battle of the gangs when he obtained authority from the Home Office to offer immunity from prosecution to key witnesses, who eagerly testified against their former associates, just as in the Richardson affair. The evidence came in abundance, but the police could only convict on the basis of the two killings, not for any other crime such as the long-firm frauds or the Mafia deals, but this was good enough for 'Nipper' Read and his team at Tintagel House. It was Read who got all the credit, but it was the team who did all the work.

The gangs of the '50s and '60s, in the main, all committed suicide. They thought they could get away with murder, but they couldn't. It wasn't Scotland Yard that caught them out, however; it was they themselves, because they went just a killing too far.

3

TRYING TO STAY OUT OF JAIL

Joe Louis was a character. He had been the heavyweight champion of the world and was a very nice man. When we got kicked out of Manchester by the police, Joe was in the same hotel as us, along with Johnny Nash, Joe Pyle and a few others. Well, the police surrounded us and said we had to leave town. Well, I went over to Joe Louis and asked him to come over to the railway station and check our luggage, just to see if they had fitted us up with shooters. Joe didn't really know what was going on, but he agreed anyway, as a favour. So he came over and checked our luggage. As soon as we got back to London that Butler feller, from Scotland Yard, was there and I think some of the police were taking photographs. They never found nothing!

Reg Kray

When the twins were court-martialled from the army they had time on their hands and time to turn those hands to small-time crime. They robbed trucks and delivery vehicles in the East End, even doing a little trading in stolen goods, but that life didn't suit them and they were on the lookout for something special. Of an evening they would hang around on street corners with their pals and sometimes they would go and play billiards at The Regal in Eric Street, just off the Mile End Road. The manager noticed an increase in violence when the twins became regulars there; the fights increased and the police were becoming regular visitors too.

The manager bought an Alsatian dog to help guard the premises, but someone threw fireworks at the animal and it went mad. By the summer of 1954 the manager had seen and heard enough; he wanted out.

It was no surprise to friends of the Krays when Ron and Reg were pronounced the new managers of the billiard hall. They had made a deal with the retiring manager and paid him off with £5 a week. The owners were satisfied and the twins took the place over. It was a wise decision, since they would probably have taken it over anyway. The only problem for the twins was lack of ready cash to fund the purchase of new tables, which were sorely needed. Their salvation came in the form of their brother Charlie, who lent them the money for the tables and some paint so that they could clean the place up really well. They all worked hard and the place was an instant success. Unsurprisingly, the trouble stopped as abruptly as it had started.

With the billiard hall a success the twins had no need to get involved in petty crime. In fact, they had all they could handle at The Regal, since they would hide weapons for their pals, trade stolen goods and keep items hidden for customers who did not have a safe hiding place of their own. Business was good, the money came rolling in and 'The Colonel' was firmly in control.

The police kept away from the hall, letting the Krays take care of business in the normal East End way. There were the usual gang fights, such as with the Maltese gangs, and there was trouble with other gangs trying to hustle in on the Mile End Road, but the twins took care of this and settled down as masters of their own universe.

For more than two years the Krays ran the business and stayed out of trouble. The police didn't bother them and the Krays didn't bother the police. It was a long time for the twins not to be involved in conflict with the law, but this was because they were running their own business with their own rules and no one said that they couldn't do it. It worked well, and even Charlie enjoyed himself at The Regal, without the fear of violence; well, almost without the fear of violence.

Inevitably, it had to change, and the reason had to be Ron. The twins had already started their protection rackets and they were making more money than ever, but Ron was still building up a personal arsenal at home at Vallance Road, where the twins were still living with their mum and dad. One day there was some minor trouble at a car dealership that was paying protection money to the twins. A dissatisfied customer wanted his money back and threatened to get some help from south of the river. When Ron heard about it he rushed to the scene and shot the customer, wounding him in the leg. It was silly really, as the customer had returned to the car dealer to apologise and Ron's shooting fit was a complete waste of time. Reg rushed over to the place, calmed everyone down and got the man treated. No police were involved, but the rumours began to spread.

There were other incidents involving Ron and guns. On one occasion he rushed into a pub and let go three shots from his Mauser handgun. He hit no one, but when Reg heard about the incident he went crazy.

'You must be raving mad!' he said, as he tried to get his brother to calm down; but Ron was getting used to the high he got from firing his gun, usually in a public place and with witnesses galore. Reg, together with brother Charlie, always had the task of talking to Ron's victims, or the witnesses, and getting them to stay quiet. Neither Reg nor Charlie liked doing it, but they did it for their brother.

Shortly afterwards, on 5 November 1956, Ron was convicted of causing grievous bodily harm and sentenced to three years' imprisonment. He caused the police no bother and went quietly. This gave Reg three years to work on the business and to prepare for his brother's return. He grabbed his chance.

By the spring of 1957 Reg, together with Charlie, had opened the Double R Club, just off Bow Road and, typically for the Krays, right near Bow Road Police Station. It was a great success as a club and was something new to the East End. Reg sorted out the internal arrangements and the boxing ring upstairs while Charlie took care of the drink and amusement. It was one of those times in Charlie's life when he would say: 'It's going so well, something's got to happen.'

By the spring of 1959 Ron was back on the scene and everything changed – for the worse. They had had two great years, with Reg going frequently to the West End and turning into a bit of a playboy, while Charlie kept the club going with slick panache. It all now lay in ruins as Ron swept back into their lives.

With Ron back, so too came the police. They had kept an eye on the club ever since Ron had made his escape from Long Grove Asylum, near Epsom, discussed later in the book. They visited the club on a regular basis, looking for thieves and goods, but Reg protected his twin and Charlie didn't have a say in the business any more. While Ron had been in prison it had been OK for Reg to share with Charlie, but now, with Ron back in his life, he only wanted to share with his twin brother.

This time, though, it wasn't Ron who caused the downfall of the Double R Club, it was Reg and his moral code: the one that said 'don't grass'. It wasn't really anything to do with Reg, but the police didn't see it like that. Ronnie Marwood, an acquaintance of Reg's, was wanted by the police for killing a policeman. It was a very serious offence, as it still is today, but Reg couldn't betray his code; he simply couldn't tell them what they wanted to know. He knew where Marwood was hiding and everyone knew it, but he still couldn't grass on a fellow East Ender. The police couldn't do anything about it at the time, but when the club's licence came up for renewal they opposed it and the renewal was refused. Reg couldn't betray a killer by telling the police of his whereabouts, so the club had to close. It was something else that made Reg hate the police and authority in general. His brothers agreed.

It had been great while it lasted, at least for Reg and brother Charlie, but, whilst it was usually Ron who spoiled everything with his aggression and madness, this time it was the moral code, held strongly by both twins, that ruined the business and put their progress into decline.

Soon Reg would be behind bars, convicted of extortion. He just happened to be there when the incident occurred but, because of his track record, he was immediately guilty in the eyes of the police. A man by the name of Shay, who ran a car dealership, asked for a discount on a briefcase he had purchased. It wasn't the fact that he asked for a reduction in the price that upset the owner of the shop, it was the use of the words 'or I'll cut you to pieces' or similar that he objected to. The police arrived just in time to arrest

Shay together with Reg Kray, who was just along for the ride. It was totally out of character for Shay, so Reg got the blame and an 18-month prison sentence; 1960 was beginning to be another bad year for the Krays.

This scenario was to play itself out on many occasions during the late '50s and throughout the '60s, like a game of chess between the Krays and the Metropolitan Police. The Krays had many reasons for hating the police and the police tried in numerous cases to convict the Krays, but with limited success. It was a cat-and-mouse game, but who were the cats and who were the mice?

With Reg back out and, surprisingly, Ron still at large in the East End, the Krays took over Esmeralda's Barn in Wilton Place in Knightsbridge. The Krays had moved up a gear and were entering the big time in a big way and the police didn't bother them. They were men of property and therefore to be respected, though still to be kept an eye on. As long as the twins didn't overstep the mark and do something really stupid then the police would leave them alone.

'They didn't want the aggro,' Ron told me once in Broadmoor. But he couldn't let things lie; he had to push everything and everyone to the limit.

The skirmishes with the law continued, including being arrested on suspicion of burglary and even loitering with intent to commit a felony. Ron made the most of these incidents to get much-wanted publicity and to make it look as though he was being persecuted by the police. His newspaper adverts telling his side of the story were very convincing and the twins were acquitted of all crimes – they even managed to get costs. It was simply a case of us and them to Ron, although Reg tried not to take it so personally. He had learned his lesson from the Marwood case, and wasn't prepared to go to jail for anyone ever again. On the other hand, Ron felt that his propaganda had worked and he was now invincible. Charlie just looked on in amazement, trying to stay out of the way of Ron and getting on with his own concerns at Esmeralda's Barn, where he had many responsibilities, including organising the amusements laid on for the gamblers and drinkers.

More clubs opened and more interest was taken by the police

in their concerns. There were more knife attacks by Ron on so-called friends, for various long-forgotten reasons. He became more and more unpredictable and depressed, and Reg and Charlie could do nothing about it. Ron had been taking pills even before Long Grove Asylum, but the mixture of booze and tablets didn't always have the desired effect. As the Krays struggled to hold things together, the police looked on, waiting for their chance. It was all just a matter of time.

They were investigating the Krays when the Lord Boothby case, to be detailed later, surfaced and was spread across all the national newspapers. A denial by Scotland Yard, stating that they had not been keeping tabs on the Krays, meant that they were free to continue their business, almost unimpeded by the police. In fact it was a lucky break for the Krays, but not so for the police, who had to scrub the slate clean and start all over again. Because of the denial, no evidence against the Krays gathered in this period could be used in a court of law.

However, when the Krays were arrested for demanding protection money from Hew McCowan, at The Hideaway Club in Soho in January of 1965, 'Nipper' Read thought that he had won at last. It was the Krays' old pal 'Mad' Teddy Smith who called at the club on their behalf demanding money. When he didn't get any he started smashing up the place. McCowan, seeing what was going on and fearing the Krays' involvement, immediately phoned Scotland Yard and 'Nipper' Read arrested the twins.

Although they tried very hard, the twins were refused bail. Their next move was to hire a good legal team and Reg, always keen to learn from past mistakes, took on the lawyer who had beaten him back in the Shay case. They also hired private detectives to dig up any dirt on the unfortunate McCowan and soon found him to be a homosexual. They used this in court to ridicule McCowan and to make his testimony unreliable in the minds of the jury. Whether the Firm had already intimidated and/or bribed the jury has never been proved. In any case, the Krays were found not guilty and walked free. That very same evening, they bought the club from a despondent Hew McCowan. The Krays had won again.

The photos of 'Nipper' Read drinking with the twins that appeared the next day in the national press did, however, cause a bit of an uproar. He was invited into the party held at The Hideaway to celebrate the victory, but newspaper photographers were also there with their flashing cameras. Although it ended in a police inquiry, Scotland Yard were now sure that the Krays were getting too big for their boots. One day, they felt sure, the Krays would pay for it.

When the twins helped Frank Mitchell, known as 'The Mad Axeman', to escape from Dartmoor in 1966 the police thought, once again, that they would get a conviction. Even though they couldn't find the body, they arrested Ron and Reg, together with their old pal Freddie Foreman, for Frank's murder. It took some time for the police to build a case strong enough to prosecute and this involved getting witness statements. However, when Albert Donoghue gave his statement to the police they thought their case was secure and they went to the Old Bailey armed with testimonies from both Donoghue and Mitchell's girlfriend, a hostess known as Lisa. Unfortunately for the police, the jury didn't accept the testimony of a known villain and found that Lisa's evidence was not reliable. Once again, the Krays had beaten the law of the land and walked free.

'Nipper' Read was furious and immediately put the Krays at the top of his 'Most Wanted' list. It wasn't long before his own investigation into the Cornell shooting in 1966 took an unexpected turn, when information concerning the killing found its way on to his desk. He couldn't prove it yet, but he was at last beginning to get the big picture by putting all the pieces of the jigsaw into place. Read was a man who worked by the book and he did his homework in a routine and logical way, so, when he finally arrested the twins on 9 May 1968, it was totally out of character. Scotland Yard had had enough of the Krays. The twins had overstepped the mark and the police had to take action to secure a decision in their favour. This time the Krays would not be getting away from the Old Bill.

Even when the police were closing in on the Krays, the twins managed to maintain their activities right to the very end. They knew they were in danger, and that they had gone too far down the slippery slope to total villainy. This was somehow symbolised with the purchase from Harrods of two pet pythons, which they called appropriately Gerard and 'Nipper', after the two most prominent Scotland Yard chiefs who were after their hides. Ron and Reg wanted to feel the power of being totally in control, hence the charade with the pets. I am sure it made them feel better, but it did them no good at all.

The twins made one last attempt at fooling the Old Bill when they tried to get their Firm to take the rap for the Cornell and McVitie killings.

'We'll look after you,' the members were all told. 'We'll even take care of your families, and there'll be something for you when you get out.'

But the loose assortment of crooks and criminals that made up the Firm were not so easily fooled by the twins any more and knew that they were only interested in looking after number one; the Krays were always more important than anyone else, or at least that was the way the twins saw it.

By denying the murders, however, the twins guaranteed that their own brother Charlie would get a long sentence for his involvement in the killings, even though he was nowhere to be seen on either occasion. Charlie got a ten-year stretch because the twins pleaded not guilty. Being a Kray he, too, felt that he couldn't grass to the law and, as a result, had to serve several years in prison for keeping to his moral code.

The statements made by the majority of the Firm made sure that Scotland Yard would get their victory over the Krays, but even here not everyone joined in. Tony Lambrianou, who was present at the McVitie killing, lived by the same East End code that meant that you did not grass to the police. For being quiet and honouring that code of conduct he received 15 years in jail, a harsh sentence for behaving with dignity.

At higher levels the situation has changed now, even in the East End of London. It is no longer a sign of morality or respect to say nothing in a difficult situation when approached by the police to give evidence. It is now called stupidity, and the current gangs in the East End are not stupid. They may be nasty, corrupt, deceitful, dishonest and dirty criminals, but they can in no terms be called stupid. They have the money to buy the brains, just as the Krays had the cash and know-how to lure Leslie Payne and

Freddie Gore. The Firm only started to fall apart when the twins decided they didn't need the business acumen of these two men. As a result, the downfall of the Krays was all their own doing. The Old Bill didn't destroy them – they did it all by themselves.

4

PLAYING THE CELEBRITY GAME

Of course Barbara Windsor, Joan Collins and Sylvie Burton all used to come to the Double R Club in the '50s. It was quite a nice club and all the villains from all over London were going there. It was still a nice club!

Reg Kray

'Judy Garland made us welcome at her party,' said Reg Kray, reminiscing about the old days at the height of the Kray empire. 'In the early hours of the morning she sat there on the floor and broke out into song – all her old songs.'

He had been used to mixing with the great and famous US showbiz personalities who were sent over to the UK with just a little help from their friends, the Mob. When the Mafia in the USA wanted their pals to get the best protection and assistance that money could buy they always turned to the Krays, but Judy Garland was different from the rest.

'I took her to parties in the East End,' he told me. 'I liked her.' When Reg's wife Frances died, it was Judy Garland who came to the rescue by offering to let him stay at her home in Hawaii. Reg was shattered that his wife had taken her own life and he was almost prepared to give up a life of crime for Judy; well, almost. Reg still had pleasant thoughts about those times, long ago. He still had stars in his eyes.

The Krays had always made a habit of meeting the rich, the famous and the notorious. From boxers to film stars, athletes to politicians, and singers to songwriters, they had mixed with them all, or almost. To hear Reg talk of the stars they had met was like a reading of *Who's Who*. Boxers such as Rocky Marciano, Joe Louis, Sonny Liston and Muhammad Ali; singers and entertainers such as Sophie Tucker, Joan Sutherland, David Essex, Frank Sinatra, Nat King Cole, Billy Daniels and Johnny Ray; politicians such as Tom Driberg, MP, Lord Boothby and others, whom I am not allowed to mention here; actresses such as Joan Collins and Barbara Windsor; actors such as George Raft, Robert Ryan, Richard Harris and Lee Marvin. The list is endless.

But was this all planned, as in some kind of grand scheme? Or did it just happen?

Ron, affectionately known as 'The Colonel', had always imagined himself as the Al Capone of British crime. He even dressed like him. To reinforce this image he had photographs taken of himself, suitably dressed, with celebrities of the time. This was an out-and-out effort to make himself a celebrity by association.

No one was spared the camera trick. Lord Boothby said yes, much to his regret as this was what started 'The Case of the Brighton Peer'. Christine Keeler said yes, and in doing so inadvertently created a connection between John Profumo and Ron Kray. Henry Cooper said yes, although he has always denied meeting the Krays. George Raft said yes, many times; but then he was getting paid for it by the Mob.

The Krays, and Ron in particular, made a serious attempt at creating larger-than-life images of themselves by being photographed and being seen out and about in the company of 'stars'. Ron was into image building long before the marketing and PR companies even knew it existed. No other British criminals have been able to emulate this extraordinary feat.

The Krays were the first gangsters in the UK to genuinely seek media attention. They were mesmerised by fame; it was, to Ron in particular, a reason for being alive. Ron always considered himself the best at whatever he did. Whether it was slicing someone up with a cutlass or a sword, or charming celebrities at his clubs, he thought big and aimed high. To Ron, mixing with stars was the norm; no low-life mediocrity for him.

Although they met showbiz folk of all kinds and sizes, there were not many who made a lasting impression on the Krays. One man who broke all the rules was George Raft.

'Where is he?' asked Ron, as he descended the stairs leading to the Colony Club. Reg and Charlie followed behind. 'The Colonel' always led the way.

'He's here,' said 'Big' Eddie Pucci, one of the Mafia's best bodyguards and the man who handled Mob business in London. 'You'll be meeting him soon.' Eddie chased after the Krays into the plush surroundings of the club.

The George Raft Colony and Sporting Club, to give it its full title, was the latest creation of Meyer Lansky, who had assembled a syndicate of fellow well-connected mobsters to establish casinos in the USA and overseas. The man who oversaw the gambling was the best man in the business, Dino Cellini, and the manager was Alfred Salkin.

As the Colony Club was not yet open for business, there were all kinds of workmen and delivery people in the club trying to get it organised for its grand opening night. And that was the reason for inviting the Krays.

The Mafia knew well that the Krays were the people to talk to in London if they wanted the right kind of protection for their establishments; this was bread-and-butter work for Ron and Reg – even Charlie sometimes got in on the act.

The month was March and the year was 1966, and George Raft had just been given a 12-month visa for entering and working in the UK. Initially he did some boxing commentary for US television, but the serious business was for the Mob. He was chairman of the club, with a flat in Mayfair, a Rolls-Royce, a chauffeur and even a dog. His job was to see that the punters had a good time, and he was very good at it.

His movie career had long been over and, at 70, he was no spring chicken, but he was a tremendously fit person who enjoyed people's company and was therefore well suited to the job. He had previously worked at clubs in Cuba, but this was his first posting to London and he wanted to make a good impression.

The four men walked across the red-carpeted floor, past all the paintpots and boxes, and into the bar. There, at a huge oval table, sat the star. Amidst all the confusion he was immaculate and appeared just like his movie image. As the Krays and their American friend approached, George Raft rose to greet them.

'I hear that you will be working with us,' said Raft as he shook hands with Ron, who was first with an outstretched hand. They greeted each other warmly like old friends and soon that is exactly what they were. Ron and Reg had just found a new subject for their incessant photo shoots.

Eddie Pucci had already explained the deal to the Krays: that they would be receiving a share of the profits for their involvement, and that suited them nicely. It was a great new club in up-market Berkeley Square; plush, posh and sweet poetry to the Krays. This was just the right kind of image that they were looking for, and it was being handed to them on a platter by the US Mafia.

All three Kray brothers enjoyed their time at the Colony Club. They were introduced to all the high-flyers of the day, both home-grown and imported. All the stars came out to meet George Raft; Joan Collins was a frequent visitor, so too was Sylvie Burton. They came in their droves to meet the ageing idol.

On one particular evening Charlie Kray was having a quiet drink with Raft over by the bar. Charlie had just arrived and needed to wet his whistle while he settled into his normal routine. This was mixing; with drinks or with people, it made no difference to Charlie. He wanted a good time and he knew that Raft could give it to him with ease.

'Come and meet a few of my US pals,' Raft said casually to Charlie. 'They are over at the tables.'

The two men made their way into the gaming room, which was fully fitted with plush carpets, velvet wallpaper and golden chandeliers. Soon Raft spotted an old friend.

'Charlie,' said the actor, 'let me introduce you to Charles Bronson.'

Charlie welcomed the American to the UK and to London, but before he could engage him in further conversation Raft had seen another friend from across the pond.

'And this is Richard Jaeckel,' he said. Charlie once again put on the style; instantly he felt taller than his normal six feet. But again he was dragged away by his host to yet another table where some guests were hard at work playing roulette.

'Another couple of pals for you to meet,' said Raft. 'This is Telly Savalas and Donald Sutherland.' Charlie's hands were beginning to wear out, but he played his part well, as usual, and drinks were ordered all round.

'There are plenty of you guys here tonight,' said Charlie. 'It's like an invasion. What's going on?' He looked at the two actors in eager anticipation.

'We're making a movie,' said Telly Savalas. 'I believe they're gonna call it *The Dirty Dozen*.'

Later in the evening actors Lee Marvin and Robert Ryan also arrived at the club to play at the tables and to socialise, that great game enjoyed so much by Raft himself. That, he often told people, was his purpose in life. No more films for him. But then, that was his job and the US Mafia expected every ex-film star to do his, or her, duty.

And this he did, right up to the time he was refused re-entry into the UK by the Home Office. They said he was an undesirable, but the powers that be let all of Raft's old Mob pals into the country just the same. It was only this amiable old actor who was refused admission to the UK; a man who, unlike his Mafia friends, could do no evil. Why this happened is still a mystery, but when it happened the Mob just carried on its business as usual. Raft never visited Britain again and died in Los Angeles in 1980. Ron and Reg were denied meeting their good friend ever again, an event that reinforced their hatred of authority in this country.

Raft had toured all over London with the Krays, visiting boys' clubs and boxing tournaments, even inviting ex-world heavyweight champion Rocky Marciano along with him to see the youngsters at work in gymnasiums and sporting clubs. He was always a great hit with his Rolls-Royce parked outside and his uniformed chauffeur, and he never caused anyone any harm. He may have been employed by the Mob, but he was pure Hollywood.

It was through the clubs and the Mob business that the Krays met many of the stars of show business. Even artists such as Lucian Freud, brother of Clement Freud, frequented Esmeralda's Barn, along with actress Honor Blackman and magician David Berglas. I remember at this time, back in the '60s, being asked by David Berglas if my twin brother and I were available for shows in London. The idea was to put one in a box, all tied up, only to produce the other one from behind a screen and call it magic. Naturally, the twin would be released from the box to show that it was just a trick, but I often wondered if he had ever asked the Kray twins to do the box trick with him, especially after I found out many years later that he was performing at Esmeralda's Barn when he invited us to join his show. It is still an intriguing thought.

Also regulars at the 'Barn' were Phil Everly of the Everly Brothers, Eric Clapton and the Walker Brothers. Diana Dors was also a good friend of Charlie's, and he even took her along to visit Ron when he was in Broadmoor. The talent was everywhere, even at the Wellington and the Cambridge Rooms, just off of the Kingston bypass. Ronald Fraser was a regular, so too was Richard Harris. The celebrities of the day liked to rub shoulders with the Krays; it gave them some spice to their lives. After all, they played villains on the screen and here they were with the real thing. It may have been good for character study, but the image presented to the public and the police caused some sleepless nights in high places.

When Barbara Windsor had trouble on the set of *Sparrows Can't Sing* she turned to Charlie for help. Joan Littlewood was worried about a gang of dockers who were asking for protection money from the film company, but Barbara phoned her then boyfriend Charlie at The Kentucky Club on the Mile End Road and he soon put an end to their threats.

Joan Littlewood accompanied Barbara Windsor to the club one night to thank Charlie and the twins for getting her out of trouble. Meeting the famous lady was thanks enough for Ron, who never let such a moment go by unnoticed. They all enjoyed the evening so much that Littlewood asked Ron and Reg if she could use the club as a set for the film. She needed a club for the final scene, a celebration in a nightclub, and The Kentucky fitted the bill admirably. Ron made a joke about not normally allowing shooting in the club and it was all agreed. Then she told the twins that the premiere of the film was to be at the cinema just across the road, in the East End, and that Lord Snowdon and Princess Margaret were to be the top guests. On hearing that Ron hatched a cunning plan. 'We'll throw a party afterwards,' he told them. 'We'll have a great time.'

Ron's plan was to get all the guests in to the club after the premiere, including the Snowdons. In the event they couldn't stay on for the party, but all the other stars crossed the road to the club and even Roger Moore came along for the fun of it. George Sewell, an old friend of Charlie's, was there, so too were James Booth, Joan Littlewood and Barbara Windsor herself. All their old friends came too, to meet all the celebrities of stage and screen. Lord Effingham met Roy Kinnear, Ronnie Knight was introduced to 'Hard Man' Freddie Foreman, who was later tried for the murder of 'The Mad Axeman' Frank Mitchell, and the twins had a ball.

They didn't get to meet Princess Margaret that time, but they did later on when she had a night out at one of their clubs. Even the Royal Family was not immune to the Kray treatment.

In fact, she made a number of trips to establishments run by the Krays and Ron was so pleased to see her that he even started to compile a regal dossier, something that he kept locked away from prying eyes. This was discovered by the police many years ago but the story of this file has only recently come to the notice of the press. When someone asked for permission to see the file it was quietly moved to another pile of files that are to be kept secret for 50 years. This had happened to me previously, when they invoked the 75-year rule on the files I asked to see. The Establishment are still protecting someone. But who?

It was the Lord Chancellor's department that took this action some time ago, but it shows that the Krays really did have contacts in very high places. In fact, more and more Kray-related files have found themselves on this stack to be tucked away for 50 years or more. One of these is reportedly a note that Ron wrote soon after he shot George Cornell. He admitted the killing, served his sentence and is now dead, so why all the secrecy?

All the Public Record Office could say was that they were being kept under wraps to protect informants and avoid upsetting the families of Kray victims. They did admit, however, that the files contained information that would cause substantial distress or endangerment. Now what that means is anyone's guess.

It was fast becoming second nature for the twins to hobnob with the jet set of the time and they took to it like ducks to water, especially Ron, who enjoyed the extravagance and outrageousness of anything theatrical. It was all a show to him and he excelled at it. Even his orgies at Cedra Court, his home in the mid-1960s, were filled with famous names. Tom Driberg MP was often there with his good friend Lord Boothby and an assortment of boys. There, too, were pals 'Mad' Teddy Smith and Leslie Holt, both of whom were involved in 'The Case of the Brighton Peer' discussed later on. It was a clandestine meeting place for many up-and-coming homosexuals, not to mention other interested revellers, who partied the nights away to the amusement of one and all. Ron had at last found a set that he could feel comfortable with.

The image presented by Ron and Reg Kray was of businessmen in complete control, and they played that role well when it suited them. At other times, however, they were still the vicious thugs who had risen from the ashes of the war, dirty and evil, with financial gain on their meagre minds. They could change in an instant and most unpredictably, especially Ron with his twisted paranoia. When they fought together they were invincible – they were their mother's favourite children, they were 'special'.

All of the Kray brothers were accomplished boxers. Through their boxing they met many sporting celebrities of the day. As well as Rocky Marciano, who was a very close friend of George Raft's, they met many other Mob-connected ex-champion boxers. One such man was Joe Louis, one of the greatest heavyweight boxers of all time. Through their pals across the pond the Krays got to hear that the champ was having a hard time financially, so they told the Mob to send him over to London and they would see that Joe had a good time and did some demonstration and exhibition bouts. They toured the UK, visiting both north and south.

On one particular trip to Manchester they almost got Joe Louis into a lot of trouble with the law. Ron and Reg were staying at the same hotel as the ex-world heavyweight champion, together with some close friends including Joe Pyle and Johnny Nash. Reg was afraid that the local police were trying to fit them up with guns, or 'shooters' as he called them. The Krays actually asked Joe Louis to go to the railway station to check their luggage for firearms, just in case they were right in their suspicions. This he did, eventually finding nothing, but it did reassure the Krays, who boarded their train with nonchalance. The big man had repaid a debt of gratitude, something that would stand him in good stead with the UK's greatest gangsters.

Another man who thanked Reg for his life was yet another ex-world heavyweight champion, Sonny Liston. Reg drove him back to his hotel from the Cambridge Rooms one evening while quite intoxicated with alcohol. Sonny Liston kissed the pavement as he got out of the car and thanked his lucky stars that he was still alive. Still shaking from the experience, he swore never to ride with Reg ever again. The boxer may not have known it at the time, but Reg was quite short-sighted and didn't like to wear spectacles. I remember hearing of one incident concerning Reg and a double-decker bus; the bus won the argument and Reg ended up in a big hole in the ground. Reg didn't care – he just went into a car showroom connected with their protection racket and drove out in a brand new American vehicle. But he still didn't wear his glasses.

One of the best ever British boxers whom they both enjoyed meeting was the ex-champion Freddie Mills. They would often visit Mills at his club and drink to past victories. There has always been much speculation that the twins were responsible for the death of Mills, but I have not come across any damaging evidence that would tend to confirm this fact. But I do know from Charlie that there were rumours that 'Nipper' Read was going to arrest the ex-champ for the 'Jack the Stripper' murders. Prostitutes were being found murdered in various places throughout West London but no one was ever prosecuted for the murders. Before the police had a chance of questioning Mills he had already committed suicide by blowing his brains out in a car. The Beatles immortalised this event in their song 'Day in the Life', but the real truth will probably never be known in full. One fact did emerge, however, when it came time to read his will. Freddie Mills died almost broke, so it certainly looks as though he was being blackmailed for something other than just running a nightclub.

When 'Nipper' Read wrote his book entitled *Nipper* in 1991, together with James Morton, in which he mentioned Mills's death in utmost detail, he suggested that no such arrest was imminent in the 'Jack the Stripper' case. But anyone who knows the history of boxing in the UK and the involvement of 'Nipper' Read in the Boxing Board of Control knows that he would never disgrace the name of Freddie Mills, one of the all-time greats of British boxing. In any case, Charlie may have been wrong about his involvement. It was all a long time ago and memories can play tricks on the most astute of villains, but there are many strange events surrounding his death that are looked at in more detail later in this book.

Many other boxers got the Kray treatment, including that great champion Henry Cooper. Cooper has always gone out of his way to deny any involvement with the Krays, even suggesting that he had never met them. This is quite wrong, since I have many photos in my possession of the twins in the company of Cooper, but I can understand the reasoning behind this denial. He never had any business involvement with the twins at all, but no one can stop anyone taking photographs in public places, so being a well-known boxer and celebrity he was bound to get Ron's photo treatment at some time or another. Cooper was, and still is, a twin. However, he, unlike the Krays, understood the difference between notoriety and fame and was keen to protect his public image. He knew all of the twin tricks and how being a twin can be an advantage, if used in the right way. This knowledge enabled him to outwit the Krays, and he never succumbed to their power games.

Ron, on the other hand, didn't give a damn about how he achieved the cult status of a celebrity; he longed for public recognition at all costs, and was prepared to do anything, even murder, to get it. Reg was drawn into this twilight zone by the sheer force of his twin brother, a force that he would never truly overcome.

Ron and Reg, with their brother Charlie in tow, looked after visiting American celebrities when they toured the UK. This was done through that jovial giant Eddie Pucci, a man whom they first met through their old Mafia pal Angelo Bruno, the 'boss' of

Philadelphia. Eddie arranged all the showbiz deals for the Krays, including on one occasion sending Nat King Cole's wife over to London for a shopping spree. Ron met her at the airport and took her all over London, to Harrods and other famous stores, even down the King's Road in Chelsea, and he loved every minute of it. It may seem strange for such a violent and paranoid criminal as Ron Kray to be acting as a guide for the wife of an American singer, but 'Mad' Frankie Fraser was conducting tours of Kray sites in 1997, so Ron, as usual, got there first. This simply shows Ron's other side, the good as opposed to the bad. The schizophrenic disability that he was forced to carry with him would make him seem human one minute and downright mad the next. There was a good, a bad and an ugly side to his nature that could change in an instant with his mood swings. But when it came to protecting the stars, he was totally reliable.

When Judy Garland came over to the UK it was generally Reg who looked after her. She appeared to be most vulnerable at this stage of her life and would cling on to Reg's arm in almost any given situation. Maybe it was because of her drinking and her own bouts of depression that made Ron stay away, or it may have been the favouritism shown by Garland towards Reg. As a single man, Reg took well to her shows of affection, but it was certainly embarrassing for him after he married. He became very reluctant to be embraced by Garland in the presence of either his wife Frances or photographers. Nevertheless, he continued to take Judy to the East End and to Chelsea, where she sang her heart out until the early hours of the morning at various nightclubs. Reg even took her along to some of his local East End pubs, where she sometimes sang songs on request. She was a favourite of all three Kray brothers, and they have talked and talked about her over the last 30 years. Even at his trial back in 1968–9 Ron shouted to Lord Justice Stevenson: 'I could be dining with Judy Garland, instead of being stuck here in the Old Bailey!' Something that he obviously wished he was doing at the time.

Johnny Ray was another favourite of Ron's. It may have been because they were both gay and were drawn together by that common trait, but, as with Lord Robert Boothby, it was most likely the fact that they both enjoyed the company of young boys.

73

Remember, homosexuality was a criminal offence in those days and therefore something to be hidden. Thank goodness that times have changed and that we are more tolerant these days.

They all enjoyed the club scene, though, which was remarkably drug-free at the time. That has all changed now and drugs appear to be a normality. Although the twins themselves never dealt in illicit substances, some say that things would have been very different in the UK now if the Krays had not been put away in the '60s. True, they didn't deal in drugs, but the Mafia was very keen on influencing their decision in this respect. Maybe the lure of the stars would have persuaded the twins to import cocaine, heroin and crack through their Mob pals; maybe they would have resisted these pressures. But that is all pure speculation.

Barbra Streisand, Billy Daniels, Frank Sinatra and Tony Bennett – they all paid respects to the Krays. The twins from the East End of London had made it; they were household names who could command respect, if not for their business dealings, then certainly for their money. But it wasn't only these foreign showbiz names that entertained the protection of the twins. British home-grown celebrities also flourished under their wing.

The house at 178 Vallance Road was not the kind of place where anyone would expect to see showbiz stars; well, it wouldn't be if it hadn't been the home of Violet and 'old man' Charlie Kray. Ron changed that by introducing his mum to Edmund Purdom, who was a popular film star at the time, with a highly popular television programme behind him. Ron took him home to meet Violet in her East End home, where he was introduced to all the neighbours. He wasn't the only celebrity to visit the terraced house in Bethnal Green.

Sophie Tucker was a regular visitor who popped in from time to time to talk to her good friend Ron. Even though Ron was openly homosexual, he was a most charming person to women when he wanted to be, and when his illness allowed. He would entertain these visiting showbiz folk in the living room, while mum made the tea. They would talk until the small hours, with Ron giving good advice, just like a marriage guidance counsellor or your friendly financial adviser; he was well respected for his judgements, another fact that would seem to disappear over time, overshadowed by the darker side of his character.

Because of all their connections in film and theatre, it may appear obvious that the Krays found much time for meeting the stars both in the clubs and at the theatre. Lionel Bart was a friend who invited them to all his shows in the West End, even inviting them backstage to meet the stars afterwards. This happened regularly and, once again, gave the press a host of photographic opportunities. Photos appeared in the newspapers on such a common basis that every policeman in the country could identify Ron and Reg Kray on sight, something that greatly pleased the twins.

Here were two violent hoods who openly sought publicity, without thought to monetary gain. They even posed for photographs free of charge. David Bailey didn't ask them to pay him for the famous photos that he took of all three Kray brothers; he didn't dare, and they didn't ask for payment from him. After all, his photos helped the twins to establish their own immortality. They are some of the most famous photographs ever taken, and they have stood the test of time incredibly well. Everyone knows the Kray brothers, if not because of their deeds, then because of those photos and the many parodies of them. Long after the Krays' crimes have been consigned to the history books, Bailey's photo of Reg, head askance, looking over Ron's shoulder will remain an icon of '60s popular culture. That is probably the closest thing to immortality you can get.

One surprising fact to come out of my investigations into the Krays' preferences, pastimes and hobbies, was the enjoyment both twins obtained from the opera. Reg and his wife Frances, even on their honeymoon, found time to take in La Scala in Milan, where they saw Renata Scotto in *Madama Butterfly* and, when they returned to London, they all went to see Joan Sutherland at the Royal Opera House in Covent Garden. Whether they did this for the music or for the chance of meeting the stars cannot be proved, but it does show a willingness on the part of both twins to seek the brighter, lighter and more cultural side of life and that, under different circumstances, the world could really have been a good place for the twins and their brother Charlie, one that they could have enjoyed to the full.

The Krays' fame has not diminished; indeed their notoriety has gained through the years with T-shirts, films, books and even records made of or about them. Their celebrity status is assured, and history will tell their story for many years to come.

It is not, therefore, surprising that Ron and Reg remained in contact with celebrities and sports personalities throughout their imprisonment and right up to their deaths. Just because they were banged up in jail was no reason for their pals to forsake them. After all, if the Mafia could stay in touch, then their showbiz allies could also show a little respect. Over the years this was mainly in the form of letters, assuring the Krays of everlasting friendship and assistance. They would have been censored by the authorities, but nonetheless it was possible to recommend go-betweens to handle deals and maintain connections. The unfortunate thing for the Krays was that they would not forego control by letting others organise and negotiate on their behalf, so this limited the deals that they were able to do and the old contacts that they were able to maintain.

Once, when I was visiting Reg, he told me about his good friend Don King in New York. King was the manager of the ex-world heavyweight boxing champion Mike Tyson, but his other claim to fame was that he was well connected with organised crime – the Mob.

'If you ever need to get around in New York, then he's your man,' Reg told me, quite casually. 'You know, it can be dangerous over there.' I felt as though he was trying to sell me insurance. Or maybe he would have called it protection?

Throughout their years in custody the Krays waged a media war, with incessant displays of loyalty appearing in the press from old friends and articles about the twins' good and charitable deeds, all performed in the name of decency. Garry Bushell constantly told us in *The Sun* of how it had always been safe to walk around in the East End when the Krays were around. Maybe that is true, but you have to ask yourself why. Why should people like the Krays have such control over our everyday lives? The comedian and actor Mike Reid joined in the celebration of the Kray name, saying that 30 years was too long for murder. When comparing latter-day cases with the Kray trial, it must appear illogical that the twins were given 30-year sentences, but as normal everyday citizens do we really have all the facts about the Krays? And what have we still to discover?

This media hype served them well and kept their names alive in the modern television age. It is still so alive that we could perhaps be forgiven for calling it a virtual-reality life, since we know so little about the facts. The media have trivialised that part of their lives that made them kings of the underworld, in favour of the image so carefully created by Ron, which portrayed them as showbiz icons who ran foul of the law and had overpaid their dues.

It is possibly this sensationalism and celebrity worship that enticed people like Jon Bon Jovi, the rock star, to write to them, or maybe it was just a case of following orders for the singer from New Jersey. It is well rumoured that Bon Jovi, too, has Mob connections, just like the music companies Warner/Reprise, Elektra and Atlantic of WEA fame (Reprise was, of course, founded by Frank Sinatra), but, just like in the '50s and '60s, it is difficult to tell who controls whom, since no one goes around wearing a badge saying 'I am a member of the Mafia'.

A frequent visitor to see Reg was the singer and actor Roger Daltrey. It was through his perseverance that the film *The Krays* was actually produced, since he was the first to show an interest in the project and to start developing a script. Bill Curbishley, the manager of the band The Who, which featured Daltrey on vocals, was also a regular, and Daltrey and Curbishley advised Reg on the project, culminating in the deal that secured £297,000 for three jailbirds who had been convicted of heinous crimes. As a result of the movie the Krays became even more famous (or should that be infamous) and next time around they wanted to make £2 million. That was the price they had set on their fame and fortune and, next time, they wanted bigger stars! This never happened, of course, mainly due to squabbling among their so-called pals. Everyone wanted a bit more and a bit more and a bit more until, in the end, no one got a damned thing.

Of all the love–hate relationships that Reg Kray had to endure, the most peculiar is that which existed between him and a certain actress. The mere fact that he was her godfather has meant little to her at times but the connection has been eagerly and actively sought and confirmed by her at other times. It is an on–off relationship without par. The lady is, of course, Patsy Kensit, and her story is told in greater detail at the end of this book where I delve into the love lives of the Krays, seeking that knowledge which explains and analyses the fatal attraction that they all seem to have had to members of the opposite sex. Patsy wrote, apparently, to her godfather, asking for forgiveness for her sins, since she had denied all knowledge of the Krays in major interviews, something that had deeply offended and infuriated Reg. In the case of Ron, of course, it was not the opposite sex that had him dreaming at night, but he somehow managed to endure two marriages – to women.

But why are the Krays themselves still 'stars'? Why do we talk of them in the same way we talk about film stars and pop stars and even royalty? I believe it all started when they were born twins. Their mother called them 'special', and special they became because of their twin-ness. Others called them special too, so they grew up believing it. Indeed, at school they did well in boxing, winning championships, which again proved to them that they were special. The Kray twins were no ordinary little boys from the East End of London.

Everyone knew them because they were twins and referred to them as 'the twins'. It was only later that their individual identities, Ron and Reg, were used around the area of Bethnal Green. I can hear their mother Violet calling out Ron and Reg in the same voice and at the same time, when addressing only one of the twins. My own experience as a twin shows that a mother is not always sure which one of them she is talking to. Even in my middle age, on the telephone, my mother couldn't distinguish between my voice and that of my twin brother. The Kray twins were stars in their own right even from birth, so it was only natural that they should become stars later on in life.

5

IN BED WITH THE MAFIA

And then I met Angelo Bruno, the Philadelphia Mafia boss. There was a term he used to use regularly when I met him in London. It went something like: 'if you kick the dog then you kick the master'. What he was saying, in effect, was that if you upset any of my friends then you upset me. I liked Angelo Bruno.

Reg Kray

'Frank Sinatra would like to meet you backstage after the show,' said the amiable giant Eddie Pucci. Eddie had been a football player of some repute, but to the Krays he was known as one of the best bodyguards in the business. They had first met him when he came to England with Mafia boss Angelo Bruno, who had employed the Krays to look after his gambling establishments in London, and they had continued as associates when Eddie arranged for the Krays to act as protectors for American stars who came over to perform in the UK.

Ron was always excited when his Mafia pals sent over a 'star'. He would wine them and dine them, even take them shopping. But this time it was no ordinary celebrity he had come to meet. It was the one and only Frank Sinatra, a king among men, and he had brought the whole family with him.

Ron, Reg and Charlie sat with their mother and father, Violet and old man Charlie, throughout Frank's performance. They sat in the best seats in the house, the best that Mob connections could buy, and were absolutely delighted when invited to join Frank after the show. Ron, in particular, just couldn't wait.

But wait he had to, since the meeting was not to be, as reports began to arrive at the Apollo Theatre that Frank's son, Frank junior, had been kidnapped.

The year was 1966 and this was at least the second successful attempt at snatching Sinatra junior away from the protecting eyes of his Mafia-connected father.

The first kidnapping had taken place at Sinatra's own hotel, the Cal Neva on the California–Nevada state line, in 1963. Young Sinatra had been performing with the Tommy Dorsey Band at Harrah's Casino on Lake Tahoe when he was grabbed for ransom money. Sinatra senior soon recovered his son and most of the money. Exactly how this was done still remains much of a mystery, although Mafia involvement cannot be ruled out. Sinatra was also cited, by many, to have organised the kidnapping himself – for publicity.

This second time, however, was a college prank. It was of no particular importance at all, save that it stopped the Krays from meeting 'Ol' Blue Eyes'. The fact that the meeting never took place is also of no importance; not, that is, to any outsider. But the fact that it was even proposed did show the status of the Krays – all three brothers – in the eyes of the US Mafia. These were allies across the pond; men of substance, to be treated with respect.

The life of Frank Sinatra will always be inextricably linked with the Mob. Indeed, for anyone trying to make a name for himself in Hollywood, it was almost impossible not to meet or have dealings with the Mob in one way or another. They controlled all the film unions; they controlled money lending; they controlled gambling. One of Frank's oldest and dearest friends, Sammy Davis Jr, was always in debt to the Mob. He would borrow for gambling purposes but, because of his friendship with Sinatra, was always treated kindly. But the Mob always collects on a debt. It can sometimes be in cash or possibly in other ways, such as asking a favour or two.

When John Fitzgerald Kennedy was running for President of the United States in 1960, it was Sinatra who organised fund-raising events throughout California and Nevada, including at his own Sands Hotel in Las Vegas and at the Cal Neva, with his many celebrity pals. But among the stars of the day, such as Dean Martin, Sammy Davis Jr, Peter Lawford and Marilyn Monroe, there were other very special guests, such as Chicago Mafia boss Sam Giancana.

Giancana had made a deal with Joe Kennedy, Jack's father, to get presidential backing for his protection, prostitution, gambling and extortion rackets after the election of Jack Kennedy to the White House. Giancana wanted to be around to see that everyone had a good time and to make sure that his man was elected president. To secure their cooperation he even had the hotel rooms bugged. If he couldn't get what he wanted then he would release the tapes to the press or elsewhere, wherever it would do him any good and get him the favours he so desperately needed.

Sam Giancana was one of the most important Mafia bosses of all time. He was on the *Commissione* – the Mafia's very own troubleshooting organisation – along with old Kray pal Angelo Bruno and rival supremo Vito Genovese. It was a club for *capos* and the most powerful criminal organisation ever. It still exists.

Frank Sinatra and Sam Giancana were very good friends and close business partners. But even close business partners don't always see eye to eye.

In July 1962 Sinatra was getting ready to marry again. His intended bride was none other than one of Giancana's most intimate of friends, Marilyn Monroe. Monroe had been going through a bad time and Sinatra wanted to help. But maybe there were other reasons why Sinatra wanted to protect Monroe. It just may have been that Sinatra knew that the Mob had been asked to silence Marilyn Monroe, for good.

Having had close relationships with the Chicago Mob for many years would naturally have made Sinatra privy to many of the Mafia deals. And Mob deals include that art of assassination known as killing for money. If Sinatra had married Marilyn Monroe just a few days before her death on 3 August 1962 then she may have lived through her ordeal. However, she didn't marry Sinatra and so died, as many believe, on orders from the CIA.

The CIA, FBI and other organisations were all afraid of the knowledge that Marilyn had of their business dealings. Having slept with both Jack and Bobby Kennedy, she had listened to many hours' worth of pillow talk; and that kind of talk can be dangerous. She had to die. Her death was arranged by her close friend Sam Giancana, with orders coming from the CIA. The Mob, it is believed, often handled dirty business for the government.

The trouble between Giancana and the Kennedys really began when J.F. Kennedy was elected president. When father Joe Kennedy saw his son Jack and family safely installed in the White House and his other son Bobby made Attorney General, he changed his deal with the Mob. In fact, he cancelled it altogether.

Giancana actually visited Jack Kennedy in the White House to try to get him to honour his father's debt, but it didn't work. Giancana was barred from ever again visiting Jack Kennedy.

The result was that father Joe persuaded son Bobby to set up a task force and to go after organised crime in a big way. This he would soon regret, since the Mafia are all about honour of a kind. It means that you don't back down from arrangements made in an honourable way, and Giancana was of the old school and an 'honourable man'.

So it was Jack Kennedy who paid the price for his father's double-dealing when he was shot and killed in Dallas on 22 November 1963. Although there have been many theories about the killing, this author believes that Lee Harvey Oswald was telling the truth when he proclaimed that he was a patsy. He was set up by Sam Giancana, who not only wanted to settle a private score but was also paid by people within the US government who wanted to see a different president in the White House: one with a different attitude towards the Russians and Cuba.

But even this didn't change the attitude of Joe Kennedy. He asked Bobby Kennedy to get Giancana and all of his Mob friends. The problem, in those days, was that a close friend of Giancana was probably also a close friend of Joe Kennedy, since Joe had dealt in bootleg gin in the old days of Prohibition alongside the Chicago mobsters.

It was at this time that Frank Sinatra was barred from visiting the White House. Being a close pal of Giancana's, however, made him a go-between for trying to reach some kind of a deal with the Kennedys. It didn't work, and in 1968 Bobby Kennedy was also killed. Some say that it was Giancana who ordered the hit.

Giancana was later to die at the hands of his own people, the Chicago Mob. So, as with many of the Krays' old Mob pals, they all ended up with a bullet in the head. All, that is, with the exception of Frank Sinatra.

The Krays first had dealings with the US Mafia when they helped to 'protect' a gambling club in London belonging to Angelo Bruno, the Mob boss of Philadelphia as well as that indelible den of iniquity known as Atlantic City. This had always been prime real estate for the Mob, even rivalling Las Vegas. The big difference, of course, is that all Mafia families are welcome in Las Vegas, whereas only one family ran Atlantic City. Things have changed slightly in recent years, but not enough to bother the current Philadelphia 'boss'.

Bruno sat on the *Commissione* together with Sam Giancana, Vito Genovese and other top-flight Mob bosses. It was an organisation put together by the entire US Mob to sort out any difficulties that might occur with regard to territories or rights or such. Mob business had strict boundaries then; it still does now.

Through Bruno the Krays had got to meet Sinatra and began acting as bodyguards for other visiting US celebrities. By the early 1960s the Mafia, with the Krays' help, were firmly entrenched in London.

Bruno was such a top *capo* that he shared bodyguards with Sinatra, one such man being Eddie Pucci, the giant American ex-football player and good friend of the Krays. Pucci was always with Sinatra when he visited the UK, and he also accompanied many other top US stars when they visited Britain.

It was probably Angelo Bruno who involved the Krays in the most lucrative venture that they were ever to undertake – selling stolen US bearer bonds on the European financial markets.

With Bobby Kennedy hot on the trail of the Mob in the summer of 1965, stolen negotiable bearer bonds to the value of some $2 million were burning a hole in safety deposit boxes and other safe places all over the USA. They had been stolen from security deposits by pals of the Mob, for a price, and they were ready for sale. The only problem was that they were too hot to sell in the USA.

The solution was to negotiate their sale in Europe, using the Krays as go-betweens. The deal was simple: the Mob gave the Krays the bonds, the Krays sold them and kept half the money for their trouble. They had to cover their own costs, however.

Ron and Reg could look forward to becoming millionaires on this one deal alone. It was simple, quick and clever, but they weren't clever enough to handle it themselves; they needed help.

The man they chose was Ron's personal business manager, Leslie Payne, and in July 1965 he took a flight to Montreal, Canada to do the first trial run with the Mob boss of that city, Don Ceville. It was only a small amount of bonds, to the tune of some £25,000 or so, but it was the start of the big time for the Krays. Payne collected the bonds with all their certificates of origin and smuggled them back into the UK in his briefcase, just like a pack of sandwiches.

Ron and Reg were pleased with the deal. It had worked just as the Mafia had said it would, but there were problems with the rest of the securities: they had no paperwork. Certificates of origin were necessary if these bearer bonds were to be sold openly, just like the real thing.

The man chosen to handle these forgeries was an American banker known as A.B. Cooper. Cooper had a small private bank in the City of London; a private bank for private business. Exactly how he was recommended to the Krays is somewhat unclear, but he appeared, to Ron at least, to be the right man for the job. As usual, it didn't matter what his brothers Reg and Charlie thought about the matter, 'The Colonel' was always right.

Cooper was a man of mystery, someone who had apartments everywhere, including London and Geneva. He spoke with an anglicised accent, was almost bald and stuttered badly, especially when under pressure. He had a Rolls-Royce and spent money like there was no tomorrow. He even had a dog. But Cooper's credentials pleased Ron. He said that he had been involved in gold smuggling, weapons deals and money laundering. To Ron he was the perfect choice.

Cooper explained that forging the certificates of origin was no problem at all, but they would have to be sold throughout Europe without setting up a regular supply source. These could be traced, he explained to Ron and Reg, so couriers should be used to carry the bearer bonds to their ultimate destination. These destinations were the major banks and exchanges in mainland Europe.

The twins chose their brother Charlie to be the chief courier, much to the annoyance of Leslie Payne, who had done the first pick-up in Canada, but he had to toe the line, just like all the others in the Firm.

In August, news reached the twins that more bonds were gathering dust in Montreal and the Mafia required collection immediately. The news had come from Gordon Andersen, an old friend of Charlie's. Andersen had certain business dealings with the Mafia boss of Montreal, Don Ceville. He dealt in insurance.

The others selected for the trip to Montreal were: Charlie Mitchell, a bookmaker; Bobby McKew, a printer; and Leslie Payne, Ron's business manager. Payne had been there before and could easily recognise the Mafia boss Don Ceville. Anyway, the Krays thought that Payne not being there would appear a little suspicious. They didn't want anything to upset their plans.

The trip was set for early September and the twins asked their brother Charlie to bring the bonds back into the UK in his briefcase, just like any other businessman. Charlie was looking forward to visiting Canada, so he agreed.

At the airport they ran into a party of Bunny Girls, who were being trained for work in the newly opened Playboy Club on London's Park Lane. The girls were surrounded by reporters and cameramen and Charlie thought at first that the press posse was there for him and that they were all being arrested, but he soon realised his mistake and settled down on the flight to Canada in the company of these gorgeous girls. What a sacrifice to make. The trip was uneventful and the party consumed a lot of booze, as usual. Soon they arrived in Montreal, fresh from their journey and in good humour.

What awaited them in Montreal, however, was anything but good news. They were arrested the moment they stepped off the plane. Surrounded by red-coated Royal Canadian Mounted Police they were taken individually by car to the 'Tombs', Montreal's top-flight prison.

They were told nothing but to leave their belongings in paper bags, for collection (maybe) later. Charlie, Gordon Andersen, Charlie Mitchell and Payne were all put behind bars. Charlie speculated as to the reasons for their arrest but he couldn't figure it out. After all, they had only just arrived. They all spent a long and frightening night in the 'Tombs'.

The next day they were all dragged into court, but the Mafia *capo* had sent them a lawyer who argued their case. Gordon Andersen had actually seen Don Ceville at the airport, while they were being arrested, so Ceville was fully aware of the precarious situation. The lawyer did her job well, and it was agreed that the party would be deported. Again flanked by the Royal Canadian Mounted Police, they were taken back to the airport and put on the first flight back to London. It was a sorry and humiliating story to tell, one of deceit, confusion and ultimately evasion, but they were all really quite relieved when they were deported. Charlie, in particular, could imagine spending the rest of his life in that cell, so being thrown out of Canada wasn't such a bad option. The only problem with the whole affair, as far as he was concerned, was that he would have to explain the entire debacle to the twins.

Back in London, the Krays held a meeting to determine what had gone wrong and who had squealed to the police. But they couldn't reason it out. Charlie thought that Mitchell had set the whole thing up to try to get the bond business for himself, but no one could be sure. In the end, it didn't really matter as, a few days later, Don Ceville took a flight from Montreal to London Heathrow and delivered the bonds personally to Ron and Reg. He had no trouble getting into the UK. It was just a formality.

The Krays were in business and, for several months during 1965 and 1966, Charlie travelled throughout Europe, collecting and delivering instantly negotiable bearer bonds for and on behalf of the US Mafia. He got to know Geneva quite well, so too Hamburg, where the banking facilities came in handy. It was all conducted legally through the official banking system and the money arrived back in London at Cooper's bank, ready for the twins. Half went back to the USA through Gordon Andersen and the Krays kept the other half for their trouble. As Charlie always said: 'It was no trouble at all.'

After the Canadian trip, Charlie Mitchell went back to his money lending and bookmaking business until he was shot dead at his Costa del Sol home. The murderer was never found. Bobby McKew inherited a fortune and settled in South Africa, well away from the Krays and their impending trouble with the law, while Gordon Andersen continued in the insurance game and acting as coordinator with the US Mob. None of these men was ever tried for these crimes. In fact, none of the Krays was ever convicted of dealing in stolen bearer bonds.

One fortunate outcome of the ridiculous Canadian adventure was the simple fact that the Mafia in the USA and Canada knew that they couldn't rely on the Krays coming to collect the bearer bonds. So the Mob was forced to set up safe routes to Europe in order to deliver the bonds in person to Charlie. Because of this, Charlie was the only one of the Kray brothers to deal man to man with some of the biggest names in the history of the Mafia. The chosen routes were to Paris, Hamburg, Geneva, Amsterdam and Frankfurt. For Charlie life was a merry-go-round, full of leisure and luxury, all paid for by the US Mafia. These men from the USA really knew how to live: the best hotels, the best women that money could buy and the best champagne.

One particular occasion, though, was to become a nightmare for Charlie, one that he would never forget, even after many years in jail with only his memories for company. This was the time he had to burn $250,000 of instantly negotiable bearer bonds in a dustbin at his mother Violet's home at Vallance Road.

It was November 1965 when Charlie received a phone call from Reg informing him that there were bearer bonds to be collected in Paris. Charlie quickly drove to his mother's house for the meeting, in eager anticipation of the trip. Greetings over, they settled down to business and Reg laid out the plan. Charlie, together with Leslie Payne and accountant Freddie Gore, would take the flight to Paris, stay at Le Claridge Hotel on the Champs-Élysées, meet their Mafia contacts, collect the bonds and then smuggle them back into the UK. It was simple enough, they thought. How could anyone mess it up? And with Freddie Gore bringing them back in his briefcase they would have enough criminal evidence on Gore to make sure he kept his mouth shut.

The three men travelled to Paris as planned. There were no problems on the outward trip; after all, it was beginning to become routine. They all knew what they were expected to do and all had agreed the plan.

The meeting with the two 'wise guys' (American slang for Mafia) went ahead as described by Reg back at Vallance Road; there were no mistakes and the bonds were delivered in a plastic carrier bag. The men then all went out on the town, from Pigalle to Montmartre and from the Étoile to St Germain, with money being no object for any of them. The twins were paying.

Charlie hid the bonds behind a wardrobe in his room and didn't even bother to look at them. He was sure it would be the normal $25–50,000 worth of bonds, so no need to make a fuss. They all enjoyed their late evening and early morning in Paris.

The following day Charlie got dressed and checked out the bonds. To his amazement there was $250,000 worth, much more than normal – and to think he had left them stuffed behind a wardrobe all night. He quickly went down the main stairway to the dining room to meet the others for breakfast, taking the bonds with him in a carrier bag.

'These are yours,' he said to the accountant Freddie Gore, as he handed over the bonds. He was pleased to get rid of them, as having a lot of money had always been a problem for Charlie; he didn't know how to handle it.

Gore looked at the carrier bag and asked how much there was in securities. He was startled at Charlie's reply.

'What?!' he exclaimed at the top of his voice. 'How much did you say?' he continued in a whisper, when he noticed that everyone in the dining room was looking at him.

'I told you,' said Charlie, quietly and soberly. 'There is $250,000 in instantly negotiable bearer bonds.'

Leslie Payne's eyes lit up. This was indeed a windfall. Ron and Reg would be pleased and maybe there would be something extra in it for him. He smiled and continued his breakfast with a grin on his face.

'I can't do it,' said Freddie Gore. 'I can't smuggle that back to

London,' he pleaded. But the others weren't in the mood for bargaining. It had all been agreed back in Bethnal Green and neither Charlie nor Payne wanted to change Reggie's plan.

Ultimately Charlie knew that Gore could spoil the whole deal, so he asked Payne to take the bonds. He flatly refused. That was not in his orders; only Reg could ask him to do that. Charlie had no choice but to stuff the bonds into his own bag in order to get them home to England and into the waiting hands of his brothers. But first he had to get back home.

The taxi drive out to the airport was like visiting a graveyard. It was absolutely silent, not a sound from any of them. Gore was sweating profusely, as he knew his cowardice would be reported when they got home, and Payne sat quietly, not wanting to take responsibility for anything. After all, it wasn't he who was in charge of the party; it was Charlie. Payne was still annoyed about not being put in charge after the first trip to see Don Ceville in Montreal.

They were soon on the plane and heading home. Charlie kept to himself and consumed even more champagne than usual. Now, that is not easy on a short trip like this, but as usual he was good at his work and the time passed easily. When the plane eventually landed he only had a short walk with his overnight bag before he was out of the airport and then he would just have the taxi drive home.

He was, of course, stopped at the customs desk.

'Anything to declare?' asked the customs man. What a question for a man carrying £250,000 in stolen instantly negotiable bearer bonds, all without certification.

'Nothing,' said Charlie. 'If you don't believe me then take a look,' he said, opening his bag. 'There's only dirty laundry.'

The customs man had just come on duty and regarded Charlie's statement as simple proof of innocence.

'OK,' he said with a grin, and Charlie was on his way.

Some distance behind him followed Leslie Payne and Freddie Gore, Laurel and Hardy to the Firm; they walked straight through the customs check with ease, but then they didn't have anything to hide. Just to be careful, they kept their distance from Charlie and took a separate taxi back to the East End.

Once home, Charlie looked for a suitable hiding place for the bonds and he quickly found it behind a loose panel in his bathroom. That night he slept well but was woken by the sound of the telephone ringing. On the other end of the line was one of the Mafia guys he had met in Paris just a few days earlier.

'They are too hot, Charlie,' said the man. 'You had better get rid of them as fast as you can.' The urgency in the man's voice told Charlie that it was real and not just a bad dream.

Charlie's way out was to burn the 'hot' bonds in a dustbin in his mother's back yard. He counted them one by one as he threw them into the bin. 'One thousand, two thousand' – it never ended. To Charlie it was as though he was throwing his life away, or at least part of it. He cried. Not even a cup of tea helped the situation.

Despite this incident, the Mafia were true to their word and continued to bring over small carrier bags that they exchanged for large amounts of cash. The business was good and the twins made a lot of East End dosh out of the deal.

After the George Cornell killing in March of 1966, the Mafia began to have second thoughts about using the Krays as collaborators in the bearer bond deals. They were actively looking around, searching for new partners. They were actually considering setting up operations themselves, even though Europe was far from their home base in the USA. There was also a kind of protocol and respect to observe with regard to the Sicilian Mafia who rather regarded France, Switzerland, Germany and Holland as their own restricted territory. As is common with our European partners, the UK was regarded as a special case.

Some limited amounts of bearer bonds came through normal channels during the summer of 1966 and the early part of the following year, but by the end of 1967 the flow of dollar bonds had all but dried up completely.

In order to resume business with the Mob, Ron decided that a trip to New York was necessary. The bonds represented good money to the Krays and he hoped to meet with the *capos* to repair otherwise strained relationships. Ron wanted them both to go to New York in the spring of 1968, but he also added that it didn't matter too much if Reg decided not to go. He would just go by himself to meet the illustrious bosses of American organised crime.

Reg couldn't believe what he was hearing.

'It's a trap,' he said. 'You can't do it. We have prison records and we won't get visas.' Reg was adamant that it was all pie in the sky, but Ron wasn't finished.

A.B. Cooper had already suggested to Ron that the prospect of going to New York was not as far-fetched as many would imagine. He said that he had contacts at the US Embassy in Paris who could arrange the necessary documentation. Cooper would take care of all the paperwork – passports, visas and tickets; all Ron had to do was to sit back and enjoy the trip. Cooper said he would even arrange high-level meetings with the top Mob bosses in New York. Ron had nothing to lose and everything to gain, according to Cooper.

'If I want to go to New York, then I'll fucking go to New York,' was Ron's reply to his twin brother. Discussion over!

The argument in their flat at Braithwaite House, Shoreditch, had lasted long enough for both men, and walls have ears, so once again Ron had made a crucial decision. It was one, he thought, that would change his life forever and, in a way, it did just that.

Reg stayed on at his parents' flat while Ron returned to his country retreat, known as The Brooks, in Suffolk. His parents, Violet and old man Charlie, were staying in the Lodge House for the weekend so he would soon be able to tell them both the good news. Their little boy was going to America!

It was all set. At the beginning of April 1968 Ron Kray, the underworld boss of London, was heading for New York for what he was sure would be a historical meeting with Mob bosses. With him were the banker A.B. Cooper and an old army friend of Ron's called Dickie Morgan, who was good fun for Ron to have around as he made him laugh.

The trio flew from Heathrow over to Orly Airport, on the outskirts of Paris, and took a cab to the Frontenac Hotel, just off the Champs-Élysées. It was an uneventful flight, with the normal light conversation. Soon they were unpacking in their rooms.

Cooper told Ron that it was too late to go to the US Embassy that evening so he suggested that they all go and have dinner with an old friend, who spoke perfect English and had many contacts in the criminal world. Ron was pleased to meet someone – anyone. It was a convivial way of passing the time in Paris, and Ron was always interested in new ideas.

The evening went well with Ron and the Frenchman doing most of the talking. Soon they were back at the Frontenac and ready for a nightcap. Ron was not tired, but he was keen to be in good shape for the trip to the embassy so they all retired early that night.

The following morning was D-Day; it was now or never for Ron to find out whether or not he could gain admission to the United States of America. Cooper was sure that he could arrange it, but Ron wasn't so sure. Even if he couldn't get a visa he was still having a holiday and the expense wouldn't break the bank. It was a no-lose situation for Ron.

They took a cab from the hotel and drove directly to the US Embassy. The driver pulled up outside and the three men got out and started walking up the steps.

'Impressive, aren't they?' said Cooper, referring to the uniformed US Marines standing guard outside.

Ron was more interested in their ceremonial swords. In fact, he stopped for a moment to inspect the troops, much to the dismay of his companions. The inspection over, a smiling Ron entered the building with Cooper leading the way. After Ron came the jovial Dickie Morgan. To Morgan it was all a laugh, so he took everything in his stride and played follow my leader.

Cooper led the way through the corridors, finally coming to a stop at an unmarked door. He didn't knock, just walked straight in. At a desk sat a lone woman, who didn't appear to be expecting them.

'I've come to collect some visas,' he told the woman, who was eating a sandwich. 'For my two friends here,' he added, pointing over to Ron and Morgan.

She began to argue that it wasn't possible to issue visas right away and that if they had been ordered in advance then they were not ready so they could come back in the morning. This didn't please Cooper, who began telling all sorts of stories about sick relations in the USA and how important it was that the three men get to New York as soon as possible.

It worked, and within half an hour the visas were issued. Ron was overjoyed and Morgan had something to look forward to too, a visit to the USA. A.B. Cooper could breathe a sigh of relief. They partied the night away in celebration, but first Ron had to make a phone call back home to tell his brother Reg that Cooper had succeeded in getting the visas, just to gloat a little. Reg told him again that it was a set-up, but his younger twin didn't believe him. Even if it was, he thought he could control it.

The next day was one full of bright hopes for new beginnings with the US Mafia and Ron asked Cooper for the details of meetings that Cooper had said he had already arranged. Highest on Ron's list was meeting Meyer Lansky, who had set up the Colony Club with Ron's pal George Raft as chairman. But Ron already felt he had won; he was on his way to the USA, to New York, and to places that he had only previously been able to dream about. Already he had beaten the system.

'We are meeting Little Joe Kaufman at JFK Airport,' said Cooper. 'He has arranged hotel rooms and will be taking you to meet the *capos*, Ron.'

Cooper was feeling smug, since he had done what, to many, was the impossible: he had arranged for a convicted felon to get a visa for the USA. No one could take that away from him, and it would do his prestige in the UK a lot of good.

Joe Kaufman and his wife Marie were very good friends of Charlie Kray and his wife Dolly and they had even spent some holiday time together in Spain. Kaufman had often been to London on business for the Mafia, who used him as a courier for bonds and also for passing on messages, so Ron had met him on many occasions. Kaufman was to be trusted and Ron was pleased to be meeting with an old friend.

Ron's mind began to wander as they neared the USA. He had already met Tony 'Ducks' Corallo, a top lieutenant in the Lucchese family from Brooklyn, when he was over in London scouting for locations for new clubs. Maybe he would be on Kaufman's list. Then there was Lansky, a very important fish to Ron since he had connections everywhere within the Mafia, even in Las Vegas, which he had helped Bugsy Siegel set up as the gambling Mecca of the USA. Then, of course, there was his old pal Angelo Bruno, the Philadelphia godfather who also ran Atlantic City. He was surely high on the list too. And, of course, there were all the celebrities that he had met in London, sent over by his good buddy Eddie Pucci. Whoever he would meet in New York, Ron knew that it was the new start that he so eagerly wanted.

It was probably fortunate for Ron that he didn't know what had happened between his brother Charlie and Tony 'Ducks' Corallo back in London only a few months earlier. I am sure Ron was never told about the incident, but I see no reason for leaving this small detail out of the story. When Corallo was in London he told Charlie that he had a small present with him from his boss in Brooklyn. Charlie was in a good mood and, in a somewhat patronising way, told the man that the twins only wanted their friendship, not gifts, so Tony 'Ducks' Corallo never gave Charlie the present. He took it back with him to the USA. Oh, the present, you ask? Well . . . it was a suitcase full of money, some $50,000. What a proper Charlie! When it came to making stupid mistakes Charlie made them big time!

But this little event didn't even occur to Ron as the plane came in to land at JFK Airport, since he didn't even know about it.

'Now, don't say too much going through immigration,' Cooper warned his fellow travellers. Ron and Morgan nodded; they wouldn't have known what to say anyway.

The plane landed, and the group disembarked and strode through immigration as if they owned the place. The only question Ron was asked was if he could support himself and a quick flash of rolled up dollar bills soon showed the immigration officer that he most certainly could take care of himself, even in a place like New York.

'It was all fixed,' said Cooper to his friends. 'The Mob had planned it that way.' Whether this was true or not, Ron didn't worry about it. He had arrived in New York City and that was all that mattered. He had won the game and now he thought he would make history.

Little Joe Kaufman met them at the airport, just as Cooper had said he would, and they all headed east towards Manhattan in

Joe's luxury limousine. The trip to the Warwick Hotel was noisy to say the least, but Ron was enjoying every minute. He loved the pace of the city; he took in all the sights and the smells of the city streets. He felt comfortable.

The visas were for a seven-day stay and the first night they spent with Joe and his wife Marie. It was an informal dinner at an exclusive restaurant, mainly 'wise guys'. It was a place to make connections; Kaufman was a regular and therefore treated with respect, which impressed Ron. Joe was chatty and gave Ron a message from Angelo Bruno. Bruno couldn't make it up to New York but would be pleased to see Ron in Philadelphia or Atlantic City if he had the time. Ron was pleased to hear from the Philadelphia godfather so soon after his arrival. Everything was looking good and Ron started to relax, feeling that he was in the right place at the right time.

'I'm trying to get hold of a good contact I have in the Colombo family', said Joe. 'It's a little difficult, but I should be able to reach him by tomorrow.'

Ron ordered another drink. There was no need to thank 'Little Joe'. After all, it was only business.

The following day Joe phoned Ron to tell him that he had set up a meeting with Frank Illiano, a lieutenant in the Colombo family, somewhere in Brooklyn. Ron wasn't bothered where it was, just as long as he got to meet a Mob boss. Kaufman was as good as his word; he had managed to succeed where Cooper had failed. In fact Ron and Morgan hadn't seen much of Cooper after that first evening out with Joe. He told Ron that he was trying to reach contacts, but he apparently hadn't been very successful. Ron didn't care; he would soon be discussing big business with the Mob and that was the main point of his being there.

It was on the second day that Joe collected Ron from the Warwick Hotel and drove out, along Fifth Avenue, towards Brooklyn. Morgan was sent on a shopping spree along with some of Ron's dollar bills so he couldn't overhear what was said in the car or at the meeting. On the way the two men chatted about the Gallo brothers, Joe's friends in the Mob and the people who had arranged for the meeting at a house in President Street, a sleepy area of Brooklyn. 'Crazy' Joe Gallo was a feared gangster of the old school, having gotten his 'button' (American slang for killing someone) many years earlier. The other brothers were just as dangerous, but Larry and Al Gallo didn't have the reputation that their brother enjoyed throughout the USA.

The meeting at President Street, near Prospect Park, started a little coolly for Ron. He was asked to wait until his credentials were checked out with Angelo Bruno and this took some time. He had to wait in silence as the Mob went about their business; this was not easy for a man like Ron Kray but he did his best and after a while the Mob boss appeared. He was in good humour, since Bruno had spoken highly of Ron. It is always good to have friends in high places.

Discussions started almost immediately. Their talks covered almost every aspect of Mob business, from protection to prostitution, from drugs to murder and from stolen bearer bonds to gambling. They discussed virtually everything and built a friendship of sorts. Even the Gallo brothers relaxed and gave advice to Ron on setting up Murder Inc, which will be examined in a later chapter.

Over the next few days Ron had many meetings with Frank 'Punchy' Illiano and 'Crazy' Joe Gallo at various locations in New York, so there was even some sightseeing included. Things were going well, until Frank Illiano sprung a bit of a surprise on Ron.

'You are being followed by the FBI,' he told Ron. Ron just couldn't believe it, but he knew that the Mob had their way of knowing these things. But why would they be following him, he had only just arrived in the country? Frank Illiano read his mind. 'They must have had a tip-off,' he said quietly.

Morgan had previously said to Ron that he thought they were being followed, but Ron didn't want to believe him. Now he knew it to be true. But the Gallos had arranged the meetings in secret, in order to throw off any FBI tail, so Ron could meet with Frank Illiano in the peace and quiet of New York's Little Italy. He enjoyed the food and the chat; everything was just fine.

Ron and Morgan had lunch with Rocky Graziano and Tony Zale in Greenwich Village and they both enjoyed the company of these boxing champions. They met other friends and associates the Krays had done business with back in London, but they couldn't get to meet Meyer Lansky. Lansky didn't want to be seen in the company of Ron as he knew all about the FBI tail, but he did pass on his best wishes through Joe Kaufman. Tony 'Ducks' Corallo also had to bow out for the same reason. Ron was just too hot to handle, not unlike his life in the East End of London.

Cooper was still a scarce commodity, always proclaiming that he was working on his contacts, but continually with the same lack of results. 'He's stuttering more and more,' said Morgan. 'What's he got to be nervous about?'

Ron had already been successful in his own eyes; he had met and had in-depth discussions with a top Mob boss. The rest of his stay was party time and he enjoyed it all with his old and new pals.

The Murder Incorporated system intrigued Ron. He learned all about *Omertà*, the Mafia's code of silence, and about the idea of putting as many people as possible between you and where the action was to take place. This would mean giving verbal orders to one associate, who would then pass them on to another and so on, ad infinitum. This is the buffer system used by the Mob to distance themselves from events, particularly killings. Ron, however, was always a 'hands on' kind of person; he loved getting his hands on a knife, a sword, a gun, a machine gun or any other type of weapon. It was difficult for him to understand how he could build up respect in this way. It worked for the Americans, but could it work in London?

One evening Ron phoned Reg back in England. He told him of the meetings with the Colombo family and about drinking with old pals; he left nothing out. Reg was pleased for his brother, but then asked about Cooper. Ron told him straight that he hadn't seen much of Cooper but that it didn't matter since he had achieved so much in such a short time. He had beaten everyone, even the system, he told him.

'That reminds me,' said Reg. '"Nipper"'s looking all over for you.' He was referring to 'Nipper' Read of Scotland Yard who was working overtime, back in the UK, trying to collect evidence against the Krays. It was unusual for Ron to be out of the news and Read was getting anxious. Ron was delighted.

Ron's pièce de résistance, though, was the news that Kaufman had managed to do a deal on more bearer bonds so the lucrative bond business could be started again straight away. This was indeed good news for Reg as it made the whole affair worthwhile.

The rest of the trip passed with partying and sightseeing with the Mob. Ron had truly achieved everything he had set out to do but, noticeably, without the help of A.B. Cooper. Ron was beginning to have serious doubts about the man who had worked the visa deal so sweetly. Could there be another reason behind these events and, if there was, what? His only regret was not being able to meet with Lansky.

Back home in the UK, Ron was treated like a king in the East End. It was party time all over again for the returning hero. Once again Cooper did his vanishing trick and made like a tree – he went straight on to Paris. Reg wasn't surprised. In fact he was pleased, since he didn't really want the man around. Cooper had a knack of spoiling Reg's fun.

Reg was pleased to get one particular message through Ron from the Gallos. Ron had promised to pass it on, even though he didn't fully understand it. Reg explains it this way:

'When Ron went to New York, he met "Punchy" Illiano, who was an ex-fighter and a friend of Joe, Al and Laurie Gallo, the Mafia people of New York. Ron, out of curiosity, asked Punchy how many brothers there were in the family of the Gallos and Punchy said that there was Al, Laurie, Joe and me [Reggie]. I thought this was very profound because in a way Punchy was including me in the family and that was a good sign of friendship.'

Shortly after Ron returned to London the Krays were all arrested. On 9 May 1968, 'Nipper' Read sprang his trap and caught them all, but he didn't get the proof he needed until much later. But with the twins behind bars the rats started to leave the sinking ship and, one by one, they began to sing.

The Krays never had a chance of putting Murder Inc. into practice and they never received any more of the bearer bonds from the Mob. Kaufman did come over to the UK with $25,000 of stolen bearer bonds for delivery to Cooper, but he was arrested with them on him, so no new deals went through. The twins, however, never knew about the bonds; it was supposed to be a secret deal with the banker.

The involvement of A.B. Cooper has always been a little convoluted. At the trial he admitted that he was working for the FBI and US Treasury Department and he certainly did pass on information to Du Rose, Read's boss at Scotland Yard. But he also contrived to kill people and it was only due to the stupidity of some of the chosen assassins that he was never accused of murder. In fact the visa office at the US Embassy in Paris turned out to be the head office of the FBI's European Division, so it is no wonder there was no sign on the door.

The Krays came so close to setting up a Mafia-style operation in the UK but in the end it was their own code that let them down. They wanted the world to see them as untouchable kings of crime, but it was 'Nipper' Read who delivered the winning punch and knocked them out cold, for 30 years.

Read's was an outrageous gamble, but it paid off. With the Krays behind bars people started talking and soon Scotland Yard had enough on the twins to put them away. There would be no more trips to the USA for the twins, no more visits by Mob gangsters to see their pals the Krays in the UK, no more bearer bonds to launder for the Mob – or would there?

In the end the Krays will only be known as home-grown British gangsters but they came so close to being mobsters on a big scale, with business operations on both sides of the Atlantic. With only a little more care and attention to detail, they could have made it. As it happened, they had to do their own killing (or at least some of it) and so they became victims of their own foolish sense of pride. No one has come close to emanating the Krays. Perhaps no one ever will.

It wasn't only the Krays who were good at killing. The US Mafia also showed a flair for a dramatic murder or two.

The top Mafia bosses who did business with the Krays mostly met with untimely deaths, usually with a bullet in the head. It was commonplace then, as it is now. You don't retire, you get retired!

One of the best Mafia friends that the Krays had was Angelo

Bruno. As a member of the US Mafia's *Commissione* he was a man of power, along with the other bosses Sam Giancana and Vito Genovese. It was Bruno who first used the Krays in London to act as minders for his casinos and clubs. It was Bruno, too, who was instrumental in getting the Krays hired to protect US singers and performers when they toured the UK. It was no coincidence that he shared bodyguards with Frank Sinatra, and it was probably Bruno who suggested the Krays when the Mob in New York needed to get rid of their stolen bearer bonds.

Bruno was to end his days with a shotgun blast to the back of his head while sitting in his car in a Philadelphia suburb. The boss of Atlantic City, which includes Philadelphia (as far as the Mafia were concerned anyway), was a powerful man. Bruno is no more, but the family survives.

On 6 November 1997, three men were arrested outside a City of London bank. They had been in talks with the bank regarding a loan that they wanted, which was to be guaranteed by $800 million of US treasury bonds that they had in their possession. One of the men was from Taiwan, one was from the USA and one was English.

They were caught by a team from Scotland Yard who were working closely with a US secret service agent based in London. The bonds were believed to be forgeries. Money fraud is a high-priority crime with all major police forces around the world, where borrowing is used to fund drugs and money-laundering businesses. Used as collateral these loans provide a much-wanted source of cash. It would appear that money laundering, as practised by the Krays, has not stopped. It still flourishes here, today, in the City of London.

Another Kray pal was the Canadian Mafia boss, Don Ceville. He was the first person that Leslie Payne went to see in Canada regarding the importation and negotiation of stolen US bearer bonds. Like his friend Angelo Bruno, Ceville ended his days with a bullet in the head. His body was finally found some years ago buried in a peat bog, just a short distance outside his beloved Montreal.

Even 'Crazy' Joe Gallo and his boss Joseph Colombo ended up with holes in their heads in 1976, while Tony 'Ducks' Corallo got away with 99 years in Leavenworth Prison.

Eddie Pucci, Bruno's right-hand man and bodyguard to Frank Sinatra himself, was shot and killed on a golf course in Chicago shortly after the Krays were arrested by 'Nipper' Read.

The killings continue to this day as, one by one, the old guard are replaced by the young pretenders. The fact is, though, that they don't pretend any more.

Even Sam Giancana was shot and killed by a pal while cooking his favourite meal. Nothing is sacred to the Mafia!

All of this happened a long while ago, but what about the present? On 20 January 2011, in the early hours of the morning, the authorities in the US acted swiftly and decisively when they arrested one hundred and twenty-seven people, all of whom, they say, belong to the five major New York Mafia families, including some in New Jersey and New England, including Boston. It took them 30 years to decide on this action, and only when they were 100 per cent ready did they act. I certainly hope the American taxpayers appreciate all of that effort.

With so much money at their disposal, however, the Mob families can afford to get the best lawyers available. At the time of writing, they had only been arrested, not convicted, and no one could say whether or not attorneys had been appointed by the defendants for their appearance in Federal Court.

Eric Holder, the US Attorney General, was pleased with the operation. In September 2010 he decided on a change of approach with regard to the Mafia when he redirected his efforts in the fight against organised crime. As a result he has merged the organised crime division with the gang unit of the Department of Justice to create a new weapon in his armoury, an elite group of prosecutors whose sole aim is to destroy the Mafia.

After the arrests he made a statement, following his journey from Washington D.C. to New York. 'Today's arrests mark an important and encouraging step forward in disrupting La Cosa Nostra's operations. But our battle against organised crime enterprises is far from over. This is an ongoing effort and it must and will remain a top priority.'

The indictments were for, among other things, gambling,

extortion, contraband cigarettes, loan sharking and fraudulent money transfers. It was straight out of *Goodfellas* – I am surprised that they didn't arrest Martin Scorsese, Ray Liotta, Joe Pesci and Robert de Niro. There were 16 different indictments in all, many of them filed in Brooklyn. Also included were illegal card games, arson and shakedowns in strip clubs – and the peddling of Ecstasy and cocaine.

Eric Holder had more to say, however, on these charges. 'Several of those charged were allegedly involved in classic Mob hits and senseless murders.' And these included, apparently, a 1981 double homicide in Queens, which appeared to have started after someone spilt a drink. 'Our goal is to eradicate these folks as menaces to this nation. How much time that is going to take I can't predict, but that is certainly the goal we have,' he said. Well, best of luck, Mr Holder.

More than 800 FBI and police officers were involved in this, the largest round-up of Mafia bosses and their soldiers in the history of the US. The arrests occurred in New York, Newark in New Jersey, in Providence on Rhode Island and in Boston, where those arrested included boss of the New England Mafia Luigi 'Baby Shacks' (or 'The Old Man' or 'The Professor') Manocchio, aged 83. But bosses of all five New York families were hit – the Bonanno, Colombo, Gambino, Genovese and Lucchese families were targeted and many arrests were made. All these families, through the years, have dealt with the Krays in London.

But it was the Colombo family who were hit hardest. In one raid they managed to capture almost the entire membership, including Andrew 'Mush' Russo, the family's alleged street boss, Benjamin 'Benji' (or 'The Claw' or 'The Fang') Castellazzo, its underboss, four captains and eight soldiers from the same family – and two reputed senior figures in the Gambino family. They even managed to arrest a couple of part-time crooks and two police officers who were trying to tip off the Mob with regards to upcoming raids on gambling dens.

Some of the unions were also in trouble, as several arrests were made of officials of the Longshoremen's Association, New Jersey division, and arrests were made on New York building sites, where mobsters were taken in for charges of targeting unions and businesses for extortion. The Genovese family was apparently involved in a long-standing dispute with the dock workers in New Jersey, who were again, apparently, forced to hand over some of their Christmas bonuses each year.

The information that was given out by the authorities made for interesting reading – it looked more like *The Godfather*, with Marlon Brando and James Caan strutting their stuff, than modern-day crime. With terms such as '*consigliere*' and 'underboss' this was straight out of the movies. But they also added that they still had a dangerous, deadly and resilient foe to defeat.

Janice Fedarcyk, Assistant Director in charge of the FBI's field office in New York, had the following to say: 'The notion that today's Mob families are more genteel and less violent than in the past is put to lie by the charges contained in the indictments unsealed today. Even more of a myth is the notion that the Mob is a thing of the past, that *La Cosa Nostra* is a shadow of its former self.'

Experts were quick to add to comments of the day. Some said that the Mafia had been severely weakened, while others said that the series of mass arrests were part of new tactics adopted by the police to counter organised crime. They said that this type of tactic was becoming increasingly popular. But maybe this was all intended for the media, the press, the television and the Internet, rather than being a means of bringing these people to justice. Those in power have used these particular tactics before – letting people see what is going on in an extraordinary and dynamic manner, even though it will not work in the long run – simply because there is an impending election. We will have to wait and see.

In recent years all the visible focus has been on the Russian and other Continental crime groups and this is still another priority of the Justice Department in its crackdown against organised crime. So just why the FBI and police were so interested in a bunch of old men is somewhat difficult to understand.

Jay Albanese, a Virginia Commonwealth University Professor, says: 'A lot of these people have already been out of business for a very, very long time.' He went on to say that 7,000 to 8,000 organised crime figures have been convicted on a national basis since the first major racketeering indictment against the Mob in 1985. He has also said that the tactics used by the FBI are designed to turn mobster against mobster – it is their secret weapon. 'You lock them up in different places and everyone is much more willing to cut a deal because their buddies have been arrested as well.' This is, of course, in direct contrast to what happened to the gangs in London, back in the 1960s, where the decision was made to lock up the gang leaders, the bosses, in the hope that other members of the gangs and key witnesses to murders and the like would eventually talk.

Among those taken into custody and charged in a Federal Court in Brooklyn were accused members of the New Jersey-based Decavalcante family, widely recognised as the inspiration for the television series *The Sopranos*. And Andrew 'Mush' Russo, mentioned earlier, reminded us again of *The Godfather* – but do the movies really tell us the true story?

Indictments against the Mafia have changed little in recent years. The *Cosa Nostra* is ruled by the *Commissione*, they say. Well, the Krays dealt with them through their old pal Angelo Bruno, many years ago – so no change there. Each crime family is headed by a boss, an underboss and an adviser, or *'consigliere'*. They, in turn, manage their crews bossed by a captain or *'capodecina'*. Members of these families are called 'goodfellas' or 'wise guys'. So, again, still the same structure that we know from the old gangster films.

Robert J. Castelli, a Republican New York State Assemblyman and former crime investigator, said the following, after the arrests: 'A lot of these guys are heavy hitters. The arrests are very significant. Is the *Cosa Nostra* gone because of this? Absolutely not. These people have the ability to change with the times. And that is the problem with combating the Mafia. Take the bosses into custody and new bosses will appear. The businesses survive and the game goes on. It is the same old world – only the names have changed.'

But now, maybe, we will get to know who bumped off that underworld boss, Joseph Scopo. He was killed back in 1993 while sitting in the passenger seat of a vehicle parked outside his house in Ozone Park, Queens, New York. There is much news yet to come out of this operation and it is a veritable writer's paradise.

And who would not want to write about Fred 'Whiney' Alesi, John 'Johnny Bandana' Brancaccio, Anthony 'Tony Bagels' Cavezza, Joseph 'Junior Lollipops' Carna, Vincent 'Vinny Carwash' Frogiero and Anthony 'Cheeks' (or'Firehawk' or 'Nighthawk') Licata? These, and many others, have the names to go with the crimes. Whether they did them or not, it makes for fantastic reading – and writing.

This may well be a good time to explain briefly who these New York families actually are. So here goes:

Gambino: Once run by the 'Teflon Don', John Gotti, this family works throughout the US and has been by far the most influential of New York's five families. But back in the 1990s the underboss Salvatore Gravano defected to the FBI, weakening the family and making it less effective.

Genovese: Under that famous Mob boss Lucky Luciano this family worked in Sicily, Italy and New York and had friends and associates all over the USA. A peculiarity of this family is that one of its bosses, Frank Costello, survived a hit and actually managed to die in his sleep at the age of 73.

Lucchese: This family operates in the East Harlem area of New York and in the Bronx. Previously led by Gaetano 'Three Fingers Brown' Lucchese, they have been a force to reckon with. But, like other families, they were damaged by one of their underbosses turning informant.

Bonano: Joseph Bonano ran guns for Al Capone, but the family is best known for the film *Donnie Brasco*, starring Al Pacino, Johnny Depp and Michael Madsen, in which an FBI agent managed to get the boss, Joseph Massino, to turn informer in 2004. It was all true – or as true as you get in the movies.

Colombo: Joseph Colombo gave his name to this family when he became boss in 1963. They worked closely with the Krays in London and the Gallo brothers were good friends of the Londoners. 'Crazy' Joe tried to start a war between the families back in the '60s and there have been many battles for control in recent years.

Modern-day tactics are to use phone taps and to take those people incriminated thereby into custody. The super-grasses used by the

FBI have done their job for the moment, but will it stick? The once sacred *Omertà* is no longer silent – this sacred vow of silence being no match, apparently, for a plea bargain. In England they used similar tactics with the Krays and the Richardsons, but with a different emphasis; when they put gang members behind bars the threat of violence against these people was removed. This was how the code of silence was broken and people began to talk, to reveal the truth. It was a case of 'not me Guv'!' all round.

And yet more comments are being heard from far and near. One blog I have seen recently said: 'America is regressing back to a form of wartime black market economy. With 43 million Americans on food stamps and at least 4 million people with no welfare support, organised groups like the Mafia are going to fill the void left by the US government. Think back to the '60s and '70s when certain Mafia families actually helped run food shelters in certain cities.'

This draws a direct comparison with post-war London, where rationing and the black market economy existed side by side. This was partially responsible for the rise of the Krays – so America, beware.

Another said simply: 'What about the gangsters on Wall Street and in the Capitol?' I certainly agree with that one. It isn't only the Mob bosses they should be arresting – they should also put their bankers behind bars. And doesn't it remind you of the Krays and their powerful friends in the world of politics, the police and money men?

So the situation in the US has not changed much since the Krays were doing their business with the Mob families. Only the individuals' names have changed – the business goes on. And there is something else that has not changed: how the stars come out in support of these people and their families.

Immediately after the 2011 arrests, James Caan, made famous by the '70s film *The Godfather*, came out in support of one of the alleged mobsters, Andy 'Mush' Russo. But then he has a good reason for this – Russo is godfather to Caan's son, Scott, who is currently starring in the television remake of *Hawaii Five-0*. Once again, we have a direct comparison with what happened in England when Reg Kray had a goddaughter in the actress Patsy

Kensit. History, it seems, has a way of repeating itself – the countries may be different but the events are the same.

In a letter read to the court, when Russo was trying unsuccessfully to get bail, Caan said: 'He is as good a friend as any person could ask for.' The now 70-year-old actor continued: 'I've known Andrew since 1972 and in all that time I have known him only as an unbelievable father, grandfather and great-grandfather.' And then he confirmed: 'I'd be willing to put up anything of personal value that the court would accept for bail. I would not hesitate a moment to fly in and be present if the court should so wish.'

Fine words, and I am sure they were meant sincerely. Why shouldn't he support a friend in need?

Another actor, Federico Castellucio, was actually present in court that day, sitting in the public gallery. When Russo saw him they waved to each other. He was used to all of this since he had appeared in *The Sopranos*. He, too, offered support for the ageing great-grandfather.

And yet again we see a recurrence of events from the other side of the pond where the Krays were always supported by their friends in the world of film and music: Roger Daltrey, Barbara Windsor, the Tom Robinson Band, Mike Tyson and many, many others. Frank Sinatra supported them, even after they were put behind bars, since he used their bodyguard business in London wherever he could. So Ron and Reg Kray continued to have their celebrity friends all the way through their 30-year sentences.

But when the prosecutors told the court that Russo had been in touch with all of his old pals, warning them against testifying, the magistrate, Cheryl Pollack, denied Russo bail, calling him 'a danger to the community'.

So, it is now 2011 and the saga continues. Will the FBI and the police win against their opponents, the Mafia? Or will new Mob bosses appear to take over the family business? And how many well-known people will come out in support of their old pals in the Mafia? Interesting.

6

TWINS RON AND REG KRAY

What decided me to get Ron away from Long Grove nut house in Epsom was some of the stories he told me about the place. One day he was sitting there eating an apple when this nutter came along and slapped him in the eye. Of course, Ron being Ron, he retaliated. Well, I ask you, just because he was eating an apple. The whole bloody place was full of nutters!

Reg Kray

One in every fifty people in the UK is a twin and approximately one third of these are identical twins. Society presupposes that twins are special, since it is a natural phenomenon that is inexplicable in academic terms in regard to why it actually happens. We know it occurs in humans as it does in animals, but we do not understand why. That makes it special. The Kray twins, therefore, by definition were indeed special, as their mother Violet always maintained throughout her life. The problem with the Krays, however, is that one of the twins, Ron, was a paranoid schizophrenic and a homosexual so these facts distort all academic research and bring us right back to basics. So what are twins?

Our knowledge of identical twins is very sparse. Because there aren't many twins available for research purposes, even though some recent television programmes have suggested otherwise, this tends to make investigation difficult. How can a researcher or investigator get a statistically viable sample to work with in order to enable substantial evaluation of the results?

Generally, the only matter scientists can agree on is their origin: how cells and genes divide to form two identical individuals, in outward appearance anyway, but still they don't know why. Immediately we have a problem. We see a set of twins, as in the case of Ron and Reg, but they are two very different people. They look the same, they behave the same and society tends to treat them the same. But the fact is, twins are individuals.

History has treated twins in many varied and interesting ways. Sometimes they have been regarded as cherished individuals; sometimes they have been hated. They have been considered as a godly apparition, but also as the personification of evil. They have been killed and discarded and they have been worshipped and pampered. The world of the twin can sometimes be a dangerous world indeed.

There are the stories of Castor and Pollux and Romulus and Remus from Roman mythology. Plautus used the mystery and secrecy of twins in his plays *Menaechmi* and *Amphitryon* and Shakespeare twice explored twin-ness in *Twelfth Night* and *The Comedy of Errors*. In more recent years Alexandre Dumas exploited this mysticism in *The Man in the Iron Mask* and Patrick White in *The Solid Mandala*. Even Bruce Chatwin wrote about a pair of farming twins in his Welsh novel *On the Black Hill*. So what is it about twins that supports and exemplifies this mysticism? To understand that, we must start at the beginning, by defining what twins are from a scientific viewpoint, and that means looking at the egg.

When the cell divides and becomes two individual new cells, the result is monozygotic twins. These are so-called identical twins, as if they were cloned. Ron and Reg, especially in their earlier years, before Ron's illness changed his features, were typical monozygotic twins. Often one is right-handed and one left-handed. One may be quiet and unassuming, the subordinate twin, the other the leader who makes up all the rules. It is not necessarily the elder twin who becomes the dominant of the two; in the case of Ron and Reg it was the younger, Ron, who was the stronger willed and dominated both their early childhood and later adolescence.

When the cell splits into two like cells, the genes are also divided, so each is a real copy of the other. The main difference is that chromosomes do not split; they simply go with one or other gene and therefore give different personality profiles to the twins. This cannot be seen from the outside, in the way of facial features, bone structure and such, but can be witnessed in behavioural patterns and mental ability. Reg was the organiser of the two, who liked everything in its place; logical and orderly. Ron, however, was the dreamer who looked at each day as a chance for fame and fortune; the adventurer. In Ron's case this was also accentuated by the fact that he was afflicted with schizophrenia. It was only later, when paranoia also set in, that his condition caused the whole family and the Firm much discomfort, since he became uncontrollable. Even his brother Reg, the control freak, could not control him. Not being able to go against his brother, he made the only decision that was possible for him: he joined him in his madness.

Science cannot tell us much about the illness that afflicted Ron, as far as his twin behaviour was concerned. His fits of extreme jubilation and deep depression did not reflect his twin-ness. He was a sick man and his brothers did all they could to protect him. Personally, I found Ron to be a very charming man who could tell a good story with a lot of wit; a man who knew he would never be free, even though he loved to talk about all the travelling he would do when he got out of Broadmoor. He was a true gent in the best East End traditions. He was also a mean killer who killed at least one man in his time, but history will probably forgive him his transgressions and put it all down to his paranoid schizophrenia, which so surely was the case. His story is a twin story, of goodness and badness, and of his own twin's efforts to help, no matter what.

When I first went to visit Ron in Broadmoor in 1992 I was a little reticent. I had heard all the stories about the twins and I was about to meet the mad one of the two. Charlie Kray had arranged for the meeting, where I was to talk to Ron about a possible future film on the Krays. The previous film, released in 1989 and called *The Krays*, had been a success and the twins were looking for more money, so I was called in to provide a plot.

The trip to Broadmoor was just like any other trip to Broadmoor, an area I knew well because I have family who live nearby. I hated the drive but I had promised to make the journey, so I felt obliged to keep the appointment. And that is what it was, an appointment to meet the most notorious gangster in the country.

Through the front office, through the maze of locked doors, conveniently opened for me by one of their over-sized guards, along the paths and through more doors and I was there in the meeting hall. It was not a nice place, a little old and shabby for my liking, but the pleasantness of the staff made up for all of that. Over at a table, along with some hospital friends and his wife Kate, sat Ron Kray. I approached the table and Ron stood up to greet me.

'Nice to meet you,' he said, slowly and kindly, as though he really meant it. Then he stared right through me with those intense deep-set eyes of his, as he reached out his hand in welcome. I had been warned about those eyes and I had been warned about that fierce handshake, so I was almost prepared for what was to happen.

We shook hands vigorously and I said hello. 'I have heard a lot about you,' I said confidently, staring into his eyes. Strangely I felt immediately at ease with the man, no sign of nerves or doubt. 'By the way,' I said, 'I am also a twin.' That was it. I had obviously said the right thing.

'I knew it!' said Ron. 'I knew we'd get on all right when I saw you at the door.'

He continued to shake my fragile hand with what looked like the utmost of pleasure and I am able to confirm, here and now, that indeed, when he found it useful, Ron had one of the strongest and most overpowering handshakes that I have ever experienced. And I consider myself no slouch when it comes to having a strong grip.

I was relieved. The journey to Broadmoor was worthwhile after all, but then I knew we'd get on. That 'twin thing' is like a magnet, it draws people together; only twins can really understand twins.

'Sit down,' he said, smiling a wry smile. 'What do you want to know?'

That was it. The ice was broken and we spoke like long-lost

friends, trying to make up for lost time. We each recounted stories only twins can tell, of mistaken identity and jokes played on the unsuspecting. Ron was very articulate and funny with it; he could certainly tell an amusing tale.

We were now ready to begin serious discussions, and I was keen to get into some of the twin stories in a more detailed and absorbing manner. My first choice was obviously a good starter.

'Tell me about the escape from Long Grove,' I asked. I had already heard the story from Charlie, but I needed the inside track if I was to use it for publication purposes or for a film.

Ron looked at me with delight written all over his face; he was enjoying every minute. His eyes sparkled as he began to explain about the incident.

'It was all Reggie's idea. He told me about it some weeks before when he came to see me and I was ready,' he replied, all keyed up and ready to go. 'I wore a blue suit and waited for him in the visitors' room, where we could talk and have a cup of tea.'

The plan was indeed simple: Reg would walk into the room, put his overcoat on a chair and then sit down with Ron who would have a photo album with him which they would look at and laugh about, just like any other visiting day. Ron would then pick up the overcoat brought in by Reg and leave his spectacles on the table, before asking to be let through to the main corridor, outside the secure area, on the pretext of getting the tea. Ron would simply take on the identity of his twin brother Reg. Reg would put on Ron's spectacles and Ron would continue walking through the long corridors of Long Grove Asylum to freedom. It was a plan that only a twin could devise, using their uncanny similarity to great effect.

In June 1958 Ron had had enough of life in Long Grove Asylum. He had been treated kindly by the doctors, but not by the other patients. 'They're all mad in here!' he told his brother Reg. He wanted out and that meant using the six-week rule that was law at the time. This stated that if a patient was to escape and could stay at large for more than six weeks without committing any crime, then on recapture he would be sent back to the prison where he had been serving his sentence to serve out the remaining period of that sentence, in Ron's case a stretch of 12 months. At least then

Ron would have a time for release from his incarceration, whereas he could be held in the hospital indefinitely.

Reg and an old friend by the name of Georgie Osbourne drove to the hospital on the busiest Sunday of the year. This was no coincidence, since Reg had, as usual, done his homework well. They left the Lincoln by the gatekeeper's cottage, in full view of anyone at the gate, and proceeded to walk into the grounds and along the path leading to the main doors of Long Grove. No one realised that there was another car, a Ford, parked nearby but out of view of security at the gate, where three men sat patiently waiting for the return of their favourite patient. These men were Billy Nash, Bernie King and Mick 'The Hammer' and they were all old friends of Ron's.

The twins greeted each other in the visitors' room, as planned. They were both wearing identical blue suits, as planned. And they began the charade of studying the photo album, as planned. It was working out well so far. Ron put his glasses down on to the table, and Reg picked them up and put them on in a very casual manner. There was no rush, no haste and no panic. Ron rose from his chair when the security people had their backs turned and picked up the coat.

'I want to go and get some teas now,' he said, as he neared the only door to the room. 'Can you unlock the door for me?' he asked confidently.

A man looked at him from outside the room, through the glass in the door; he was one of their regular visitors so there were no problems. He had seen the man before and he always went to get the teas. Ron was let through into the corridor as Reg sat with Georgie Osbourne and laughed and joked about the photos in the album. They were also joking about the success, so far, of the cunning plan to free Reg's twin brother.

'What did it feel like to be free again?' I asked Ron, trying not to get too caught up in the euphoria of the moment. Ron had confirmed everything that Charlie had previously told me, and more, so the story was really taking shape in tremendous detail.

'It was incredible,' he told me. 'I had a long, long walk down the gravel drive to the main gate. I thought it would never end. And I was getting so hot in that bloody overcoat, but it was all part of changing places, so I had to put up with it. There were people all around the gardens, but nobody noticed me. I walked out through the big gates and found my friends sitting in a car, waiting for me.'

He was smiling. It appeared somewhat strange to see Ron Kray smiling, since I had already heard so many tales of his vicious character and of the terror he induced in people. But here was a man enjoying himself by telling a story of the old days.

Reg and Georgie Osbourne stayed on until somebody realised that a switch had taken place, but they couldn't hold Reg as he was not a patient at the hospital. Reg and his pal walked back along that same gravel driveway to their car and drove off as though they were just off for a Sunday drive in the country. The plan had worked in every detail; the only problem now was how to keep Ron in hiding until the six weeks were up.

At first Ron was kept in a caravan in the Suffolk countryside, but he didn't like it too much. It was just like being in prison. So he persuaded Reg to let him come to London. This was not a problem, since they had numerous good hiding places and friends who would help to conceal Ron, so there shouldn't have been any difficulties. But there was one main problem that no one had thought of – Ron was an ill man and he needed medicine.

While Ron continued to take the tablets prescribed at Long Grove he didn't have bouts of depression and was easy to handle, but six weeks was a long time and the pills in his possession would not last that long. Reg had to do some hard thinking, as did Charlie. They even thought of getting their own medical opinion, by taking Ron to see a specialist. Before the pills ran out, though, Ron managed his own twin trick.

'How did you do that?' I asked him.

'I just walked into the pub, sat in a chair normally reserved for Reg and ordered his favourite drink. Everyone thought I was him!' he joked. He really did enjoy these twin tales. 'Someone even asked me how Ron was doing. So I told him that Ron was doing fine. I didn't tell the man that he was talking to him.' Again he laughed about his reminiscences. These were the good old days and that was all he had left, his memories.

Other tales followed of how they used to use each other's driving licences. For example, if Reg was on the run from the police or was wanted for questioning, then he would take Ron's driving licence with him to prove he was Ron. Ron did the same when it suited him. They could swap places with ease, something that came in handy when it came to alibis. But Ron's story about Long Grove was not yet finished.

When the tablets ran out Reg and Charlie got their second opinion and the doctor diagnosed paranoid schizophrenia, something that needed urgent attention and constant medication. But, fortunately for Ron, the six weeks were up and he returned voluntarily to Long Grove, from where they sent him straight back to prison to serve out his time. Their plan had worked well, they had cheated the system and soon Ron would be a free man. Being a twin certainly did have its advantages for Ron and Reg Kray.

Through those sessions with Ron at Broadmoor I came to learn much about the way being a twin affected both their lives. They were competitive, each trying to outdo the other, whether it was in boxing or business. At one time Ron even asked for protection money from a club that was part owned by Reg, one that he had taken on while Ron was inside. This was not the attitude of a compliant twin. Ron was aggressive by nature but he knew instinctively that his twin would always stand by him, in a fight or in a court of law; it made no difference to the Kray twins. Their brother Charlie could never come between them and he never tried – he knew better.

Ron and Reg always were, and even now after their deaths always will be, twins. The memory lives on of those 'terrible twins' who dominated the underworld in the '50s and '60s, and I am sure their stories will be told for many more years to come.

The phenomenon known as twins consists of both monozygotic (identical) twins and dizygotic (fraternal) twins. The Krays were monozygotic, as previously stated, and the behavioural patterns of such twins have been researched and studies undertaken at the Institute of Psychiatry in London. The institute has undertaken to study the development of twins, through their twin register, but results are inconclusive since the research only started a few years ago with infant twins and not with adult twins who could relate and recall real-life incidents. Only time will tell if this research is of any use or whether they have missed the boat. After all, twins have been used for research purposes for many years, starting with the evil Dr Josef Mengele.

Back in the time of Nazi Germany's Third Reich, Dr Mengele took twins from all ethnic backgrounds and performed experiments on them to determine the effects of gas, poison, injections of toxic substances and so on. The vast majority of these twins were of Jewish origin. The Krays also had a Jewish background, although they were also influenced by gypsy and other ethnic stock. They were lucky that they were born in the UK and not in mainland Europe.

Mengele would take one twin and inject a poison, using the other twin as control for the experiment. He would then cut up both and see the results. Since he reckoned that the insides of the twins would be the same, he could then determine the success of the drug. This was a very crude experiment but thousands of twins had to suffer in this way. And all in the name of science.

This leads us on to a tricky topic, that of cloning. This has been performed recently in the UK and the sheep known as Dolly is a prime example. Scientists can perform these experiments on a daily basis and the results will be the same, time and time again. It is now possible to clone sheep, so when will we be able to clone people? Twins are the nearest we can get to clones, but they are not pure reproductions, since all the tests show that two individual twins have two different psychological profiles. These profiles can be distorted, however, if one or the other has an illness such as schizophrenia, and that is the problem in the case of the Krays. Ron was a paranoid schizophrenic and so out of control with regard to the rules. But then he never paid any attention to the rules.

Research is being carried out all over the country on sets of monozygotic (identical) twins, to try to determine the depth of human characteristics such as telepathy, extra sensory perception (ESP), language abnormalities such as in the case of the so-called 'silent twins', thought patterns and processes and many, many more topics of interest, especially in the field of medicine. Cloning is itself only one area of twin study and this has been developed mainly in the field of genetic engineering, where doctors and scientists are now able to clone to order, so that identical embryos can be produced for fertility treatment. This could mean that only one embryo is used initially, so one or more could be kept in cold storage for use later. This will then produce a family of identical children. The question is really whether or not this is justifiable morally and scientifically and many fear misuse of knowledge in genetics.

Dr Jerry Hall, of the George Washington Medical Center, is just one scientist experimenting in genetics and cloning. He splits the egg to produce exact copies of embryos that are used in laboratory conditions for implantation, retaining one or more embryos in case of their need later on in life. If, for example, the child dies, then a new child with exactly the same looks can be born to the same mother, providing an exact replacement. It is a dangerous game and many fear the knowledge gained in this way. It can so very easily be misused, as in the case of Dr Mengele's experiments.

Other scientists fear this experimentation and talk openly of 'family farming'. 'The public feels uncomfortable with meddling in the life-producing process,' warns Dr David Meldrum, of California's Center for Advanced Reproduction. 'They will see this as one more step along a slippery slope.'

So nature supplies us with natural twins, whereas science produces clones in a more unnatural way. But here we are dealing with 'what you see is what you get' and this is only the outward appearance. We are still left with the internal problems of twins, such as schizophrenia and other mental disorders where the chromosomes have been infected or mutated for one reason or another. If science produces clones with mental disorders, then maybe the world will turn away from this method of scientific research. Only time will tell.

Dr Susan Blackmore, at the University of the West of England in Bristol, has researched twins for some time with regard to telepathy. But again, the results are inconclusive. However, any twin can relate stories of telepathy, and this is not uncommon. Even in the case of the Kray twins there are incidents where Ron and Reg were in contact mentally, if not physically. These cases are generally put down to having the same genes and gene research appears to be telling us that our physical and behavioural attributes are determined by these genes alone. Culture and social class, it would appear, have very little to do with our development. If this is the case then the development of twins cannot be changed, even if the two are kept apart for long periods of time. In the case of the Krays, then, Reg could not have changed Ron's way of being, even if he wanted to. It is all decided by our genes, even before we are born. Dangerous ground indeed, since it means that Reg would have killed anyway and didn't need the encouragement of his brother. There can be no one else to blame, since our genes pre-determine our characters.

Violet always talked of the telepathy between her boys; even their letters revealed similar thoughts and thought patterns. 'If I got a letter from Ron, then I would soon be getting a letter from Reg full of almost identical plans and points of view,' she would say. 'It was uncanny, but they always said the same.' Any twin will understand this, since it occurs almost randomly throughout their lives.

The telepathic sympathy between twins is something that we hear about on a regular basis, but proof is difficult to establish. Dr Blackmore has not been able to show telepathy between twins, although she is aware of all the stories. But these stories cannot be verified, although for twins themselves this is not necessary.

I myself have such a twin story, one of telepathic thought travelling long distances to reveal the mental and sometimes physical status of the other twin. When I was living in Copenhagen, in Denmark, back in the early '70s, I had a terrible night tossing and turning in my bed, which resulted in me breaking out in a cold sweat. Before anyone says that I must have been enjoying myself with female company, let me explain the reason for my difficulties. I was having a nightmare concerning my brother. He was in pain and I couldn't help. I felt helpless. It was devastating. When I awoke in the morning I immediately telephoned my brother in Salisbury to tell him of my experience, as I thought I was going mad. 'Are you all right?' I asked, cautiously, not wanting to appear a right prat and silly with it. He then, without any prompting, went on to explain about the treatment he had had only the previous day to extract a wisdom tooth, treatment that had left him in terrible pain. 'It was the worst night's sleep I have ever had,' he told me. I sighed in relief. I wasn't going mad after all.

Language is an often-quoted topic when discussing the phenomenon of twins. Most twins appear to have their own special way of communicating with each other, and the Krays were no exception to this rule. One twin only had to give a certain look for the other to realise what he was thinking. Reg and Ron understood their own sign language and their own body language, something that is really only now beginning to be understood, especially in the field of business. The Firm always talked of their lack of visible communication; it wasn't necessary for them to talk to each other as each instinctively understood the other's thought processes. This is something that accentuates the difference between twins and non-twins.

Others can't understand it and so it becomes something to fear. The Krays used this to their advantage on more than one occasion, such as the fight with the dockers in the pub on the Mile End Road. Everyone in The Regal knew that the twins were going to meet the dockers, but Ron and Reg never talked about it. They seemed to know what was going to happen and didn't need to communicate openly with one another. When the time came for the meeting they simply put down their cups of tea, straightened their ties and walked out of the billiard hall. Not a word was spoken. Even when the time came to fight, they didn't need a coded message or sign; they knew it was the right time and that the other would join in immediately. They beat off the dockers, using fists not words, and walked home to see their pals at The Regal. Silence, it would appear, is a language of communication between twins.

But are the genes to blame? Or is it just that twins have already found a friend, even before they are born? They have nine months together in the womb to establish a firm relationship and not even a mother can break that bond. They can't talk to each other during this period so they must develop some other way of communication. Call it instinct or call it telepathy, the difference is the same. Twins are hard to deal with because of this sixth sense.

Two people who look the same and don't need to talk to each other to understand how the other feels is a quandary. It isn't only the sight of two identical people that threatens; it is also the lack of visible or audible communication that exposes witnesses to the paranormal. It all makes 'outsiders' fearful and the Krays were indeed feared by everyone.

Probably the most interesting research into twins that could help us considerably today is the work done in the USA at the National Institute of Health in Washington DC by Dr H. Clifford Lane. Here he has chosen twins with unusual characteristics: one is heterosexual and healthy whereas the other is gay and HIV positive. He has been studying 12 sets of twins, all taking part in this pioneering hospital project. Because their genes are identical, doctors hope to cure the sick twin through replacement treatment. The HIV-positive twin is bombarded with billions of healthy cells taken from his monozygotic counterpart. 'We are optimistic that this could lead to a positive advance in the fight against AIDS,' Dr Lane has said repeatedly. Research is not finished yet, but so far, so good. There may yet be a cure for AIDS, all through the study of twins.

The strange fact that makes the above research possible is the remarkable coincidence that there are at least 12 sets of twins in the USA that fit the bill for the research programme. So is it then normal for one twin to be heterosexual and one homosexual? The simple answer is that we don't know. And then again, what is normal? There could be so-called normal heterosexual twins just as easily as twins where both are gay. There are no research details that would conclude anything of this nature. The only conclusion is that the similarity between twins is all in the genes; it is nature and not nurture.

Ron Kray, being a homosexual, created a curious picture. He was both macho and gay, both a twin and a separate individual, both a crook and a philanthropist, both generous and greedy. The study of Ron is an extensive look at both his background and history, whereas Reg would appear to present a more normal picture of your everyday male, even though he was more bisexual than heterosexual. Whether or not these contradictions also apply to him is pure speculation. But twin research shows that the genes are there and it seems that nothing we twins can do will change the nature of our make-up. Twins are tied to each other by an invisible bond, one that will always take the strain of the ups and downs of such a close relationship and one that will always be there, even in death.

Medical faculties all over the world are studying physical and mental similarities between monozygotic twins to try to determine whether or not these twins have the same weaknesses, the same strengths, the same disorders. It is also important and interesting to note that, even in death, Ron was a tool for such study, when his brain was removed before he was buried and taken for research purposes to Cambridge University. The problem here, however, was that no one saw fit to tell the Kray family, and that is a diabolical and disgusting thing to do. The authorities that be let Reg bury his twin brother not knowing that Ron's brain was missing. When the brain eventually turned up, Reg had to have the coffin dug up and the brain put inside, once again reunited with its owner.

Meanwhile the research also continues at the Minnesota Center of Twin and Adoption Research in the USA. Professor Thomas J. Bouchard has for many years carried out research using twins that were separated at birth. Here he has proved, once and for all, that nature beats nurture every time. The genes would appear to have the upper hand in all statistics and no matter the social background of the families that the twins enter, however dissimilar, the twins develop in an almost identical way. This would tend to indicate that no matter what the sexual preference of the twins or illness that one of them may have, their pattern of life is determined even before birth through their genes. So, in a way, it was quite inevitable that Reg should kill someone after his twin had killed George Cornell. So Jack 'The Hat' McVitie was just in the wrong place at the wrong time. Destiny took control.

The Krays were never, to their knowledge, involved in any academic or medical research, other than being scrutinised in various recent papers and books by sociologists such as Professor Chris Jenks and Dr Dick Hobbs. Maybe Violet Kray could have benefited from the knowledge gained since 1978 by the twin organisation in the UK known as TAMBA (Twins and Multiple

Births Association). The association helps parents to understand the needs of twins, especially in infancy. The peculiar fact is that all the twin books available only concern themselves with infants; there is no guide to twins in adolescence. I, for one, would like to see this undertaken. Maybe then we would begin to understand how the Krays, through their twin-ness, came to dominate crime in the UK. There were other brothers in crime, whole families even, but no twins – until the Krays.

Dr Hobbs suggests that 'when issues emerged from beyond the parameters of these concerns, then offences were committed that the police could no longer ignore.' The concerns in focus were trouble, toughness, smartness, excitement and autonomy, and when the Krays altered these boundaries, because of Ron's homosexuality and mental illness, the police had to arrest them both. But the study of twins tells us that genes and genes alone are the decisive factor in the development of twins and that illness and sexuality only play a minor part. It does, however, appear almost certain that if Frances, Reg's wife, had not succeeded in her third attempt at suicide, then Reg would have been able to stop his brother from totally dominating his life. It wasn't only the actions of the twins, therefore, that changed their lives; it was also the actions of all the main protagonists, including their own immediate family.

'The symbolic core of the Kray enticement, and clearly central to their own sense of identity, purpose and belonging, is their very "twin-ness". This birthright multiplied by the privations of working-class, 1930s, East End life rendered their survival and maturation into adulthood if not remarkable then at least not commonplace,' says Professor Chris Jenks. So, also in a sociological sense, this twin 'thing' was at the heart of the twins' success – and downfall. He continues by saying that 'the personality development and public persona(e) of twins is very different to that of non-twins. Infant twins charm and attract attention of other mothers in the street [as in the case of their mother Violet when she was out walking the twins in their pram], they create a halo through the synergy of their needs, demands and delights; they fascinate others through the verisimilitude of their hairstyle, their eyes and their matching outfits – they both mirror and contain like facing bookends. Their significance is simultaneously ancient and modern.'

Again we have the paradox of complexities that is twins, so how can they be expected to grow up to feel like any other normal human being? The fact is that they don't and they can't be expected to be like any so-called normal person. They are indeed special and they will always remain that way.

Some twins would like to be like any other ordinary man or woman, while others accept their similarity, such as in the case of the film *City Slickers 2*, where Jack Palance, who plays Duke, looks in the mirror every morning to see the face of his twin brother Curly who died in the first *City Slickers* film, so he is with his twin even after death. I wonder if Reg had the same experience when he shaved every morning after Ron's death? Any twin will know what I mean.

'These same traits,' says Professor Jenks, 'in adult twins are appealing, but not in the same ways. They can arouse the vicarious appeal of a "freak show" – people sharing physical features, mannerisms, and wearing the same clothes – these are all transgressive and thus threatening images stalked by the conceptual menace of clones, cyborgs and replicants.'

These trends and traits are present throughout the lives of the Kray twins, where their later lives were virtually dominated by power in the form of violence and the fear of violence. The following, taken from the academic paper 'The Kray Fascination', sums up the complexities and confusion of identity that twins alone must carry with them throughout their lives: 'In adulthood their identicality generates a confusion between the natural and the intentional, the compulsive and the wilful. The tension contained in this confusion both conceals and discloses a monstrous power that is experienced externally but sourced wholly within the dyad. The ultimate and particular power exercised by twins is that of exclusion, the symbolic rebuff that is generated by "oneness" manifested in the cryptophasia (or private language) identical twins often assume; a community of inner sanctum that defies all and any other membership.'

Reg summed this all up with the wreath to his brother laid on his grave at Chingford Mount Cemetery in Essex. It said simply:

'To the other half of me'. He even placed a painting of himself and his brother on the grave to symbolise their uniqueness and constant companionship. Unfortunately, the souvenir hunters do not respect any man's private wishes and feelings of sadness in bereavement, since, as soon as the gathering left the graveside, they swooped and stole the painting laid there with such precision and sense of loss by Reg himself. He had been allowed out of prison for the funeral, but he was not allowed to see his twin when the illness took hold. He had pleaded with the authorities to let him visit his sick twin brother in the hospital at Ascot, but permission was refused. Ron's dying thoughts would have been with Reg; it is such a pity that the two couldn't have been together at the end. Alone now for the first time, Reg was left in his prison cell to grieve, to remember the good times and the bad, to reflect on the past and the possible future, and to think about burying his twin brother Ron.

Chris Jenks also notes that: 'A further intimidation that is presented to the collective by the experience of twinning is the threat of loss or abandonment of identity and purpose. The real secret of twins, which holds our imagination, is their fusion of free will and the tacit disregard for the achievement that is our individual difference. We may struggle to constitute our own characters through experience but the very oneness of twins is utterly dismissive of that struggle.'

True, there is a dual feeling of common purpose within the two individuals that tends to make them very supportive of each other. But this can be both helpful and advantageous. When I needed to talk or think or reflect, for example, my brother was there to advise and the discussions could be deep and intense. There was no room for anyone else in these discussions or arguments or disagreements; no 'outsiders' were allowed. But, ultimately, we made our own final decisions and these could be varied indeed. There was no need for a common purpose, or a similar way of doing or achieving things. We each had our own way and often took choices at different ends of the spectrum. But this only brought us closer together, since we each realised the individuality of the other. It united us with a common singularity of purpose and diversified us with the assistance and acceptance of the other half, and both polarised simultaneously. Another paradox.

The twin-ness alone cannot constitute a basis for their existence, but it complements the emergence of the Krays as a feared duet within their own particular society. Their social and geographical details helped to form their mindsets and this, together with their appearance in the time scale of things, in the 1930s, provided the background for their dominance within the criminal fraternity.

Complementation was itself complemented with opposite polarity, providing contradictions to the norm. As stated earlier, Reg was generally dominated by Ron, but Ron was the younger of the two. As boxers it was Reg who dominated, with his stylish and effective boxing against Ron's rough-and-tough tumbles in the ring, reflecting his street-fighter image. Reg was a businessman first and foremost. He would have liked to have continued to drive his Mercedes to the West End, as he did back in the '60s; he was even planning an office in a plush part of London, just like the Richardsons. His perspective was wide and he could see a clear vision of the future within the world of glamour, business and sport. But Ron was the psychotic who could not leave his brother alone. Ron wanted to win at all costs and he never gave in to sound commonsense. Even as a child he thrived on his tantrums and this, for him, became a way of life. This was his control mechanism and guns and swords became an extension of that control. To him it was like a fix, by which he could maintain control over people and events. These unconscious thoughts from his early days came to dominate Ron as they did his brother Reg. He, and he alone, made the decisions that mattered and those decisions were to haunt both him and his twin to their graves.

'Their seeming capacity for parthenogenesis enabled an almost seamless tapestry to emerge comprised of contradictory, bathetic and incommensurable images. The "many" Krays were irreconcilable to the Twins themselves and to their burgeoning public. They became gentleman/thug, philanthropist/extortionist, respectable/low-life, calculating/unpredictable, kind/brutish.'

These words from Professor Chris Jenks sum up the thoughts that I myself have had through the years regarding the Krays. There are too many contradictions in their lives, too many similarities and too many paradoxes for anyone other than the Krays. Theirs was a special life. It was a metamorphosis into image and lives lived through image. Today we understand the idea of 'celebrity' through film, music, television and so on, but back in the '30s, '40s and '50s this was still an almost unknown phenomenon, apart from the Hollywood films that so greatly influenced the twins themselves. But the Krays changed all of that. They became twins of mythical proportions and lived their lives through a sense of mythology, which made icons out of killers.

7

THE KRAYS AND THE BEATLES

From my own experience, I have numerous stories of meeting celebrities and stars of stage and screen, simply through the fact that I am a twin. One such story includes a popular band of the time that was also known to the Krays. My brother and I were working during our school vacation, back in the early '60s, at Heathrow Airport. We were both serving at the bar and also working in the rear of the premises making sandwiches. Noticing that my brother Rod wasn't attending the bar, I walked out and asked the first customer if he wanted a drink. The customer, a young man of about my own age, said: 'We'll have two teas please,' and gave me a rather odd look. Nevertheless, I went back into the rear of the premises, where I noticed that Rod had just made a new pot of tea. Happily I poured two cups and went out to the bar to deliver them to my customers. Rod was already there talking to the two lads, who had two cups of tea sitting on the bar in front of them.

The lads looked at my brother, and then at me, and then back at my brother. 'Christ, you're twins!' said one of them.

'I've never seen such identical twins in my life,' said the other.

They both stood there, mouths open. There wasn't much they could say that we hadn't heard before.

'And I've never seen such identical haircuts as yours,' I said quickly in reply. I now found myself looking at their hair, curiously cut in the same extraordinary fashion. 'But what shall I do with the teas?' I asked.

'Don't worry,' said one of the lads. 'George and Ringo will be along in a minute. They'll have the teas.' It took me some time to translate from the Liverpudlian to Middlesexian, but I got there in the end. We were talking to John Lennon and Paul McCartney and the two they referred to, and who joined them a few moments later, were George Harrison and Ringo Starr. Together they were The Beatles.

The Kray Files (Colin Fry)

It all started when Angelo Bruno, the godfather of Philadelphia, suggested that the Krays in England did what the Mafia did so successfully in the USA – get involved in the music and film business. He also suggested that getting The Beatles away from Brian Epstein would be a good way to start and he urged them to set up a meeting, any way they could. He had a long list of artists that he thought would be of interest to the Krays in order to help them build up a celebrity clientele like the Mob had in America, which included Frank Sinatra, Nat King Cole, Judy Garland and many others.

It was not hard to set up a meeting with Brian Epstein as he was well known in London's illegal gay clubs. Ron, in particular, had many useful allies on that scene, including Firm member 'Mad' Teddy Smith, who had written plays for the BBC. There was also, of course, Lord Bob Boothby and Tom Driberg MP, who were always at Ron's parties, or orgies as they were known in the Firm. Leslie Holt, Boothby's live-in lover, was also a good contact as he was well acquainted with the smart set, albeit in a very different way, as he was one of the best cat burglars operating in the West End at the time.

Eventually a meeting was set up at a gay club in Soho, London. It was the early '60s and homosexuality was illegal, but if you had the money and the contacts then you could do anything and, in the main, get away with it. It was Epstein who chose the setting but it was the Krays who chose the agenda.

It was one of Ron's associates who organised the meeting, as he helped to run the club and, for the purposes of this book, I will call him Sydney. The twins arrived at the club with a few friends who stayed in the car, parked around the corner. The twins were alone when they entered and signed the guest book, but Sydney was there to help with the proceedings, which were strictly adhered to in a club where secrecy was king.

The meeting started innocently enough with Epstein talking about what it took to keep a band like The Beatles operating – all the hard work, the marketing, the accounts, the obligations and the problems associated with being on the road for long intervals of time.

Ron was becoming increasingly frustrated with Epstein's condescending attitude and Epstein knew he had gone too far when Ron slowly stood up and performed his nail trick. Ron didn't care who his assistant for the trick was; he just knew that he had to show Epstein who he was dealing with. Tough business usually meant tough tactics to Ron, and his tactics were usually very bloody.

Ron reached out and randomly grabbed a young man as he walked past and pulled him into a corner. He then took a six-inch nail from his jacket pocket and rammed it into the youngster's cheek, pushing it all the way through and out through the other cheek. The terrified man said nothing – he couldn't. He just stood wide-eyed as the nail went through his face. Ron then bent the ends over so that the youngster couldn't easily remove the nail.

Ron's demonstration worked and he now had Epstein's full attention. As the lad was taken away by his friends the discussions continued.

No deal was agreed at this meeting, but they all agreed to think about it and consider the options. The problem was that there weren't many options for Ron and Reg.

The Krays had come to realise their over-dependence on Leslie Payne, Ron's business manager. In fact, they were so disillusioned with him that they were already considering getting rid of him, permanently, and that meant killing him. But, without Payne, where would they get the expertise necessary to manage a band like The Beatles? They knew they could not trust anyone apart from Charlie. But even there they were afraid they could be cheated, as Charlie was, in fact, quite a clever businessman. So, who else did they know who could help?

A few days after the meeting with Epstein, Reg phoned one of his old pals in Glasgow, Arthur Thompson. The twins had worked with the Glasgow crime boss for a number of years, even getting him to send heavies down to London to take care of their opposition when the need had arisen. Arthur was full of encouragement but he had a stark warning for the twins: 'This is legitimate, hard work. Are you prepared for that?'

Ron and Reg met up with Arthur a few weeks later when they were in Glasgow scouting for business. They met up at The Cockatoo Bar in Govanhill and chatted about the possibilities. His advice was simple: why get involved in all that aggro when it was only the money they wanted?

He suggested that it was far easier to dig the dirt on Epstein and blackmail him. He had already shown his cards by meeting them in a gay club, so he should be easy pickings. And there was also the possibility that if it were known that the Krays, gangsters from the East End of London, had taken control of The Beatles, then the band could be finished when the news hit the street.

In the end it was no problem putting pressure on Epstein. They knew about his association with young boys, his drinking and his drug taking. In particular, they knew about his relationship with a young singer, a young man very much in demand in the entertainment world.

Arthur Thompson had been right, he was easy pickings. Over the next few years, until his death in 1967, Epstein made regular payments to the Krays. He was terrified and completely out of his depth. Epstein's vulnerability had made blackmail the easiest option for the twins, but it would have been interesting to see what would have happened if the twins had decided to take control of The Beatles instead.

When the club closed some years later, Sydney went over there to make sure that he got his share of the takings, and maybe a few souvenirs. When he saw the book that the twins and all the club's regular clients had used to sign in at the club, he quickly put it in his pocket. There were names in there that he thought could be a good source of income in the future and it would also protect his pals the Krays. As far as I know he still has that book; I wonder what other names are in there?

The Krays did not stop with John, Paul, George and Ringo, however. Soon their attention was drawn to The Kinks, another popular band of the '60s. Singer Ray Davies has told of how one of the Firm called on their managers to discuss a takeover.

Their managers at the time were businessmen of the old school who were more at home in the stockbroker belt than dealing with gangsters. Meeting a pal of the Krays was a different ball game for them, especially when they were told that Ron wanted to date the band's drummer, Mick Avery.

Ray Davies is not sure why the deal did not go through, but he was glad that it didn't. The fact is, the Krays were not true business people. Arthur Thompson had hit the proverbial nail on the head when he said that, in reality, they were only after the money. Whether or not they collected from The Kinks on a monthly basis, as they did with Epstein, is not known. But it wouldn't surprise me.

Just think of it – Ron Kray and The Kinks? Now that would be kinky!

The Krays' attempts to get into the music business didn't end with their bids to take over The Beatles and The Kinks, however. In 1975, when Charlie Kray was released from prison after serving a seven-year sentence for disposing of bodies for his brothers and had to find something to do, he almost immediately became the manager of a band called Stray.

The band did reasonably well, but there were no major hits. They did, however, write a few songs that were picked up by other artists. Iron Maiden, for example, covered their song 'All in Your Mind', but this was not enough to save Charlie's management career and he quit after only a short time in the position. He had quickly come to realise that it was a lot of work running a band and that Brian Epstein was right when he said it was not all fun and games.

In the mid 1980s Charlie was once again contacted by the Mob in New York. This time they wanted to start a new record company in London and they wanted Charlie to be involved. When he was told that there was £2 million available to start things up he immediately accepted.

He contacted his old pal Joe Pyle and they set about getting people together whom they thought they could trust, who could handle the business and who could make them lots of dosh.

A crooked lawyer from New York contacted them, on behalf of the Mafia, asking Charlie and Pyle to create a business plan, which they needed to complete their paperwork. They quickly put a proposal together and had a few artists record new products for the label. They even managed to persuade Billy J. Kramer to record a brand new album for release through the new company.

But, once again, the company never came to fruition. The principals couldn't agree on the way to proceed, the people they took on were not trustworthy and the money never materialised. It had simply all been an effort by the Mob in New York to launder their ill-gotten gains in the UK.

Charlie tried to get things moving by getting private investors to join the company and he was reasonably successful with this, but the big money never arrived, and ultimately Charlie lost interest. And when Joe Pyle and his pals resorted to guns, Charlie said enough is enough and got out rapidly.

Pyle and his cronies tried to get more money out of the investors by, amongst other things, threatening to collect their children from school, kidnapping their wives and holding them to ransom, breaking their bones and getting rid of their bodies at sea, just like in the old days. This worked for a while, but it couldn't last.

The investors got together and threatened the company with police action and that was enough to make Joe and his pals put their guns away and admit defeat. They almost got away with it though. But for the greed of the crooks in the East End of London the Mafia would have set up their company in England and they would have had a great ready-made company through which to launder their money.

Billy J. Kramer had also been given the 'do it, or else!' treatment. He told me that he had had a phone call from one of Charlie's friends telling him that he had to do what he was told and be quiet about it, or they would pick up his wife and children and he would never see any of them again. It was his choice, they said, but in reality there was no choice at all. When the company collapsed he was a very happy man and, let's face it, he didn't deserve all the trouble, the threats and the aggravation.

Charlie never tried to get back into the music business again, although his brother Reg, while he was in prison, did try to write some songs. He even managed to get some of them recorded, but they were not successful; it was all done to placate Reg, to keep him happy, and it allowed the artists to stay on good terms with the old 'Godfather of Crime'. They all knew what would happen if they said they didn't like the songs, so they just got down to it, recorded them, and threw them away.

Reg didn't really care, as he had made his point and could tell his friends that his songs had been recorded, and how many of them could say that? Reg could now call himself songwriter, author of books and writer of articles and that was what he wanted. He did anything that he thought would get him some kind of recognition and this ultimately became his *raison d'être*, his reason for living.

It made him feel good about himself; no longer would he try to commit suicide in prison and he realised that it made him, in a way, more respectable and someone to be reckoned with. It wasn't his fists doing the talking any more and this got him thinking that maybe Charlie was right after all.

8

THE KRAY MYTH

It started when we beat off them Maltesers at The Regal.
They didn't like it when the knives came out. They've got
no bottle.

Ron Kray

Events such as the death of Diana, Princess of Wales, or the trial of British au pair Louise Woodward in Boston, USA, have brought about an intense debate regarding the media and the reporting of such tragic incidents.

The words 'synthetic media attraction' have been used frequently in this debate, suggesting that there has been an over-exploitation by the media solely for the purposes of making money out of tragedy. The televising of trials and even Parliamentary proceedings alters the perceived nature of justice; emotion takes over from reason. Sentiment becomes key, with enthusiasm, or negativity, whipped up by the press and television alike.

These tragic affairs attract sympathy. People become emotionally involved and a feeling of solidarity takes over; we allow our prejudices for one side of the debate to dominate. So is this a legitimate human response, or just tasteless drivel with little or no regard for the truth?

With more than 30 years in jail, Reg Kray came in for a similar level of scrutiny. Why, people asked, should he still be behind bars when others, who have committed much more serious offences (in the eyes of the general public, at least) were already free after much shorter sentences? Had we become sympathetic towards Reg, with an apparent loss of memory regarding the violent offences he undoubtedly committed?

To many, Reg has become a kind of Robin Hood figure, an icon. He carried on his charitable work from inside prison and contributed regular articles to the media, provoking even further discussion. Colleges have named societies after the Krays; football teams asked for Reg to be their manager. So have we forgotten the truth in favour of exploited emotions? And if these emotions have taken over completely, then how do we consider today the rough justice performed by Justice Melford Stevenson when sentencing the twins to at least 30 years each in jail?

Does, then, human virtue rest on emotion? And if so, is it right that the media should have such a great part to play in our perception of justice? People are, after all, vulnerable and no one lives in isolation. But the law should be seen to be just, without emotion entering the fray. The cold and merciless system of justice, therefore, is tempered by human emotion. But in the case of the Kray trial, did this factor work against the Krays and not for them?

Certainly, in recent years, there has been much controversy surrounding the Krays. We have been inundated with books (sorry, here is another one) and with films and gossip, so has society changed through this revolution within the media? Are we becoming more compassionate, with a higher regard for feelings and emotion, as a balance to the cold heart of the law? Is this the reason why we appear to remember the positive sides of the Kray experience, although there do not appear to be many of these at all? Or is it simply that Reg had been so long in jail that the majority of the country, and certainly the younger generation who were not even born at the time of the trial, had forgotten the events of the '50s and '60s? And does forgetting mean forgiving?

This emotional tug of war continues.

So, is it all a media illusion? And if so, then who is responsible for it?

Do we really know or understand the Krays and should we know or feel the need to know all about Princess Diana and Louise Woodward? This apparent need to know could be considered a reaction towards the harshness of modern society, with emotions taking over. Right or wrong does not matter any more; it is all about what we perceive as being right or wrong.

This emotion, however, leads us to make irrational judgements on the basis of philosophical and romantic associations. The need for empirical proof flies conveniently out of the window. The science of law requires proof, but the verdict of emotions comes from within and is therefore biased.

Can we really be manipulated by the media through mass hysteria? Does superstition become a popular culture, replacing old rational values? Certainly journalists manipulate, but then so do those who leak stories to the press and certain Internet sites. Even Ron and Reg used the press to their own advantage.

This dissatisfaction with reasoning and the leaning towards emotion and sympathy, even towards villains, cannot, by definition, be objective. This is a very dangerous and difficult area of debate, since we get down to one common denominator – who controls whom? The will of the people is important, but it must not override the truth. This surely must be sacrosanct.

The truth is also objective. The academic elite also manipulate, as in the universities. But here, in the main, it is emotion in the form of passion that drives you on. It is the emotional search for truth that is the guiding light. There is no conflict.

Heart over head is an urge towards irrational behaviour. They are opposites. They deal with different values, one blinded by rationality, the other blinded by emotion.

At the heart of all of this controversy is the actual justice system that we have in this country. It is one of sides – the defence against the prosecution. We learn to listen to both and then to make up our minds. But how can this not be emotional? Our judgements are made on what we perceive to be the facts and not necessarily the truth. This is part of a far wider debate and I will not delve into this subject matter. The adversarial system has, throughout history, caused many men and women to be sent to prison quite unjustly. Even in the case of the Krays, the sentence of 30 years does appear to be unjust, although some might say it is emotional.

Ronnie Biggs, that fugitive from justice who had been living reasonably well in Rio de Janeiro in Brazil, had been pardoned by the Brazilian authorities. His case was more than 20 years old, so he had been allowed to stay in Brazil. This precedent would be dangerous to take on board in this country, but it does show a certain compassion. Feelings towards crimes and towards those who commit those crimes have changed, to a degree. This is possibly something that the British judiciary should contemplate further.

To understand how the Krays tried to influence the media to their own particular advantage we have to go right back to the beginning. And the beginning is Hoxton, then a much deprived area of the East End.

'The twins' tale is and always will be inextricably bound to the signs, symbols, rituals and folklore of London's East End.' So says Professor Chris Jenks. His argument stems from an analysis of the types of media necessary for sustaining myth within a social memory, one that immortalises the past in a symbolic and selective way. He cites the five main media types as: oral histories; written records; images and the pictorial; actions and rituals; and, finally, social framework of space. Although he says that the Krays were just as much about psychic space as social space, the confinements of the East End have helped to develop cultural mnemonics through geographical realignment. Selective memory then creates an illusion of history, establishing these larger-than-life figures through metaphors of grandeur and power. The myth takes control but only when the main protagonists are themselves worthy of such status, through their own mythogenic prowess.

This is most clearly seen through written and pictorial representations, something that the Krays were all too aware of in the heyday of their nefarious careers. Starting in their boxing days, the twins soon learned that fame meant power and they thought they could create that power not through their ability to discuss and theorise, but through the sheer forcefulness of their fists. They were becoming famous in their own village-like area of the East End, using this initial step up the ladder of fame as the basis for their thinking. They became known as twins, boxers, tough guys and ultimately gangland bosses, and they used those written and pictorial records to full effect. Ron with his camera always at hand, Reg with his ability with the pen. They helped to create their own image and the media did the rest.

Nothing illustrates the myth of the Krays better than Ron's funeral. It made every front page in the country, ousting the death of Lord Lovat, the wartime commando leader, from the pages of most newspapers altogether. Even television was full of the event, with film footage of the cortège with the glass-sided hearse, pulled by six black horses, followed by a stream of Rolls-Royces. The stars were there to pay their tribute among the 60,000-strong crowd who thronged, longing to see Ron being taken away to his last resting place.

Most of the crowd wouldn't have known the Ron Kray who had died, but they would easily have recognised the images created by David Bailey, whose photographs helped to immortalise the twins. They are the images that the media use, even now, when describing British gangsters, and when comedians of all kinds need a couple of villains for their sketches, they naturally choose the Krays to parody. Unfortunately, this also creates another image, one of comic-like tendencies, but the Krays were no comedians. This selective memory process is thus enhanced by the media through film and through written recordings, such as those by the numerous celebrities who pleaded for the release of Reg Kray. The general public cannot compose a 'big picture' in this way, as they only see certain aspects of the lives of the Krays. As a result, the myth is enhanced through this social history of remembering.

It is important to note that it is not only the Krays who came in for this treatment, since even the policemen who were trying to catch them have now become famous. Such is the case of Leonard 'Nipper' Read, who may not have been so well known today if he hadn't captured the Krays. The image of the detective became one of a specialist whose image was boosted still further by the activities of the Krays and the subsequent prosecutions. This, according to Dr Dick Hobbs, has given an elite status to Scotland Yard, no matter what methodology they use and no matter how much they bungle. It is dramatic and bizarre in every detail, finally culminating in the portrayal of the fight between good and evil, where both sides become part of the myth. This dramatic fight, which saw the imprisonment of the Krays, changed their activities from normal everyday life to one of remarkable achievements through the use of fear and the threat of violence.

The case of the Krays had everything, says Dr Hobbs, 'including the hint of police corruption, murder, homosexuality, madness, show business personalities, politicians and the aristocracy. All these cases were presented as a series of dramatic confrontations between good and evil in which the police possess the preponderance of resources, skill and virtue.' For sure, the police were more inclined to go after the big fish than to use a net to catch small fry. The detention of the gang leader was the way ahead for the officers at the time. And some would say that it still is.

But the Krays were not always corrupt and criminal, by nature, although they were forced to hear stories of the well-known gangsters and petty crooks of the Mile End Road from their father, who cherished these memories and fantasies. He filled the heads of his twins with these outrageous tales of bygone days; no wonder their imaginations knew no boundaries. They grew up with the myths of Jack the Ripper and the boxing heroes from the East End whom everyone admired. They also knew that they themselves were special, since their mother had always told them. And they could certainly trust their mother, couldn't they?

So when the Second World War came to a close, they were in the right place at the right time. They were already famous in their neighbourhood and they wanted to be known all over the country. It was Ron Kray who had this need for fame, more than his brother Reg. Whether he thought it would hide his homosexuality or disguise it in some way, no one can say for sure. But he was convinced by the films of the day that if you projected an outer image of some magnitude, then you would soon inwardly become that character. Throughout his life he always tried to live up to his own creation, that of 'The Colonel'.

But the myth really only came into being when the Krays were sentenced to thirty years in jail, with brother Charlie getting ten years for getting rid of the body of Jack 'The Hat' McVitie. Charlie Kray himself doesn't really fit into this myth, since he is only there by association. He always said that he had to create his own life despite his brothers, but in reality he tried to live his life on the back of his brothers' success and normally with their money.

The simplicity of the paintings and poems created by Reg Kray shows his own selective memory. He chose to paint childlike pictures, depicting normal everyday life, although his life was by no means normal or everyday. His world then, in prison, was one of poetic description, where he attempted to re-create history to protect his ego. He had blotted out the violence and the bad deeds in favour of the charity and kindness that he and his twin showed to many in the East End. Just like Ron, he could not face up to the reality of their deeds, so they camouflaged them to create the image they wanted, one they could live with. It is a world of make-believe just as it is a true tale of historical achievement. This is the image, one of 'faction', that was so commonly portrayed in the newspapers of the day, where their show-business pals argued the case for the release of Reg Kray.

Garry Bushell, writing in *The Sun*, was always calling for the release of Reg Kray. He remembered the good old days of the near crime-free East and West Ends of London, but here again we have the use of selective memory. Others, such as Mike Reid, the comedian and actor, had also voiced the same opinion. Talking of the days when he was a 22-year-old comic, doing the rounds of the pubs and clubs, he said: 'We were introduced [to the Krays] after a show at The Rising Sun in Bethnal Green and I was left with a lasting memory of them as absolute gents.' I wonder what the relatives and descendants of George Cornell and Jack 'The Hat' McVitie would say?

And still the tributes and the good wishes poured out from all those well-wishers, who, with compassion in their hearts, advocated the release of the best-known gangster in Great Britain. 'Locked in to crazy sentences,' said *The People* newspaper in the mid-'90s. 'Freedom day for a Kray!' said another. Yet others reported on the good deeds the twins had performed for various charities and good causes all around the country. When seven-year-old Sean Williams was brutally murdered in the mid-'90s, Reg sent the family a letter of sympathy, which they quite naturally cherished. Although I am a little cynical about such behaviour from Reg, his letter did help to ease the suffering of the parents and therefore should not be ridiculed as a callous gesture just to get publicity. In his own way I truly feel that Reg believed he was doing some good and it is good to know that he had the wellbeing of others in mind.

So newspaper coverage had magnified the Kray myth. 'Publicly polite, patriotic, devoted to their mother and dressed in sober suits, the Krays developed an uncanny double act replete with controlled menace; it spawned a whole genre of fiction, and gained them a cult following,' said the *Daily Telegraph* on Ron's death in 1995. This is a far more objective view of the legend of the Krays, full of death and violence and intrigue. The balanced picture, however, is not the stuff of myths.

Keith Waterhouse, writing in the *Daily Mail* on 20 December 1993, was concerned about the current status of children's books from the publisher Puffin, replete with all the violence of a blockbuster Hollywood film. Clive King, the hugely successful author, told him that authors were told to use simple sentence structure and tabloid-style headings, catering for 'the couch potato child surfeited with violence on the little screen', who Puffin obviously believes can't be persuaded to look at a book unless it is kept simple and written in short word-bites. Mr Waterhouse used the suggestion of 'Charlie and Reggie Kray meet *The Borrowers*' as an example of this category, which reinforced the myth. Puffin, he said, tells of the violence that is around us in these modern times and that we cannot hide it from children. This is, of course, true, but wouldn't it be nice to see this child-like unawareness extended, even if it does simplify life? After all, there is plenty of time for growing up.

No matter what happens from here on in, the Krays will be there forever, imprinted on our minds in one way or another. The film *The Krays* helped to create a new generation of youngsters with extravagant and, some would say, outrageous views on the Krays. The twins have become working-class heroes and are still admired in many parts of the East End where they are now icons of the Establishment; that same Establishment that they tried to corrupt. Despite the inaccuracies of the film and the short memories of some of our journalistic commentators, the Krays will always be gangsters, but the myth is now firmly in place and it will take a whole book full of revelations to change that contrived impression. But maybe that isn't even enough.

9

THE DEATH OF 'THE MAD AXEMAN' FRANK MITCHELL

I like to think of him roaming the Outback in Australia.

Ron Kray

I knew otherwise, and he knew it too. Reg had given the order and Ron had just looked the other way because Frank Mitchell had become an embarrassment. But Ron didn't want to talk about it any more. He was relaxed and on his medication, sitting at the head of the table in the visiting room in Broadmoor, surrounded by his gay lovers and other 'friends'.

'The Mad Axeman' Frank Mitchell escaped from Dartmoor Prison on 12 December 1966. Escape, however, is a far too dramatic word for what really happened, as he just casually walked out of the gates of one of Her Majesty's top-security prisons and disappeared into the mists of the moor and away to freedom.

It was another madman, 'Mad' Teddy Smith, who had suggested the caper to the twins. Smith was, amongst other things, a playwright, but his imagination often got the better of him and he had a difficult time telling reality from fiction.

The plan was to break Frank Mitchell out of Dartmoor as a protest about his treatment; it would be, according to 'Mad' Teddy Smith, a bit of a media event and it would be good public relations for the twins. 'The Mad Axeman' had phoned the twins for help and Ron, in particular, was interested in doing something, especially something big like breaking a man out of the 'Moor'.

Mitchell was a giant of a man with big hands, big feet, everything big. He was 37 years old and was serving a sentence of 18 years.

Albert Donoghue and 'Mad' Teddy Smith drove down to Dartmoor and found the pre-arranged meeting place. Mitchell had already been informed of the plans by telephone and already knew the location of the telephone box as he regularly roamed the moor, having been given complete freedom by the guards. Not only a huge man, he had once been certified insane, so he wasn't a man to argue with.

As 'Mad' Teddy faked making a phone call, 'The Mad Axeman' slowly walked over the hill and to freedom.

Mitchell quickly got changed out of his prison gear and into something more suitable as they were afraid of roadblocks once the escape was discovered. Soon Mitchell was in the car and the three men turned their minds towards London. While they drove they listened to the radio in the hope of hearing news about the escape and of any police roadblocks, but they heard nothing; nothing, that is, until they were already safely in London and on home territory. The escape was a complete success.

The twins had, however, underestimated the newsworthiness of the story. For once Ron's sense of media manipulation had let him down.

Mitchell wrote a letter to *The Times*, protesting his harsh treatment in Dartmoor Prison, and, suddenly, it was all turning into a farce; gradually it became a nightmare.

The problem for the twins was that the whole underworld knew of the escape and of the predicament that Ron and Reg faced. It looked as though they were losing their grip; their reputation was on the line.

To keep Mitchell happy at a friend's flat in Barking, the twins brought in a hostess in the shapely form of Lisa Prescott. But 'The Mad Axeman' fell in love with her, something that no one could have anticipated, and that only further complicated an already complicated situation.

Something had to be done and quickly. Mitchell wanted to escape and to take his hostess with him, but what would the twins have to say about that kind of scenario?

Their answer was the gun!

According to Albert Donoghue at the trial in 1968–9, the twins decided to cut their losses by getting rid of Mitchell once and for all. They just didn't know how to handle the situation, so their recourse was to kill the problem by killing Mitchell.

Donoghue was told to get Mitchell out of the flat and into a van. Mitchell didn't like the idea of going anywhere without his new love, but he was persuaded that she would follow once he was safe and out of the country.

Unknown to Mitchell, there were three other occupants of the rear of the van. The hit men were already in position and armed. They were Alfie Gerrard, a South London villain by the name of Gerry Callaghan and 'Hardman' Freddie Foreman. None of the three were members of the Firm, as the twins wanted to keep the outcome a secret – at least from their own gang. To be actually seen disposing of a problem in this way would have done nothing to enhance their reputations.

Mitchell got into the van, which was parked on the Barking Road. Once inside he was told to sit by himself on one side of the van, opposite the other three men. As the driver, Donoghue, drove off the first gunshots rang out from the back of the van.

Mitchell wasn't dead, so the three unloaded their guns again into the huge man. He was still groaning as another bullet entered his brain. 'The Mad Axeman' Frank Mitchell died at the hands of his rescuers.

Lisa Prescott, back inside the flat, heard the shots and was convinced that they would then come after her but no one paid her much attention.

Donoghue stopped the van and got out. He couldn't stand the stench of death. He walked away from the van, half expecting to be killed himself. But nothing happened.

Later Donoghue reported back to the twins that the job was done, supposedly with just four words: 'The dog is dead.' It is well reported that Reg wept when he heard the news.

The date was 24 December 1966, Christmas Eve.

Following the arrest of the Krays in 1968, 'Nipper' Read pulled Lisa Prescott in for questioning about the 'Mad Axeman' affair. The police car carrying Lisa drove towards Tintagel House and away from Scotland Yard and, fearing that it was the Krays who were having her killed, she pulled herself free from her captives and almost threw herself off one of the bridges over the River Thames. Eventually she was convinced by the policemen that they were genuine and they continued their drive.

Donoghue was later asked by the twins to deliver £1,000 in cash to Freddie Foreman in payment for the killing. In January 2000 Foreman openly admitted in a TV documentary to killing Frank Mitchell but, as he has already been acquitted of the murder, he cannot under UK law be tried again for the same crime, which leaves a self-confessed killer free to walk the streets.

And so it was that the Krays were responsible for another killing in 1966, which they were never convicted of, but this time they didn't pull the trigger themselves.

The twins were now being openly encouraged by the US Mafia to use hit men, something that didn't exactly appeal to their sense of honour and respect. To the Krays, men should be men, and they should be seen to be so.

'What actually happened to Frank Mitchell?' I asked Ron during one of my regular visits to Broadmoor.

'I like to think of him peacefully settled in Australia or South Africa,' replied Ron, head down, peering into his lager.

I thought at the time that this was a somewhat peculiar way in which to reply to a question, but now that I have learned the facts about the case, I can understand why. Even then, Ron would not own up to his part in the killing. And now that they are all dead, there will be no more questions to answer.

In the eyes of psychologists this behaviour by Ron is called 'splitting'. In his case, being a paranoid schizophrenic, it is quite understandable, since he has replaced his bad memories of Frank Mitchell with a vision of what could have happened. This is a typical schizoid defence mechanism, whereby the traumatic event becomes an internal object, thought or phenomenon; it becomes 'split off' from the conscious side of the mind, the ego. Bad thoughts, events or acts are denied or repressed in favour of something that is more acceptable to the ego.

It is the emotional implications that demand splitting in the minds of the Krays. Both the twins are guilty of this, since Reg also denied any involvement in the murder, of which he was apparently justly accused. The anxieties of both men are too much for their egos, therefore the splitting from reality to unreality. In the world of the Krays there is a fine line between the truth and make-believe, between the image and the man.

As time went by, Ron humiliated his twin brother so much, by mocking him over his inability to kill, that the inevitable was sure to happen sooner or later. This was to be the ridiculous stabbing to death of Jack 'The Hat' McVitie in October 1967.

10

THE END OF FREDDIE MILLS

Freddie Mills was a great champion, but he couldn't run a club. At first it was a restaurant, but Freddie wanted the limelight, the smart set. Ron and Reg tried to help, but Freddie started to get ill, maybe because of all those punches he took in the ring.

It was only a matter of time before everyone wanted out, except Freddie. And then there was the 'Jack the Stripper' murders around London. Now, I don't know if it's true, but I was told at the time that the police wanted to question Freddie about the case and my brothers didn't like that. He knew a lot about what was going on, so they were quite relieved when he blew his brains out!

Charlie Kray

The case that became known as the 'Jack the Stripper' murders started in June 1959. The place was Notting Hill. In those days it was a cheap bedsit area mainly frequented by London's small Jamaican community. It was a warm night and most people were sleeping with their windows wide open, trying to get the feel of fresh air on the breeze. Others were in the drinking dens and local seedy clubs, getting fuelled up on booze and bad company, trying to find an ear or two to bend. But what they got was a terrifying scream, shrill in the night.

This was not the usual shouting or loud noise from a street fight, which were common in the area at the time. The woman's scream echoed around Westbourne Gardens, waking normal people from their sleep and making them rush to the windows to scour the rooftops and streets for the source of the disturbance. No one reported seeing anything suspicious, although many saw what was going on.

Nearby a man struggled with a young woman, a local club hostess-cum-prostitute, in the front seat of a parked car. Her shrieks were constant and alarming, but this was a dangerous part of London and not a place for well-wishers or do-gooders to venture out at night to make discreet enquiries, or make a nuisance of themselves. So no one went to her aid. Everyone in Notting Hill knew that they had to mind their own business and no one would disturb them in theirs.

Some six hours later the half-naked body of Betty Figg, a 21-year-old prostitute, was found strangled on a Chiswick towpath. Her underwear had been removed and her stockings had been ripped off. She had scratch marks around her face and she had been strangled with bare hands.

Her murder was front-page news at the time, and the press made much of her lifestyle and that of her lover, 'a coloured man friend'. But the police could find no evidence, nothing to support an arrest – they were clueless.

Four years later the murderer struck again. Exactly how the police concluded that it was the same man is not exactly clear, but the near identical circumstances must have played an important part in their coming to this conclusion. Throughout a period of twelve months, between 1963 and 1964, six more murders took place, with six more prostitutes being killed. Everyone in London followed news of the 'Jack the Stripper' case, almost on a daily basis.

The second victim was 22-year-old Gwyneth Rees, who was found strangled in Mortlake. Three months later the naked body of Hannah Tailford was fished from the River Thames. She was well known to the police as a drug dealer and prostitute, and she had been drowned in a bath before being thrown into the Thames, near to the same towpath where the body of Betty Figg had been found. London's 'goodtime girls' were worried, and they had a right to be.

In April, Irene Lockwood, aged 29, was dragged naked from the River Thames, again at Chiswick. And, later in the same month, Helen Barthelemy, a 22-year-old stripper originally from Blackpool, was found naked and strangled in Brentford. Earlier in the evening she had been spotted at a club in Westbourne Grove, Notting Hill, and the police complained at the time that they had not been getting any assistance from the local community there. Cooperation was sadly lacking, they said, as they continued on the case. But they did discover that Helen had been in trouble recently with her pimp, a 'coloured' man. He had beaten her and had, in fact, knocked some of her teeth out.

But still the police had nothing to go on. They were baffled and desperate for a break. They even sent women officers, dressed in low-cut blouses and tight skirts, into the clubs of Notting Hill and Soho, in an attempt to get the girls to talk. They even went as far as interviewing Christine Keeler, in jail for her part in the John Profumo affair. But their trip to Holloway Prison provided no results.

The *London Evening News* wrote an open letter to the murderer: 'Perhaps you can't help yourself,' they said, 'when in the midst of your obscenities with a cheap, bought woman, the red mist comes down and your hands tighten and tighten and tighten. But you cannot win.' The newspaper journalists were sincere enough, but it didn't work.

Mary Flemming, a 31-year-old prostitute, was the next victim, found dumped beside a garage in Chiswick. The police stepped up their enquiries and launched one of the biggest investigations ever seen in the capital, where they actually visited some 2,000 clubs. But again, it didn't work.

In November 1964, the killer was at it again. This time he chose Margaret McGowan, a high-class call girl, who had also been involved in the Profumo scandal. She was found naked near Kensington's Civil Defence underground control centre. Even though she carried a knife, the strangler managed to subdue her and kill her. And then, as suddenly as they had begun, the murders just stopped.

It was Charlie Kray who told me about the possible involvement of ex-world light heavyweight champion, Freddie Mills, but other gangland mobsters such as Charlie Richardson and 'Mad' Frankie

Fraser agree with Charlie. This, of course, may just be their way of saying that, if it was ever proven that they were involved in his killing, they were right to do it, because he really was 'Jack the Stripper'.

One thing is for sure, as I have stated earlier, Freddie had been robbed of all his money by the gangsters he had befriended. They bled him dry with protection demands and it was believed they were about to help plot a complete takeover of Freddie's club, along with his old partner Andy Ho. It was a good location, a good place to launder money and a good place for dealing drugs.

Old boxing pals of Freddie were openly talking about his problems with depression, brought on by taking all those punches in the ring. His speech was now slurred and he was getting dizzy spells. Freddie was not a well man.

Freddie was often seen on television in those days, and he was a real British boxing hero. He had been in films, he had written for newspapers and he had opened a restaurant in Soho. He was charming, wealthy and successful, or so everyone thought. So why should he blow his brains out, while sitting in the back seat of his car, in July 1965?

The police said suicide; the gun was still there in the car. But his wife, Chrissie, was convinced that this was not the case and told the police that she thought it was murder and named the Krays. She also told of Freddie being systematically robbed by gangsters demanding money for various reasons. She also claimed that, a few weeks before his death, her husband had been visited by a former professional wrestler. When Freddie didn't pay the demanded protection money the man smashed the place to pieces. She also told of another club owner having his club doused in petrol and being threatened with having it set alight.

The police had other theories at the time. They knew that Triad gangs were actively involved in trying to buy into the area, and there were plans to make the club a restaurant once again. But the police kept to their suicide theory.

They heard that Freddie had tried to get a gun from a number of crooks who frequented the club. He told them that he thought his life was in danger, but no one could help him. So he eventually approached a friend, Mary Ronaldson, who ran a rifle range at

Battersea funfair. He said he was going to a charity event and that he wanted to dress as a cowboy. This was the gun found in his car when he was found dead, a bullet through the eye.

When he was taken to Middlesex Hospital, Professor David Wingate, the resident medical officer, carried out a full examination. He was convinced at the time that someone had taken the gun off Freddie Mills and that he was then murdered with it. But he was never asked to give evidence at the inquest, and his comments have been largely forgotten.

So, was it suicide or was it murder? Everyone agrees that Freddie was in trouble with the Krays. He knew his days were numbered. And then there were the headaches and the depression. He was ill, he was broke and, like in a boxing ring, he had nowhere to hide.

A few days before his death, Freddie had a visitor from the Kray Firm. Freddie was told that the twins were not happy and that there was going to be real trouble. He told him to be smart and let the Krays have the club. The odds were against him, and he knew it. There was no getting away and no one to help him in his hour of need. Freddie started complaining about his partner, who he said had been stealing from him, and he couldn't understand why Ron and Reg weren't willing to help him.

Ron Kray always said that he had nothing to do with the death of Freddie. But he and his twin had plenty to do with the reasons for his death, whether he pulled the trigger or ordered the death or just played a waiting game. We may never know the truth about the death of Freddie Mills, a great boxing champion, but the Krays have a lot to answer for in this respect. They are all dead now, so this secret, along with many others, has gone with them to their graves.

11

LORD ROBERT BOOTHBY AND RON KRAY

'Sorry, dear boy,' said Lord Robert Boothby. 'It's all gone!'
Boothby smiled as he closed the door on Charlie Kray.
Boothby had spent all the money he made from the libel
case, some £40,000, on repaying his gambling debts, so
there was nothing left for Charlie.

The Kray Files (Colin Fry)

It was called 'The Case of the Brighton Peer', but it also involved
Boothby's live-in lover, cat burglar Leslie Holt, and his pal Ron Kray.

Robert John Graham Boothby, Baron Boothby KBE, was also
known to his friends as Bob. The only son of Sir Robert Tuite
Boothby, KBE of Edinburgh, was educated at Eton College and
Magdalen College, Oxford.

He stood as MP for Orkney and Shetland back in 1923 but was
unsuccessful, eventually becoming a member of parliament in
1924, when he won the seat for East Aberdeenshire. He held the
seat until 1958.

From 1926 to 1929 he was Parliamentary Private Secretary to
the Chancellor of the Exchequer, Winston Churchill, and held
other offices later in his long career in Parliament. In 1940, he
became a junior minister as Parliamentary Secretary to the Minister
of Food, but was forced to resign his post for not declaring an
interest when asking a question in Parliament.

During the Second World War he reached the rank of Flight
Lieutenant in the Royal Air Force Volunteer Reserve.

Robert Boothby was a keen advocate for being in Europe, and he served his country as delegate to the Consultative Assembly of the Council of Europe from 1949 to 1957. Later, he was involved in economics, agriculture and much, much more. He became Rector to the University of St Andrews from 1958 to 1961, Chairman of London's Royal Philharmonic Orchestra from 1961 to 1963 and President of the Anglo-Israel Association from 1962 to 1975. He became Baron Boothby of Buchan and Rattray, Head of the County of Aberdeen, on 22 August 1958.

Boothby was a well-known figure around town, with his deep voice, bow tie and colourful clothing. He was a good storyteller, a likeable drunk, a good liar and a compulsive gambler. He was also bisexual. This was the man known to Ron Kray as Bob.

Robert Boothby was only interested in boys at Oxford, earning himself the nickname 'Palladium' because he could do it 'twice nightly'. It was only when he was in his mid-twenties that he suddenly found himself also enjoying the company of women.

In May 1964, Leslie Holt set up a meeting between Lord Robert Boothby and Ron Kray. The topic of conversation was a project in Nigeria, detailed in the next chapter, that the Krays were interested in getting Boothby involved in, on a charitable basis.

Leslie Holt was a well-known cat burglar and former boy boxer. Some say it was in his boxing days that he had met Lord Boothby and they became 'good friends', but in reality he met Boothby at a gambling club owned by Ron and Reg Kray, Esmeralda's Barn, and was introduced to him by Tom Driberg MP. Boothby couldn't take his eyes of him. However it happened, it was perhaps unfortunate for Boothby that Holt was a very good friend of Ron Kray. Because homosexuality was illegal at the time, Boothby had kept his relationships with Holt and others secret from most people, but Ron, himself a homosexual, knew of these relationships and wanted to exploit them to the full.

When the project in Enugu, Nigeria, first came up in the spring of 1964, Ron met an architect who just so happened to be the son of a lord. The project was the architect's dream child and, through his father, Ron was wined and dined at the House of Lords. Lord Robert Boothby was soon to be another feather in the cap of Ron, and potentially a good image builder for him in the eyes of the media.

Holt was one of nine children from an East End family. As a young boy he was sent to reform school where he developed an interest in animals and boxing. He was dashing, popular and, to many, glamorous.

Holt was bisexual and had a long-running affair with Boothby, and it was Holt who introduced Boothby to crime, prostitution and gay clubs. Their liaisons took place at Boothby's flat in Eaton Square, London, and Holt shared the flat on a semi-permanent basis. Their clandestine get-togethers were most secretive, but not to Ron Kray.

Ron needed a figurehead for the African scheme, and he had decided that Boothby was the right man for the job. Through Leslie Holt, who was a regular member of the Kray Firm, he set up a meeting with Boothby at his London flat. Also there that day were Boothby's lover, Holt, photographer Bernard Black, who was there to record the event for posterity, and 'Mad' Teddy Smith, another homosexual gangster and a friend of Labour MP Tom Driberg. Driberg was a friend of Boothby's, and together they enjoyed the company of boys, preferably young boys between the ages of 16 and 18.

They discussed the business of the Nigerian project and Boothby told Ron that he would think about the plan. A few days later, however, Boothby telephoned Ron to tell him that his busy workload meant that he didn't have time for the project.

He might not have had time for the Enugu project, but Boothby could still find time to enjoy himself, and Ron did all he could to supply him with young boys, for his pleasure. Boothby and Driberg attended many 'parties' that Ron held at his flat in Cedra Court. Reg was usually there as well, indulging in his own homosexual activities, while his wife, Frances, stayed alone at home in the flat below Ron's at Cedra Court.

Boothby, Driberg and Ron only wanted boys, and Ron would arrange for sex shows to be put on for their benefit. It was perverse and they loved it. Ron got a real kick out of it, enjoying seeing these powerful politicians doing unspeakable things in the company of his boys. Boothby didn't care though, and neither did Driberg.

It was at this time that Scotland Yard were beginning to take a serious interest in the Krays, and an investigation was underway into their roles in protection rackets, extortion and fraud.

Bernard Black took many photographs that day in early 1964,

and later, on 12 July of the same year, he handed a complete roll of film to the *Sunday Mirror*. Earlier in the day the newspaper had run an article headed 'The Peer and Gangster', in which they didn't name names but hinted at a homosexual relationship between a well-known peer and a top gangster from London's underworld. Black was after some easy money.

Later that same day, however, he had a change of heart and asked for the photographs back. He pleaded that they were not his to sell, but it did no good. The *Sunday Mirror* refused to hand them back.

Other newspapers at that time were taking an interest in the activities of Scotland Yard, and rumours were rife about corruption in high places. Alec Douglas Hume, prime minister at the time, ordered an investigation of his own and sent the Home Secretary Henry Brooke to talk with Boothby, who denied all the stories. He lied through his teeth.

The Home Secretary then had a quiet chat with Sir Joseph Simpson, the Commissioner of Police. On the following Tuesday, 14 July 1964, Sir Joseph Simpson of Scotland Yard issued a statement in *The Times* saying that he had asked the Yard to look into allegations recently made in the *Sunday Mirror*; allegations regarding orgies and homosexual conduct between a peer and a man with a criminal record. There was also talk of clergymen being involved.

The statement of 14 July read as follows:

I have today asked senior officers for some enlightenment on newspaper reports that:

1. I have ordered an investigation into, among other things, allegations of a homosexual relationship between a peer and a man with a criminal record.

2. I shall give the Home Secretary details of reports submitted by members of the Metropolitan Police resulting from this investigation.

3. An investigation embracing relationships that exist between gangsters, a peer and a number of clergymen has taken place and that blackmail is alleged.

None of these statements is true and beyond this fact it is not my intention to make any report to the Home Secretary. My duty as Commissioner of Police in serious criminal cases is to put the facts before the Director of Public Prosecutions, for him to decide whether prosecutions should take place.

In saying that I hope it will be understood in the press that I am not going to disclose information about the many inquiries being conducted into various aspects of underworld life. Inquiries of this kind are in fact going on almost continually.

The *Mirror* followed up the story on Thursday, 16 July, with the heading 'The Picture we Dare not Print', where they added lots of detail to the bones of the story, but again without divulging the names of those involved.

However, on 22 July 1966, the German magazine *Stern* came right out and named Lord Boothby as the peer in the story – and Ron Kray as the gangster.

Lord Boothby, who was on holiday in France at the time, telephoned his friend Tom Driberg in London. They were in a mess and needed help quickly. That help was to come from none other than Harold Wilson, then leader of the Labour Party.

Boothby had always been fond of boys. He had once said: 'I'm not sure if I like the boys better than the girls, or the girls better than the boys.' He was a well-known bisexual, even at university, but his charm normally kept him out of trouble. Apart from boys, his favourite hobby was gambling. And this brings us once again to Ron Kray.

Ron wined him and dined him in the West End of London, introducing him to many young boys who caught the eye of the peer. Ron once told a poor young man: 'You will go home with Mr Boothby. You will do anything Mr Boothby wants. Or I will hurt you badly!' There are no prizes for guessing the result.

Boothby frequented casinos owned by the Krays and still carried on his relationship with Leslie Holt, who was always on the sleeve of the peer. That is, whenever he was not carrying on his trade as a cat burglar. Boothby couldn't understand why he couldn't stop, but Holt did it for the fun of it and just wouldn't stop.

The relationship between Boothby and Ron isn't difficult to understand. Boothby always lived on the edge; he loved excitement, and Ron gave him plenty of that. He also gave him other gifts, apart from the boys.

Wilson was a worried man, since he knew all about the stories involving Tom Driberg MP, who was one of the elder statesmen of the Labour Party. Driberg was a homosexual who had a peculiar sideline in setting up people for robberies. He even got a cut of the loot in return for all of his hard work. Driberg was also involved in the African business.

Harold Wilson assigned Gerald Gardiner QC and lawyer Arnold Goodman the task of getting both Driberg and Boothby off the hook. There was an election coming, and Wilson did not want a scandal that could open up a real Pandora's Box, a real can of worms. Their solution was for Lord Boothby to write a letter to *The Times* denying all the allegations.

It was published on 1 August 1964 and read as follows:

Sir, On 17 July I returned from France and found, to my astonishment, that Parliament, Fleet Street and other informed quarters in London were seething with rumours that I have had a homosexual relationship with a leading thug in the London underworld involved in a West End protection racket; that I have been to 'all male' Mayfair parties with him; that I have been photographed with him in a compromising position on a sofa; that a homosexual relationship exists between me, some East End gangsters and a number of clergymen in Brighton; that some people that know of these relationships are being blackmailed; and that Scotland Yard have for months been watching meetings between me and the underworld thug and have investigated all these matters and reported on them to the Commissioner of the Metropolitan Police.

I have, for many years, appeared on radio and television programmes; and for this reason alone, my name might reasonably be described as 'a household name' as it has been in the *Sunday Mirror*. On many occasions I have been photographed, at their request, with people who have claimed to be 'fans' of mine; and on one occasion I was photographed, with my full consent, in my flat (which is also my office) with a gentleman who came to see me, accompanied by two friends, in order to ask me to take an active part in a business venture, which seemed to me to be of interest and importance. After careful consideration I turned down his request, on the grounds that my existing commitments prevented me from taking on anything more; and my letter of refusal is in his possession.

I have been since told that some years ago the person concerned was convicted of a criminal offence, but I knew then and know now nothing of this. So far as I am concerned, anyone is welcome to see or to publish any photographs that have ever been taken of me.

I am satisfied that the source of all these sinister rumours is the *Sunday Mirror* and the *Daily Mirror*. I am not homosexual. I have not been to a Mayfair party of any kind for more than 20 years. I have met the man alleged to be a 'king of the underworld' only three times, on business matters, and then by appointment in my flat, at his request and in the company of other people.

I have never been to a party in Brighton with gangsters, still less clergymen. No one has ever tried to blackmail me. The police say that they have not watched any meetings, or conducted any investigations, or made any report to the Home Secretary, connected with me. In short, the whole affair is a tissue of atrocious lies.

I am not by nature thin-skinned; but this sort of thing makes a mockery of any decent kind of life, public or private, in what is still supposed to be a civilised country. It is, in my submission, intolerable that any man should be put into the cruel dilemma of having to remain silent while such rumours spread, or considerably to increase the circulation of certain newspapers by publicly denying them. If either the *Sunday Mirror*, or the *Daily Mirror*, is in possession of a shred of evidence documentary or photographic against me, let them print it and take the consequences. I am sending a copy of this letter to both.

Your obedient servant

Boothby

House of Lords, 31 July

It worked, and Boothby even got £40,000 from the *Mirror* in compensation. The case was over, and both men could sleep easy at nights, together with their 'boyfriends'.

Leslie Holt continued to visit and sometimes stay at No.1 Eaton Square, and 'Mad' Teddy Smith continued his relationship with Tom Driberg. Nothing had changed, other than the *Mirror* losing a lot of money. If they had continued the fight, then they surely would have won. But then, this was a political game.

Lord Boothby was, however, having a change of mind. The visits to Ron Kray's pad at Cedra Court continued and he still enjoyed the orgies, but he was now wary of the media and was convinced that a complete change was required.

Although he had been married, Boothby was not very keen on women. The only one who took his fancy was Dorothy Macmillan, and she just happened to be the wife of the then Tory Party leader, Harold Macmillan, but even this didn't stop her purportedly having Boothby's child. So, with one miserable marriage behind him and an impossible relationship with Dorothy and the child to conceal, he decided to get married.

The marriage was the highlight of the year for the media and Leslie Holt became the marriage's first victim; he was barred from Eaton Square. The story was thus finished. Well, almost.

'It was all down to Wilson,' Boothby told friends later. 'He got me out of it.' But he still managed to meet Ron secretly and carry on their mischievous games of 'pass the boy'.

Boothby ended up with the money, and Ron ended up with the notoriety that the media had so gratefully handed him on a platter. He was now a household name, just like Lord Boothby. But Boothby was also an ally. When the twins were being held in jail in connection with The Hideaway Club extortion case, Lord Robert Boothby stood up in the House of Lords and asked why they were being kept in prison. Soon they were freed, and eventually acquitted.

Some time later, Charlie Kray was looking around for some ready cash because the twins were once again in trouble with the law, again accused of extortion. He paid a visit to Lord Boothby at his Eaton Square flat and asked him for a loan of £40,000, which just happened to be the same amount that the peer had recently been handed by the *Mirror*. 'Sorry, dear boy,' said Boothby. 'It's all gone.' Boothby had gambled it all away in a matter of months. Some people in the press have stated that some of this money went to the Krays, but I have found no truth in this speculation.

Ron would not take money from his pal, Bob. That was not the kind of relationship they had. It was all about the boys, not the money.

'Mad' Teddy Smith was also getting himself into trouble, by being involved in the same case of extortion as Ron and Reg, but Leslie Holt had already flown the coop.

This dangerous liaison between high life and low life carried on for some time, but gradually it faded; in the end, it died a miserable death.

Leslie Holt had teamed up with a doctor, Dr Kells, who found clients for his cat-burglary skills. These robberies continued for a number of years, until Scotland Yard caught on to the two men. The doctor knew that the police were on to him but hadn't decided what to do when Leslie Holt inadvertently gave him the solution that he so badly needed. Holt had some trouble with one of his feet and Dr Kells offered to operate on it for him, saying it was no trouble and wouldn't take long.

Leslie Holt died on the operating table in 1979. The doctor was tried for murder, but acquitted. The man who had introduced Ron Kray to Lord Robert Boothby, the man who is pictured in all the photographs taken at Eaton Square, was dead: another victim of injustice.

No one can really be sure what happened to 'Mad' Teddy Smith, since he disappeared in 1968, shortly before the arrest of the Krays. There were rumours at the time that Ron had killed him, but Smith may have just decided that enough was enough; he may have been crazy, but even he could see what was coming. Reg, later in life, often spoke of Ron killing other people, so maybe the authorities and the press alike simply put two and two together and came up with five. But the crook, playwright and madman that was Teddy Smith was no longer around. He couldn't be tried, he couldn't give evidence against the Krays, he couldn't take any part in determining the future for all three Kray brothers. Is he really dead? Read on and you just may find out.

Lord Boothby died aged 86 in 1986, his reputation almost intact. It is only now, after his death, that the whole truth is being heard for the first time and his true relationship with Dorothy Macmillan and Ron Kray is being documented.

Dr Kells died of a heart attack, only a few years ago. So justice was finally served, after all.

Ron Kray died in Broadmoor in 1995, although his legend still lives on in the East End of London. Reg and Charlie Kray are also now dead, so they can no longer answer any difficult, awkward questions.

When Harold Wilson won the general election and became prime minister, he gave Goodman a peerage in reward for his efforts. He had managed to keep the secrets of Lord Robert Boothby and Tom Driberg MP out of the public domain and saved many more of his comrades in Parliament from being outed as homosexuals.

But he had also saved the Krays from jail, by lying his way to victory.

The story of 'The Case of the Brighton Peer' is a web of intrigue and deceit. It was covered up by the prime minister of the time and led to the abandoning of the then current case against the Krays. Because of the statements made necessary from Scotland Yard the case against the twins was put back more than two years. The Krays were free of the press; no one would touch them as they were scared of more court cases as had happened with the *Mirror*. They were free from police scrutiny, since Scotland Yard had issued statements denying investigations into the Krays and their underworld activities. In fact, they were free to do as they bloody well liked. And they did just that.

Lord Robert Boothby must be laughing in his grave at all the fuss he caused in his lifetime. He lied about the whole thing and got away with it. He danced with the devil, cheated him and succeeded. He dared to live out his devious life in the full glare of the media and was never caught in a compromising situation on camera again.

In 1964 he was featured on the TV programme *This is Your Life*. There was no Dorothy Macmillan, no 'Mad' Teddy Smith, no Leslie Holt, no Ron Kray nor Bernard Black, the photographer who took those amazing black-and-white photographs. His was indeed a black-and-white existence; partly open to public scrutiny, partly hidden from prying eyes. But he, like Ron Kray, had learned to manipulate the media, and he did it to great effect. It was a sad day for journalism when he died.

12

GETTING CHARLIE KRAY OUT OF NIGERIA

When Ron told me I had to go to Nigeria I thought he
was joking. But he didn't laugh, so I knew he was serious.
I didn't even know where it was, but I do now.

Charlie Kray

It all started simply enough with a chance meeting between Leslie
Payne, Ron Kray's business manager, and a young architect. The
two men talked of a scheme in Enugu, Nigeria. It was completely
above board, everything legal and Bristol fashion, but Leslie Payne
had a few ideas on how extra money could be made by taking
backhanders from all of the contractors trying to get in on the
build. The project was huge – there would be houses, a shopping
mall and a lot more. There was already a hotel in place and the
future looked good for the area.

Payne thought that his future was bright, too, when he approached
Ron with his ideas for raking off a surplus of money – easy money,
lots of dosh in brown paper envelopes, money to burn.

Ron and Reg laughed out loud when they heard Payne's ideas
for the scam. Just why should they want to get involved in Africa?
They had never been there, they didn't care about Nigeria, they
didn't even know where it was. And it was almost legal!

Undaunted, Payne went on to explain about the money that
could be made: money without accounts; money that could go
anywhere at any time. It would be money that they had complete
control over.

Ron and Reg weren't laughing any more.

'The Richardsons have a gold mine in South Africa,' said Reg quietly, strangely subdued.

'It would be good for our image,' said Ron, in reflective mood. The two brothers were thinking – something new for them.

It was then Payne's turn to contribute to the discussion. 'It would be good for you to be seen helping out our black brothers in Africa. This kind of opportunity for such positive publicity is rare, don't you think?'

Again the twins were quiet. They were still thinking. They were thinking of their image, of their reputation and of the money, but not necessarily in that order. Payne was thinking of fame and fortune for himself. After all, with a lot of money around some would surely rub off on him. Payne had the brains and the Krays had the power. Together they could be irresistible.

At last Ron spoke. 'Check it out,' he said quietly, after a quick glance at his brother. 'Go down and talk with them and do your sums.' Ron paused for a moment before he added: 'If it doesn't add up then we don't do it, but if there's money to be made then everything else is a bonus.' Again he paused. 'So what are you waiting for?' he asked Payne. 'Fuck off down to Nigeria and sort it out!'

Payne packed his briefcase and headed off for home. He was already dreaming about fame and fortune, trying to work out how he could make a little extra for himself and how he could explain to his wife that he had to go away, all by himself, with loads of expenses money and a stack of clean white shirts, to deepest, darkest Africa.

It was early in 1964 when Payne first flew down to Nigeria. The BOAC flight was fine and he enjoyed the company of the architect, who was along for the ride. The architect had spent some years trying to get the project started, but no one had even bothered going down there. This was his chance and it was the Krays that gave it to him.

Payne was not apprehensive about going to Nigeria. In fact, he was relishing the chance to show the twins his true character as a financial wizard, a man to be reckoned with, a man who the Krays really needed on their side. He also knew that there was no decision, as yet, as to whether or not the Krays would back the venture. So he had nothing to lose. If it went well and they could make a lot of money, then fine and he would find an extra something for himself. If it didn't work out then he would have had a good holiday anyway. It was a win–win situation as far as he was concerned, so he just sat back and enjoyed it. Why get your knickers in a twist when you can get someone else to get his or her knickers in a twist? And that was why the architect was along for the ride.

The plane touched down in Lagos and they made their way to a local hotel where they had planned to spend the night. Payne and the architect discussed the project during the evening – a shopping mall, some 300 houses, the possibility of further projects, the list was endless. The evening ended after a few gin and tonics in the bar and both men slept soundly in their beds.

The next day they took a small aircraft to the township of Enugu. Here things were very different. The air was humid and hot, the jungle was everywhere and the place was in the middle of a wilderness. There was nowhere to go and nothing to do, except discuss business and drink in the hotel bar, but this suited Payne and the architect, since this was all about business, pure and simple.

The Presidential Hotel was new and the rooms were clean. Payne was pleased to see that there was even a small fridge, filled to the brim with bottles of booze and plenty of ice to keep the drinks cold. He unpacked and met the architect in the bar for a few more drinks. If this was doing business, thought Payne, then bring it on.

Over the next few days discussions took place with various contractors and Payne was pleased with his research. He found out that things were very much the same there as in the East End of London, where they called it the 'Wild West'. Even in a place like Enugu, way out in the jungle of Nigeria, he found that money was everything. Money was all that mattered. Without it you had nothing, no life and no future, but with it you could do anything.

On his last night there, after a few more drinks in the bar, Payne did his sums. He was astounded. Even being cautious, and he had to be with the twins, who could be very demanding, he calculated that they could get around £120,000 in backhanders from this project alone. And this was only money for the Krays – he could skim off a little himself without anyone being the wiser. It was perfect. He had enjoyed the trip, had a little holiday and a bit of rest and relaxation by the hotel pool and in the bars, and he was going home with a great scam that was full of potential. What on earth could go wrong?

Payne and the architect came back from Nigeria full of great expectations for the future. The architect would get his housing development and the shopping mall and the Krays were due to get a lot of dosh out of the scam visualised by Payne. It was perfect.

On arriving back in London he immediately got together with Ron and Reg. Also at the meeting was the accountant Freddie Gore, although why he was there is not particularly clear, since the money was all due in cash, hidden from the taxman, hidden from anyone. Payne presented his assessment of the scam and the Krays were overjoyed with the prospects. It was agreed that Payne would set up a legitimate company for the scheme, so they could offset the costs of their trips, and they even talked of getting an appropriate office, somewhere nice – why not in Mayfair?

Payne came up with the idea of calling the company 'Great African Safari', and it was to be a part of a group of companies that he had already set up for the Krays called the Carston Group. They even discussed who they could get on the letterhead.

But first the twins wanted to see for themselves, and soon they were all flying down to Nigeria so Ron and Reg could be absolutely sure of what they were getting into. On landing in Lagos they checked into the airport hotel previously used by Payne and, like before, they spent most of the evening in the bar, gin and tonics all round. The twins enjoyed their first time away from home for a long, long time but Payne was anxious and drank a little too much.

The following morning the three men took the flight to Enugu. The Sikh pilot skimmed the treetops on the way, as he had on the previous trip, and Payne didn't like it. He was still feeling the effects of his excessive drinking the night before and he just couldn't wait until they got down to terra firma.

They arrived at Enugu in good time and quickly collected their luggage. To their surprise they were met at the airport. Dr Okpara, a local government minister, had arranged with Payne to provide transport to the hotel and he didn't let them down. The driver escorted them to the car and they settled into the back. They were quickly into the drinks cabinet and drank and smoked their way to the hotel, doing a little sightseeing on the way. But the biggest surprise of all was the car itself – a beautiful old Rolls-Royce.

The twins enjoyed themselves in Enugu. They liked the food, even the monkey brains that they were served as a delicacy. Ron told Dr Okpara, when he met him one evening, that he was interested in their justice system, especially how they treated prisoners. Accordingly, he arranged for Ron to be shown the local prison, where he saw the cells and talked to some of the inmates. Okpara said that he would even let Ron use his Rolls-Royce and his driver, of course.

The prison was outside of town, in the jungle. It took some time to get there on the dusty roads but soon they pulled up inside the main gates, which were opened specially for the Rolls-Royce. Ron was dressed as usual in a suit and tie, all in perfect shape. At the prison they thought he was someone of importance from a foreign country, a member of parliament perhaps, so they treated him exceedingly well and were very courteous.

There was a blackboard just inside the office, near to the main gate of the prison where they had checked in, and there were names chalked on the board. Some were crossed out and Ron asked if they had been freed.

'Yes,' he was told, 'they are not here any more, they have all died!'

Ron was not smiling when he left the prison. 'Our English prisons are like holiday camps compared with this place,' he told the police officer who had shown him around.

Payne had been right; there was money to be made here. Ron and Reg enjoyed the rest of their time in Enugu, hardly ever thinking of how things were back home in London. They even got to know some of the locals who treated them to special displays of dance and their traditional festivities. And then there were the boys. Yes, the Krays enjoyed Nigeria.

They took trips into the jungle where they saw life in the raw. They were treated like kings and often had a motorcycle escort, for their own protection, of course. There were the 'Leopard Men' around at that time, so the government and the police wanted to take special care of their guests. And they had the use of the Rolls-Royce for as long as they wanted.

After an evening of palm wine, in the company of boys whom they had befriended during their stay, it was time to go home. The adventure had come to an end and it was now that the real business had to start, in earnest. Payne, who had generally stayed well away from Ron and Reg on the trip, was also ready. He had been talking to contractors and trying to decide on a system that he could use to get the money together. He was thinking of the £120,000 that he had told the twins he could get. Had he gone too far? Was it too high? What if they didn't get it all?

Back in London everything was set. The twins, however, were not pleased with the activities of the Firm, who had been idle while they had been away. Protection money hadn't been collected in full and there were 'long firms' that were waiting to be busted. They decided there and then not to go to Nigeria together ever again. Ron would go, then Reg, then Charlie, and so on. Never again would Ron and Reg travel together to Africa or anywhere else for that matter.

They decided that Charlie would take care of business in Enugu. All he had to do was collect money and Charlie was good at that. Payne could do the business and Charlie could take care of the dosh. There shouldn't be any trouble with anyone down there, no rough stuff to be taken care of, so the two of them could easily be trusted to do what they had to do, couldn't they?

Charlie's first trip to Enugu was with Payne. He hated the trip down, with Payne incessantly talking about what he had done on previous trips as though he were a travel guide. He hated Payne, who had previously been a corporal in the army, although he always said he had been an officer. And he hated the way he talked, always trying to speak 'proper' English and pretending that he was cultured, well educated, posh.

Despite Payne, Charlie enjoyed the VC10 and the efforts of the stewardesses on the flight. They treated him well, with champagne and a few scotches on the side, and there were one or two he wouldn't have minded showing him the night life of Nigeria.

On the way down they landed at Kano Airport, on the edge of the Sahara. It was way out of town, so there was no chance of any sightseeing. But they were not there for long and were soon back on their way to Lagos. Fortunately the monsoon period was over and the weather was fine and dry, no wind at all.

Payne led the way to the airport hotel and they checked in. Soon they were unpacked and in the bar. A few glasses of bubbly for Charlie and a couple of gin and tonics for Payne and they were ready to talk business. Payne told Charlie that he had already spoken to a contractor in Enugu who was prepared to pay them £5,000 for the privilege of getting in on the project. It should be in a brown paper envelope, loads of readies, all set to take back to Ron and Reg, and there were plenty more who were willing to pay good money to get involved in the work. Charlie was optimistic. He was also thinking there might be a little extra something in it for him, away from the prying eyes of his brothers, just like Payne had thought on his first trip to Nigeria. Charlie was not impressed with Payne, but he liked the thought of all that money.

The flight down to Enugu the following morning was uneventful, except for the antics of the Sikh pilot. This was Charlie's first experience and he loved the plane flying low and the mysterious jungle below, but once again Payne was silent – he didn't like the aerobatics, not at all.

Once on the ground Charlie and Les Payne got their suitcases and headed for the exit. Waiting to meet them was Dr Okpara's Rolls-Royce and the doctor's, by now well-known to Payne at least, cheerful driver. He smiled as he greeted them both, shaking hands vigorously. He loaded their luggage into the boot of the Rolls-Royce and then they were ready for the drive to Enugu and their final destination, the Presidential Hotel.

Charlie enjoyed the drive – it wasn't often he got to ride in such a vehicle – and they were soon at the hotel. Checking in was easy, one room for Charlie and one, further down the corridor, for Payne. The unpacking was done and, before they knew it, they were out by the pool, drinks in their hands. The sun was still high and the weather dry and warm. So far, it had been a perfect day for Charlie Kray.

And so it continued. Later in the evening Charlie and Payne had a meeting with the contractor that Payne had been talking about the previous evening and Charlie pocketed a brown paper envelope containing £5,000 in used Bank of England notes. They didn't ask where it came from and they didn't care. They had it and the game was on.

Charlie was relieved to get the money. He knew now that it was a real money-spinner, not just a scheme that Payne had dreamed up over a few gin and tonics. He was pleased his brothers had already invested some £25,000 in the project, so they needed a quick return on their investment. It was still a perfect day.

Nothing went wrong; it all went right for the duo from England. The only low point of the evening was when one of the local boys, who worked at the hotel, told them that he had been robbed by a member of the 'Leopard Men' cult who were notorious at that time in Nigeria. They had stolen his weekly wage, some £3.50. Charlie took pity on the lad and stuck his hand in his pocket, pulled out a few notes and gave them to him. It was later to prove to be one of the best investments Charlie ever made.

Payne met with more contractors and Charlie did his best to keep things sweet. He bought champagne for the contractors and told stories of London. He was his normal, charming self, all while Payne was lining up his next target and talking of more brown paper bags full of money. They had a good time, but it had to end.

They were soon on their way back to London, and Charlie had the pleasure of passing the brown envelope, with all the money, over to his brothers. They were overjoyed. At last they had their hands on some cash from the scam and there was plenty more to come.

'When's the next trip?' asked Ron, putting the envelope in his inside jacket pocket.

'Soon,' said Charlie, 'very soon!'

But Ron was not finished. 'I've been looking for someone to go on the letterhead,' he told Charlie. 'What would you say to someone with a title? It would look good, give the right image.'

Charlie didn't know what to say, so he waited for Ron to continue.

'I've got someone in mind. I've been told that he could be interested. His name is Lord Robert Boothby!'

Charlie just nodded in agreement – he knew the name well and he had seen him on television on many occasions. His brothers knew many people in high places, so why shouldn't they have a lord on the payroll?

While the twins were discussing the possibility of getting Lord 'Bob' involved in their African dreams, Charlie and Payne were once again heading south to Nigeria. The plan was to collect more money and to line up a few more contractors for future payments. The project was all ready to go and the weather was perfect for the build. They even had the construction company Turif International along for the ride, all legitimate and very eager to be involved in the project.

There were others on the trip down to Enugu. Payne was, by now, a regular on these flights and this time he was joined by his friend, the accountant, Freddie Gore and an old pal of Charlie's, a Canadian businessman known as Gordon Andersen. Everything went fine until they reached the airport in Enugu.

There was no warm welcome, no Rolls-Royce, no motorcycle escort to take them to the hotel. Even when they eventually arrived at the Presidential Hotel the reception was far from cordial. However, they found their rooms, unpacked and met up in the bar. And it was here that Charlie found the reason for their poor reception in Nigeria.

Payne had been in contact with the contractor who had paid them the £5,000 while back in London, but he would not give the man the go-ahead to start construction, even though the timing was perfect. Charlie discovered that they could not agree on where to start. Payne was no engineer nor builder, so Charlie couldn't understand why the contractor just couldn't get started anywhere.

Charlie argued his case, stressing that the twins would not be happy about these developments, or lack of them, but Payne was adamant and said that Charlie should just look after the money and he would look after the business. After a few gin and tonics his attitude worsened. He stood in the bar of the hotel wearing his brand new safari suit, looking like a great white hunter from an African travel novel, telling everyone, very loudly, how the locals should run their country.

Charlie was not pleased. This was not what he expected from the usually docile Leslie Payne. The others in the group said little or nothing for or against Payne's decision and how he was handling the situation, but Charlie again tried to stress the urgency of getting the project started. After all, the only reason they were there was to collect money, not to argue about where or what to build. Again he stressed how it would look to Ron and Reg back in London.

Charlie went to his room to try and think of a way to resolve the situation, one that would please both Payne and the contractor. He was even thinking of phoning Ron and Reg, so that they could contact Payne directly. He could see the whole business just slipping away, like sand, through his fingers, like money being burned. He decided to contact his brothers the next day if he couldn't make Payne see the sense of his argument.

The following morning Charlie went down to the restaurant for breakfast. It was normally quiet in the mornings, just a few customers around enjoying their first meal of the day, but this morning was very different. Payne was in loud discussions with a man at the breakfast table. Charlie recognised the man; it was the contractor who had given them the £5,000. This was not a good start to the day.

Payne suddenly stood up from the breakfast table and towered over the small contractor. He shouted at the man, leaving him in no doubt as to who was the boss of the project. The contractor was quiet for a minute before responding. He then said slowly and softly, 'I want my money back.'

This was not what Charlie wanted to hear. Payne immediately started to laugh, while he told the contractor that only he would make decisions, only he would determine when the contractor should commence his work – only he was the boss.

'No,' said the contractor, again quietly and strangely subdued.

The boxing twins – around the time they fought each other at Victoria Park.

An early photo of the Krays – teenagers with a pal. Just who is who?

The twins with their mother, Violet, in the back yard of the house at Vallance Road.

Reg with a tribal chief
in Enugu, Nigeria.

Reg and Frances on their wedding day.

Ron and Reg Kray meet Joe Louis.

Ron and Johnny Ray – they shared similar tastes.

Reg, Charlie and Ron in 1964,
photographed outside their home
in Vallance Road after being
acquitted at the Old Bailey.

Frank Sinatra Junior in discussion
with Ron Kray, looking for a
quick exit, just in case.

The Kray twins with Judy Garland.

Eddie Pucci, Sinatra's bodyguard, holds hands with Shirley Bassey. Charlie and Ron are second and third from left respectively, while Reg is third right.

Reg and Ron at Vallance Road.

Leslie Payne is sitting in front of Ron Kray (middle left) and
next to Reg Kray. Tom Driberg MP is behind Reg. Charlie
is seen in profile at the top right of the photo.

Ron Kray (centre) at a party for Joan Litttlewood's film *Sparrows Can't Sing*.
Also present are Reg's wife Frances (far left), Barbara Windsor
(second from left) and George Sewell (second from right).

Lord Robert Boothby,
Ron Kray and Leslie Holt
at Boothby's flat in London.

Charlie, Ron and
Reg at Billy Hill's
flat, in the back
room at the bar.

Ron trying to keep his
cool in Lagos, Nigeria.

L–R: Eddie Pucci (Mafia bodyguard), Ron Kray, George Raft,
Reg Kray, Rocky Marciano and Charlie Kray.

Reg Kray, Billy Hill and
Ron Kray relaxing in
Tangiers. The Krays had
fled the country after Ron
killed George Cornell in
The Blind Beggar.

Ron Kray dining with the Mafia in New York.

Charlie Kray with his mother and father. A David Bailey photo of the brothers is hung on the wall behind them.

'I just want my money back – now.'

Payne was laughing himself silly as the contractor started to walk away from the table. Charlie could say nothing – he was in shock; he had never seen Payne like this before. The others were not down for breakfast yet, so there was no one else to help in this most precarious of situations. And then it happened, and it was Charlie's worst nightmare.

The contractor stopped, turned round and lifted his head. He aimed his words directly at Charlie.

'My cousin is the chief of police,' he told him.

Charlie woke instantly. He rushed to the man, offering his apologies and saying that they could find a compromise, but the man was adamant. If he didn't get his money then he would contact his cousin. He turned away from Charlie and, not looking back, headed off in the direction of the hotel's reception, and the telephones.

Shortly after the contractor had left, Freddie Gore and Gordon Andersen appeared at the breakfast table, completely unaware of the morning's events. They sat down cheerfully and got on with their meals, leaving a silent truce between Charlie and Payne. No one spoke about the project. Discussions were simply of the food, the weather and how well they had slept.

Charlie was in deep thought. He had heard all the stories about Enugu Prison from Ron and he didn't want to be locked away in a place like that. As he drank his morning coffee he heard the sounds of sirens. Back in London it would have been police cars, but here it could be anything.

It turned out to be police cars after all, as, within only a few minutes, there were three armed police officers and a large man wearing an officer's uniform with a lot of gold braid on his shoulders standing at their breakfast table. As if on cue, the contractor also entered the restaurant and stood beside them. The officer told them all to stand and immediately pronounced that they were all under arrest and would be taken away to Enugu Prison.

Charlie jumped into action, telling the man that he was not a part of the group, that he had nothing to do with the project and that he was only there for his health. On checking with hotel reception, the police officer found that he was right. Charlie Kray was not registered in the name of 'Great African Safari' and neither was the Canadian Gordon Andersen. They were not employees of the company, or so it appeared, and had nothing to do with the building of the houses and the shopping mall. After a short while Charlie and his Canadian friend were told that they could stay, under house arrest at the hotel, but the others, Payne and Gore, would be taken to Enugu Prison.

Charlie pleaded for the release of his friends, but as no one had £5,000 available, there and then, to give back to the contractor nothing more could be done. As they led Payne and Gore away, Charlie shouted after them: 'I'll get hold of Ron and Reg. They'll sort it out, don't worry!'

Payne was almost crying as they took him away. Freddie Gore was sobbing his heart out. Gordon Andersen and Charlie were left alone to finish their breakfast.

Somehow, Charlie was happier now that Payne and Gore were no longer with them. He enjoyed the company of Andersen and they took their time over breakfast – plenty of food, lots of coffee and bucketfuls of fresh orange juice. Whatever the twins had to say, it wasn't his fault. He hadn't caused the trouble, but he had to sort it out. It was his chance to shine!

Reg slammed the phone down on the table as Ron finished his cigarette. The Widow's, their local pub on Tapp Street, near to Vallance Road, was quiet; no one said a thing. Reg and Ron strolled over to the window and looked out into the street. They discussed the problem between themselves, trying not to let on to the other members of the Firm at the bar that there was trouble in Nigeria. Gradually the pub noise resumed as the gang members started to talk and drink as normal.

The twins had a big problem – how to get the money. As Payne controlled all of their bank accounts then they couldn't just go to the bank and withdraw enough to send down to Nigeria. And it was also Saturday, so the banks weren't open anyway. The Carston Group did not carry cash, and they never carried cash themselves, apart from a few notes, since they never needed to spend money. Being the Krays, they always just took what they wanted.

Reg phoned Charlie's wife to see if she had any money lying around – she didn't. He then phoned Payne's wife to ask if she had any money in the house – she didn't. They phoned everyone they knew, but no one could help. It was now time to pull out all the stops – they had no option but to send the whole Firm out to collect protection money. And then there were the 'long firms', which were set up to fail – they could crash some of these and raise extra cash.

Their next move was to wait to hear from Charlie so they ordered more drinks and waited by the phone. It was a nightmare, and the brothers were not in a good mood. This was supposed to be their great adventure in Africa, but now it was all falling apart right in front of them. Worst of all was the simple fact that they had to give all the money back. They weren't worried about the money they had invested in the project, some £25,000, as they could always get more given time, but, to the Krays, giving money back was just not right and to raise the money over a weekend was downright stressful, but Charlie had to be brought home, no matter what.

Charlie went to see Payne and Gore in Enugu Prison on the Saturday afternoon. They didn't like it there. The chief of police wanted Charlie to get the money, and fast. He had already told him that he wanted the money by the end of the weekend and he insisted that they could all be kept permanently in Enugu if the money did not arrive in time. So Charlie decided to phone again, as planned, and come to an agreement with his brothers. It was not just a question of getting the money; it was also a question of how they could get the money from London to Enugu.

The telephones in Nigeria were not very reliable in those days and, once again, the phones at the hotel were not working. So Charlie had a friendly chat with the youngster he had helped when he was robbed by the 'Leopard Man'. The lad told Charlie of a local field telephone, just outside of town, and that he could show him the way, but they would need transport. This gave Charlie an idea.

He asked the youngster what a car would cost, one that could get him a few hundred miles or so, one that could reach the coast.

The lad knew where he could get one and they decided to stash the car at the back of the hotel as Charlie was still under house arrest. He gave the lad some money and they agreed to meet in a couple of hours, out the back, where the car was to be parked ready for a quick getaway if needed.

The lad got the car and they met up in the parking lot, normally used for the staff of the hotel. It worked fine and no one saw them as they drove off to find the field telephone. Charlie was smiling as he put the old car in gear; he was in control and it was all going to plan.

They soon found the telephone and Charlie was able to call Ron and Reg. He explained about his plan B, but said that they needed to raise the money or else Payne and Gore could end up in jail for a very long time.

'Let them rot in jail,' said Ron.

'We don't need them, forget them,' said Reg.

But Charlie reminded them about the bank situation. Payne was the only signatory and, like it or not, they needed him, at least for a while.

The twins agreed that finding the £5,000 should not be a problem, but how were they going to get it to Charlie? Charlie told them that he would sort it out with the chief of police and they agreed to let Charlie handle it. It was all settled, and Charlie felt better on the ride back to the hotel. The young lad who was with him on the ride had enjoyed helping Charlie and the two slipped back into the hotel. The lad went back to his work and Charlie joined Andersen in the bar to tell him what had been going on. A few glasses of champagne later and Charlie felt much better. It was now time for the twins to do what they were good at – raising cash. And Charlie had to do what he was good at – drinking champagne.

Ron and Reg sent the Firm out to collect protection money. They had the 'nipping list', where they would just nip into a pub and take away some whisky, or nip into a shop and take away some cigarettes. And they had the 'pension list', where they would collect cold, hard cash. The 'pension list' was the list they chose, and Ron put a figure by every name on it. He then told the Firm to go and collect. He wanted no excuses, no reasons for failure – all he wanted was the money.

Reg told a few of them to 'hit the floor' with some of the 'long firms' that had been fraudulently set up by Payne. They had bought stocks on credit, but it was now time to cash them in for real money and empty the warehouses. The directors would be gone, the goods would be gone, nothing would be left. It was all normal business for the Krays and they were good at it. Whatever they got out should be brought to The Widow's in Tapp Street, where Ron would be in his counting corner, by the phone.

A quick phone call to the Nigerian High Commissioner's office in London confirmed Charlie's story. They even told the twins that they would be available over the weekend in case Ron needed any help with getting the money to Enugu.

Ron and Reg sat drinking as the Firm left to start collecting the cash. They weren't drinking because they were happy with what they were undertaking; they were simply drowning their sorrows.

As Charlie waited for the money to arrive, he had to sort out the procedure for getting the money paid back to the contractor. The chief of police didn't want the money himself; it had to be paid to a local judge, acting on behalf of the Nigerian government. The only problem here was that the judge had his office a long way out of town, through the jungle, in an area completely unknown to Charlie.

Charlie asked around the hotel and eventually found a local solicitor who was willing to help. This man would accompany Charlie to see the judge and hand the money over. He would also organise the collection of the £5,000, in cash, through his bank. All Charlie had to do now was to wait.

Sure enough, Ron and Reg did what they said they would do and raised the £5,000, plus a little bit more for themselves, just to ease the pain. On the following Monday they found a friendly banker and soon the money was on its way to Nigeria. The money would soon be there, and all Charlie had to do was deliver the dosh.

This was easier said than done. The solicitor got the money from the bank and contacted Charlie telling him the good news, but how would they get it to the judge? Charlie contacted the chief of police, who suggested that they use the Rolls-Royce belonging to Dr Okpara. He would have no problem with this as it would do his image a lot of good in the local community. The driver knew the judge's house so there would be no problem finding it, even though it was way out in the jungle.

And that is what happened. The driver took Charlie and the solicitor through the Nigerian jungle to the judge's house where the transaction could take place. The ride out was not pleasant. Charlie had the money on him and all he could do was think about the 'Leopard Men' and all the other gangs that could be roaming the dark, damp places they passed through. It took a long time, but eventually they reached the house and the rest was simple formalities. The job done, they headed off back to Enugu.

Now it was time to collect Payne and Gore from jail. Charlie was looking forward to it, seeing Payne and Gore in jail that is, with the smell of rotten flesh and the constant fear of not ever being seen again. The chief of police laid on the transport, taking all of their belongings with him. He had their suitcases from the hotel and their passports, so he could drive straight to the airport from the jail and put them all on a plane to England.

Andersen was nowhere to be seen. He had gone his own way and was still in Nigeria, courtesy of the chief of police, but Charlie was there to make sure that everything was done by the book.

Payne and Gore were in a terrible state. They had not eaten, they had not slept, and they had not been outside their cells. They had not been told of their imminent deportation, so Charlie was able to deliver the good news himself. Their relief was obvious and Charlie was their hero.

They were given a police escort to the airport where there was a plane waiting to take them on to Lagos. The cars pulled up beside the plane and they quickly embarked; everyone was in a hurry. As they climbed on to the plane the chief of police had one last instruction for them: 'Don't ever come back to Nigeria!'

They were quickly in the air, and Charlie was laughing and joking about the whole business, but inwardly he was relieved that he was now on his way out of Africa. Payne and Gore were quiet and said nothing all the way to Lagos. In fact, they said very little all the way home and, remember, they were still in the same clothes that they had worn in jail. Even Charlie made sure that they were sitting well away from him on the plane, as he didn't want their smell to sour his flight back home.

At last they landed at Heathrow Airport and their ordeal was over. Some time later, someone tried to kill Leslie Payne and this led to him testifying at the trial of all three Kray brothers. Freddie Gore, part of the Laurel and Hardy team that he was, shortly left the Firm and disappeared into obscurity.

13

THE MAGIC BULLET

> Ron was a laugh when he spoke with Joan Littlewood. She asked us if she could shoot some scenes for her new film in The Wellington, she said it was just the right place. But then Ron told her that we didn't normally allow shooting in the club. We all roared with laughter; even Ron was smiling.
>
> *Reg Kray*

When it comes down to sheer luck and escaping the malevolence of Ron Kray, there can be no better example than George Dixon.

Dixon was a small-time criminal, more a hanger-on than a true member of the Firm, although he had been involved with the Krays for a time and was usually welcomed by them. He had, however, made a few unwise remarks about Ron and his homosexuality, which was not something that was talked about at the time. Not, that is, in front of the man himself. Ron had, as a result, barred him from all Kray establishments.

Now, most men would have thought themselves lucky not to be cut up at the pig farm or thrown into the sea or into an open grave, but George Dixon just couldn't take a hint. Maybe he was pushed into it by his pals, maybe it was just bravado on his part, but then maybe he was just hard of hearing.

So when he heard that Ron was at the Regency Club in Stoke Newington he decided to have it out with him once and for all. It was almost the last thing he ever did. After all, who would willingly go up against Ron Kray on his own turf, in his own club, where he ran protection, and with other members of the Firm around him? And, don't forget, Ron was known to be a paranoid schizophrenic.

On charging into the club, Dixon made directly for Ron, who was sitting with some friends at a table in a corner. He then vehemently asked Ron why he had been banned from the clubs. Now, seeing that this was only a short time after the Cornell killing, when Ron had shot dead the Richardson henchman in cold blood at The Blind Beggar, this was not a very good idea.

Ron, however, was enjoying himself and not in the mood for a battle of words. He therefore slowly stood up, pulled out a gun and aimed it at Dixon's head. He fired at point-blank range. By all rights, Dixon should have been a dead man, lying on the floor in a pool of blood, but nothing happened, apart from a quiet 'click'. The gun had failed to fire.

Dixon stood there motionless. As did everyone else in the club. There was no sound at all; you could have heard a pin drop. No one knew what to do or where to go. It was simply unbelievable.

It was Dixon's lucky night, although he didn't know it at the time. He was still waiting for Ron to shoot again and he was positive that the gun would fire next time.

But, instead of firing again, Ron just laughed. He stood and stared at the gun in his hand for a moment before pulling out the dud bullet. He looked at it for a few seconds before giving it casually to Dixon as a souvenir. The rest of the evening continued as if nothing had happened, with Ron and his pals enjoying themselves on the free house booze and Dixon having a few drinks to calm his nerves and to toast his lucky escape.

History isn't clear as to whether or not George Dixon was ever allowed back into a Kray establishment, but after treatment like that, why would anyone risk an unlucky bullet?

Whatever Ron had done before in his criminal career, that evening he made George Dixon's day!

14

MURDER INCORPORATED

Ron talked to our friends in America about all sorts of things. They had lots of ideas, things we could do to expand our business empire.

Reg Kray

When the banker A.B. Cooper took Ron on a guided tour of New York in April 1968, one of the hottest topics of conversation and discussion between the top Mob bosses and Ron was the idea of setting up Murder Inc in the UK. All Mafia families were involved, throughout the USA, and Frank Illiano of the Colombo family in New York outlined the whole idea to Ron. It would be a simple matter to organise Murder Inc in England, and Ron and Reg would get all the contracts and therefore all the money. The key was to get outsiders in to do the killings. The Krays would become even more powerful with the backing of the Mafia. They would become true allies.

Ron thought much about this idea and presented it to his brother Reg when he returned to the UK. There was also the promise of more bearer bonds and that, too, guaranteed substantial earnings for the twins.

Ron had, during the summer of 1967, already tried various ways of killing people. The idea of Murder Inc was nothing new to him, but somehow he just couldn't manage to pull it off. There was always a problem, and perhaps that problem was A.B. Cooper.

It was Cooper who had supplied the machine guns, the handguns and even the crossbow that is now housed in Scotland Yard's Black Museum. He had even supplied the syringe hidden in a briefcase. But none of them worked. And none of the killers he selected could do their job properly.

It was also Cooper's idea to kill President Kaunda of Zambia and other political leaders, for money naturally. Ron made his own hit lists, but we cannot be sure how many he actually killed or had killed. Needless to say, many of the old Firm disappeared at that time, including 'Mad' Teddy Smith, whom many were convinced had been killed by Ron.

Even the diamond mine in South Africa that Ron wanted, not least because the Richardsons had one, never materialised.

The common denominator here was always A.B. Cooper, but still Ron did not wise up. Reg was never keen on the stuttering American, and neither was Charlie.

'Who could trust a guy with the initials ABC?' Charlie once told me. How true!

But the strangest attempted killing was yet to come. After the trip to New York, Cooper was once again flavour of the month and could do no wrong in Ron's eyes. So, when Cooper suggested that they should kill a Maltese nightclub owner by the name of George Caruana, as a favour to the US Mob, Ron naturally said yes. It was his way of thanking his American cousins for their hospitality.

Cooper brought in a man from Scotland to do the killing, but, yet again, it all went wrong. Either there was a hex on Cooper or there must have been some other explanation.

What Cooper never told Ron and Reg was that he was working for the American FBI as an agent provocateur. He also never told them that he was dealing directly with Commander John Du Rose at Scotland Yard, 'Nipper' Read's boss, and that he was actively trying to get proof for a murder conviction that the Yard were trying to hang around the necks of the twins. And he also never told them the real reason for killing Caruana.

When the Krays were sentenced in 1969, it didn't take long for the Sicilian Mafia to arrive in the UK to take over the drugs trade. The Mafia family that arrived were called Caruana, part of the

Caruana-Cuntrera Syndicate. Now, it would really have been a coup for Cooper to kill off a Caruana Mafia boss for the FBI and, simultaneously, get enough evidence on the Krays for Scotland Yard to put them away forever. This would leave the double-dealing Cooper in the clear and allow him to take over the bearer bond deal himself, which would have been very lucrative indeed. Remember, Sicilian Mafia often used Maltese passports to enter the UK. It is not surprising that they still do.

So, was this the real reason for the intrigue surrounding the attempted Caruana killing? Perhaps we will never know, but the arrest of the Krays in May 1968 put an end to any thoughts of establishing a Murder Inc in the UK. From then on, the Mob handled things themselves.

Cooper's double-dealings were over, and he discreetly disappeared after giving a signed statement to Scotland Yard. No charges were ever brought against him and he was never heard of again. A chapter in the history of British crime was over, but the full story of the Krays is not complete. Some of you will, no doubt, be asking yourselves if it ever will be.

15

RON KRAY AND THE KILLING OF GEORGE CORNELL

I shot him in the face. He fell like a sack of spuds. It was lovely!

Ron Kray

The most important killing of all those carried out by the Krays was that of George Cornell, shot and killed by Ron at The Blind Beggar public house in Whitechapel on 9 March 1966. The importance of this killing is that it had such immense repercussions throughout gangland, as it broke all the rules that were previously standard practice.

George Cornell was the only Richardson gang member to escape from the Mr Smith's fiasco of the previous evening, and why he had to go and have a drink on Kray territory is anyone's guess. Sure, he had been visiting a pal in the hospital across the road who had been injured in a shoot-out, but he knew that The Blind Beggar was a Kray pub and he also knew that he shouldn't have been there. He was a loner and not an established part of the Richardson gang. He was also a mean man who had a reputation for being a tough customer to deal with, and Charlie Richardson was not one of his favourite people.

The East End grapevine is a mysterious phenomenon and it has ways of reaching those parts not reached by other grapevines, so news quickly got to Ron that Cornell was alive and well and drinking in The Blind Beggar. This, to Ron, was nothing short of out-and-out provocation. The fact that Cornell had apparently called Ron 'a big fat poof' at a recent gangland meeting only made matters worse. Maybe he knew his days were numbered?

What really took the biscuit for Ron was that he had been badly beaten up by Cornell a short time earlier. Ron was like an elephant – he never forgot. Whether Cornell actually did utter those fateful words is pure conjecture, but rumours were enough to sour the reputation of Ron Kray. He didn't care if it was true or not; it was time for justice, as he saw it.

Ron rushed from The Widow's to Vallance Road to collect his 9 mm Mauser handgun. He took his driver John 'Scotch Jack' Dickson and his minder Ian Barrie with him for the ride. He also supplied guns for them.

Very soon they were heading in the direction of The Blind Beggar. Ron Kray's moment had come.

Dickson was told to remain with the car while Ron and Barrie loaded themselves with weapons. Slowly, Barrie opened the door to the pub and the two men went inside. They took a side door that led them straight into the 'snug' at the back of the building. It was here that Cornell was sitting at the bar.

The snug was almost deserted, with only a handful of drinkers downing their midweek pints. Cornell and a man by the name of Albie Woods were near a partition at the end of the bar, quietly having a few beers. Cornell was sitting on a stool and Woods was standing. There was no panic or sign of alarm from Cornell.

Ian Barrie fired a few shots into the air just for the sake of it. It was a warning of what was to come, but Cornell didn't seem bothered by it at all. He remained seated, but Albie Woods moved away, holding on to the bar top as he went.

Ron approached the bar and stood face to face with Cornell. It was like a scene from a film noir, with both men standing almost eyeball to eyeball. Who would blink first?

Cornell sneered back at him.

'Well, look who's here,' he said, as he got up from his stool and raised his glass to his adversary. It was the last thing he ever did.

Ron pulled out his 9 mm Mauser and shot Cornell in the forehead. As he did so, the barmaid was putting on a new record. It was the Walker Brothers' 'The Sun Ain't Gonna Shine Anymore'.

After Cornell was shot, the record stuck on the words 'any more . . . any more', which kept repeating throughout the bar. It was rather poignant, but the playing of this particular song happened completely by accident. What had happened to poor George Cornell, however, was no accident. It was cold, bloody, deliberate murder!

Albie Woods had already moved well away along the bar, but he had slipped and was crouching on the floor, trying to bury himself somewhere in the darkness. When the shot rang out the bloodied body of George Cornell came gradually down to join him. Once again he came face to face with his old pal. But this time he was almost unrecognisable.

Ron and Ian Barrie left as quickly as they had arrived. Out of the side door and into the darkness. Woods tried to help Cornell but it was all too late, so he phoned Cornell's wife to tell her what had happened to her husband. He couldn't console her.

John Dickson drove Barrie and Ron back to The Widow's in Tapp Street, and to home territory. He still wasn't aware of any killing.

In fact, Cornell, even with a bullet in his forehead, wasn't yet dead. It was only later that night, in the same hospital he had visited earlier, that he actually died. Ron got to hear about it and he laughed out loud. And when 'The Colonel' laughs, everybody laughs. The whole Firm now knew that he had earned his button. There was now no turning back.

Reg spoke with Ron and told him how stupid he had been. Killing someone in a dark alley was one thing, but shooting a rival gang member in a pub, where witnesses could talk to the police, was a stupid thing to do. But Ron was enjoying himself and Reg knew not to push that particular topic of conversation any further.

It was some time later that the news got out, but the few witnesses who were there that evening were all ordered to keep quiet by members of the Firm sent to threaten and intimidate them, with the result that the police couldn't collect even one statement. It wasn't until Scotland Yard's 'Nipper' Read took his gamble by imprisoning the Krays that people began to talk. It was a repeat of the Charlie Richardson affair, and the police were learning fast.

In 1993 I had a memorable chat with Ron about the Cornell killing. The trip to Broadmoor had been the usual hour's drive and I was looking forward to seeing Ron and to hearing more stories about the old days. After locking away my briefcase in one of the reception security boxes, just like those seen on railway stations in American films, I made my way, escorted by a guard, through the maze of locked doors that make up the most secure hospital in the country. Before long I was in the meeting area, where tables and chairs were strewn around the room and smiling staff sat in corners, waiting to help any visitor or inmate requiring assistance.

The buildings were grey and uninviting, and the meeting place was in need of a coat of paint. The atmosphere was congenial enough, though, and I could see Ron seated at his usual table being waited on by a white-coated figure who brought him his favourite non-alcoholic lager and lit his cigarettes for him.

The normal pleasantries over, we immediately got down to business. And business that day was the story of the killing of George Cornell. Ron was very much matter of fact in his telling of events, and showed no sign of remorse or regret. In fact it looked very much as if he was enjoying it thoroughly.

'Just how did you feel that day, Ron?' I asked him thoughtfully.

He looked right through me as he said, with a glint in his eye: 'Bloody marvellous!'

The gun featured in the Cornell killing is now the prized possession of Scotland Yard's Black Museum – some years ago the police dragged the River Lea in London's East End and found the small 9 mm Mauser automatic, rusty and looking its age. Like its victim, it can't tell the story of the killing and why there was ever the need for the event to have taken place. Even John Ross, the curator of the museum back in the 1990s, didn't know the whole truth about the incident.

Ron Kray shot and killed George Cornell – it is as simple as that. There is really no need for any explanation. He did it because he wanted to, and it made him feel 'bloody marvellous!'

16

THE DEATH OF FRANCES KRAY

She was a lovely girl, Frances. But I knew it wouldn't last.
Ron didn't like her.

Charlie Kray

To understand fully the relationship that Reg had with women it is necessary to travel back in time to 1961, when Reg was already 27 years old. It was at this time that he met the only one true love of his life, Frances Shea. Even here we have contradictions, since Reg himself has always said that his wife was 18 at this time, whereas research has shown that she was a mere youngster of 16 and pure and innocent, which, even allowing for the sexual freedom of London in the Swinging '60s, was not such a rare event.

Frances was only 17 when Reg whisked her away to Milan and Barcelona, much to the dissatisfaction of her father, who was employed by Reg at one of his clubs. Reg asked Frances to marry him on several occasions but, knowing her parents would not give their permission, she rejected his proposals. The trips continued, to the South of France and to Holland, with Reg playing the courteous suitor and Frances just being her natural sweet self. She was an Irish redhead, with brown eyes framed by long eyelashes and with long hair swept back from her cherub-like face. Reg was absolutely besotted with her and treated her with the utmost of respect; so much so that he never slept with her before they were married. Some say that they never slept together even after they were married. Reg didn't like to talk seriously about sex and was always fearful of sexual ailments such as venereal disease. No, sex was almost a taboo subject for the Krays.

Reg took Frances home to meet his mother on many occasions and she enjoyed the company of the Kray family at Vallance Road, but she never took to Ron. She could see trouble in his eyes, even though outwardly he treated her kindly. Frances couldn't understand the power Ron had over Reg and why he would almost always take the side of his brother in any disagreement. And, with Ron's blatant homosexuality, it was obvious to her that there were troublesome times ahead. She didn't understand the problems of the Kray household, and Reg did little to try to understand her fears and put her mind at rest. Everything was normal to Reg, but it was a nightmare situation for Frances, who was torn between her love for Reg and her compassion and regard for her own family. She was a kid out of her depth, and Reg did nothing to keep her afloat.

Frances was still only seventeen when Reg was sentenced to a six-month jail term, and it was this that really antagonised the Sheas and turned them so vehemently against him. They didn't want their lovely daughter mixed up with a gangster who would be in and out of jail for the rest of his life. They wanted happiness and security for Frances and not the insecurity and deprivation that went hand in hand with the life of a gang boss's wife.

Not that Reg went out of his way to disappoint Frances and to complicate her life. On the contrary, he tried his best to give her everything she had ever dreamed of, but his own lifestyle always got in the way. Even after they were finally married, in June 1965, the problems continued.

Frances wanted a quiet wedding, Reg wanted to invite the entire East End of London. Frances wanted a family affair, but Reg wanted all the razzmatazz of the twins' club scene, with Rolls-Royces in abundance and David Bailey taking the photographs. When Reg gave Frances a new car, she found an instructor to teach her, but Reg was jealous and she never saw the instructor again. When she said that she wanted to work again, as a secretary, Reg refused, saying that no wife of Reg Kray would ever be going out to work. Reg was the breadwinner and that was that. Even when they went out together it always seemed to be with Reg's gangster friends and the talk naturally came around to crime, something that Frances hated. Reg just could not win, even though he meant the best in everything he did in trying to woo and comfort his young wife, who was now still only 21.

The honeymoon was spent in Athens, with Frances complaining about the food and Reg drinking heavily. In fact, rumours quickly spread back to London that Reg was impotent and unable to have sex with his new wife. This was not the right kind of impression that Reg wanted to make in the East End, where he could very easily be ridiculed for his lack of masculine prowess. The East End was, and still is, very much a man's world, and Reg knew that his position as an underworld gang boss could be in jeopardy.

The problems continued after the honeymoon, and you have to ask if the marriage was cursed from day one. When they returned from their honeymoon they couldn't move into their new apartment in the West End as the decorators weren't finished, so they moved into the Shea household for a few weeks. This was another big mistake as the Sheas could see the problems brewing between their little girl and her club-owner husband. Reg was out all day and most of the night, and he quickly became an unwelcome guest at the house in Ormsby Street, Bethnal Green.

When they finally moved into the West End apartment they didn't like it and quickly moved back to the East End. It was here that Ron saw his chance of upsetting their lives further by persuading Reg to take on a flat below his in Cedra Court, where Ron held sex orgies for his boys; this was yet another big mistake.

It appeared that no matter what Reg tried, he could not get away from his twin brother. And Ron was loving every second of it. He wanted things back like they were in the old, pre-Frances, days. He missed his twin and he would make sure that Reg was soon missing him. He was intent on coming between the newly-weds, and when Ron made up his mind about something then he would turn heaven and hell to make it happen.

Frances became desolate and depressed, and she was soon back with her parents in Bethnal Green. She had been married for only eight weeks.

The following couple of years became a routine of hospitalisation and drug abuse for Frances Kray and, prompted by her family, she even tried to get the marriage annulled. Her parents blamed it all on Reg and even claimed that he had supplied her with the drugs, but Reg has always denied this and I, for one, feel that he was quite sincere on this point. All the way through this on-off marriage her mother always maintained that her daughter was a virgin. Despite this, Reg managed to keep his reputation as a stud, with various women saying that he had fathered their children. But this was a simple trick for Reg to achieve; a telephone call would pull in favours for a suitable sum and the woman would be rewarded well for her time in court. As there was nothing to prove, then naturally Reg would win the case. Simple, but it worked. Whether or not Reg actually pulled this kind of stunt is not certain, but it is an interesting thought.

Frances's problems turned her life into a living nightmare and she became more and more depressed. Her premonitions that she would die young didn't help the situation. Reg continually tried to talk her round by telling her of all the exciting places that they would be seeing and the great things that they would do. Unfortunately, Reg became more involved in business at this time, as his services were needed at Esmeralda's Barn. Frances knew that he didn't really need her and she tried to commit suicide.

Ron, again, saw his chance of getting her out of his way for good. He hated her for coming between him and his twin and took every opportunity to demean her and to disgust her. In fact, he made her life intolerable. His plan was beginning to work.

Reg made one last effort to make things work by offering to take Frances away from everything for a holiday and Frances reluctantly agreed. On 6 June 1967 they went to a travel agent and bought the tickets, but that same night Frances apparently took an overdose and died in her sleep. At 23, her life was over.

Reg was still her legal husband as the divorce had been put on hold, and he knelt by her side all day, with her lifeless body motionless on the bed. He drank and drank until he could drink no more. The gin didn't help; nothing helped. And still the Sheas blamed him for it all. True, Reg had made many disastrous decisions, but in no way could he have known the outcome of these events – or could he? Did he know what Ron had intended for Frances? Was it his own decision to close the chapter on his marriage? Did Ron actually force her to take the tablets that led to her death?

Reg was still in love with Frances and he just couldn't believe that she was dead. The funeral was held at Chingford, Essex, with the Kray and Shea families split in an ever-increasing feud. It was the first time that Reg had had to face the music alone, as Ron did not attend the funeral. Mum and Dad were there with brother Charlie, but it just wasn't the same. He didn't have the support of his twin brother. He was confused and in agony. But the agony appears to have subsided for long enough to allow him to drive to the Shea residence and collect all the letters he had written to Frances and the jewellery that he had given her over the preceding seven years. Was this really the action of a grieving husband?

Reg turned to gin and to guns. He drank more and shot a few people just for good measure, and he put it all down to the death of Frances. But maybe it was, in reality, all due to his own shortcomings as a husband and to his own family's attitude to relationships. Whatever the truth, I suppose we will never know.

Reg told people later, when he was near to death, that Ron was responsible for the death of Frances, but did he mean it was all his brother's fault? Or did he mean that Ron actually killed her?

17

REG KRAY AND THE DEATH
OF JACK 'THE HAT' McVITIE

I always knew Ron would cause me trouble, but I just
don't understand why Reg had to kill Jack.

Charlie Kray

The date was 28 October 1967 and, for Reg Kray, it was time to kill Jack 'The Hat' McVitie, a small-time villain and pill-taker who owed money to the twins.

In a way, McVitie had brought about his own death by agreeing to kill Leslie Payne, the twins' one-time business manager. Payne was no longer part of the Firm and the twins thought that he would most likely talk to 'Nipper' Read, who was closing in fast on the Krays. In the end, McVitie didn't commit the crime, but he kept the money that he was paid for doing it. Payne, on hearing that the Krays were after him and intent on settling the score permanently, squealed all he could to 'Nipper' Read and told him all about the Kray long-firm frauds, Mafia dealings, protection rackets and anything else he could think of.

Ron had been urging his elder brother to commit the ultimate sin ever since he, Ron, had openly shot and killed George Cornell. They were, after all, twins, and, to Ron's way of thinking, Reg had a duty to kill, just like his brother.

Reg had been drinking all day, still in a terrible state since the death of his wife Frances in the early part of June. He hadn't been able to get over her death and now, once again, there was no one to counter Ron's manipulation of his brother's feelings. He was also drinking because he wasn't sure exactly how Frances had died. He knew that his brother had tormented her throughout their marriage, even before, and he suspected that maybe Ron had killed her. After all, he had access, as Frances was staying in her brother's flat – who just happened to be working for Ron at the time.

Just why Reg deemed it necessary to kill McVitie is difficult, if not impossible, to say. It may have been due to his brother's constant nagging or it could have had something to do with a psychological imbalance caused by the death of Frances. Or possibly it was all about reputation. And then maybe it was just the booze doing the killing.

Previously, during the summer, Reg had had fits of drinking that, predictably, led to trouble in the form of a shooting or two. The first was a friend called Frederick. Now, if he does that to his friends, then his enemies had better watch out. Poor Frederick had some time back said something not too nice about Frances and this, after a bottle or two of gin, made Reg crazy with a capital C.

Unable to drive, he got one of the Firm to drive him to Frederick's house where a woman with a cluster of children opened the door. First, there was the compulsory shouting and calling of names, then there was the scuffle and finally the shooting. Fortunately, poor drunken Reg only succeeded in wounding his friend in the leg.

Reg was quickly bundled back into the car and driven to a safe house where he could sleep off the effects of the booze.

Charlie Kray, on hearing the news, drove over to Frederick's house and took care of the unfortunate man. A friendly doctor was called in and the patient put to rest, in his own bed; alive and relatively well.

Shortly after this incident, Reg was involved in another shooting, where he again wounded a man.

'You can't kill anyone!' was the scornful jibe made by his brother Ron, who had already earned his button. Ron was relentless; he kept up the pressure day and night. Soon Reg had to give in.

Tony Lambrianou and his brother, Chris, were sent out to find Jack 'The Hat'. The twins had concocted a story about a party at a friend's flat in Evening Road, Stoke Newington, and the

Lambrianou brothers were told to find their target and drive him over to the flat.

On arriving at the flat, Tony Lambrianou parked his Ford Zodiac nearby and, together with his brother, led their intended victim down the stairs and inside the basement flat.

Ron and Reg were there waiting for them and, as Jack 'The Hat' pushed past him demanding wine, women and song, Ron told him: 'Fuck off, Jack!' Not exactly the words of a man intending to kill someone. McVitie didn't get the drink, he never saw a woman, but he did end up acting out his own swan song.

To everyone's surprise, Reg took out a gun and fired at Jack from point-blank range. No one could miss from that distance, but the gun failed to fire. Reg tried pulling the trigger again, and again it failed. It was really making a farce of his openly attempted murder.

Members of the Firm were there that night, but seeing Reg in that kind of belligerent mood was not normal for them. It was, on the other hand, something they expected of Ron. They could only stare in disbelief.

When the gun failed, McVitie began ranting and raving – quite natural under the circumstances. He even thrust his hand through a window, trying to escape.

'Be a man, Jack,' said Reg.

'I am a man, but I don't want to fucking die like one!' was the reply from the now terrified small-time crook.

The Lambrianou brothers, Ronnie Hart, Ronnie Bender and some young boys who had come along for the party could only look on as Ron urged his brother to finish the job. He kept taunting Reg, winding him up, trying to pull his strings. The pressure on Reg must have been intense.

Eventually Reg snapped. He grabbed a kitchen knife and stabbed McVitie in the chest. He stabbed him again, this time in the face, and then again in the chest. Soon there was blood all over the carpet. Blood flowed everywhere, McVitie's blood!

Still the gang members stared in horror, not believing or understanding what they were witnessing. No one had expected a killing. No one thought Jack worth it. But no one tried to prevent it.

Tony Lambrianou was told to get rid of the body and Albert Donoghue was asked to re-decorate the flat. Even after a thorough job by Donoghue, the police still managed to find blood six months later when they found out about the killing. It was only when 'Nipper' Read took the twins and their brother Charlie into custody that people began to talk and the real details of the murder came out into the open.

At the time of the killing of Jack 'The Hat' McVitie, Charlie Kray was safely home in bed. It was a rude awakening when he was charged with getting rid of the body. It was ruder still when he was convicted and sent to prison for ten years.

The killing of Jack 'The Hat' McVitie, who was more a ladies' man than a thug, was meaningless and stupid. Reg Kray had nothing to gain from such an action but he had all to lose. Ultimately, it gave him 30 long and miserable years in jail.

'They were arrogant, brazen killers,' said 'Nipper' Read after the trial. Indeed, they were found guilty of terrorising the whole of the East End of London.

18

LIFE BEHIND BARS

I hated every minute I was inside – all seven years!

Charlie Kray

After being kept in Parkhurst Prison for 20 years, Reg Kray was sent on a 'tour' of the UK – paid for in full by the British taxpayer under the ever watchful eye of the press. Even back in the 1990s, when I first met him in jail, Reg could not feel absolutely sure of ever being set free.

The only sure thing he had to look forward to was a regular six-monthly trip to Broadmoor Hospital to see his twin brother Ron, who was sent there after attacking a fellow prisoner at Parkhurst many years before, just into his thirty-year sentence. Then, suddenly, it was all over; finished and done with when Ron died suddenly of a heart attack in the early part of 1995.

However, the days of being a 'Category A' prisoner and constantly kept in maximum security were long over for Reg as we neared the end of the millennium. Then, he could look forward to his release in the comforting knowledge that it would, most likely, one day happen. He had been downgraded in status and shoved around the country in ever decreasing circles. At this time he was on the last leg of the tour. He even had the key to his door with him day and night; he had never attempted to escape and had been a model prisoner.

The early days had been hard. As a 'Category A' prisoner he was regarded as highly dangerous and a possible threat to both the public and the police if he should escape. Indeed, he was reckoned to be a possible threat to even the state.

He had suffered all of the hardships that accompanied this status, such as not being allowed to mix with the other prisoners, being kept in isolation whilst under constant surveillance – even being chaperoned to the toilet by a warder. His visitors and mail had been rationed and restricted, as well as being scrutinised by the authorities. The list of restrictions was almost never-ending, but he had handled it well, except for a few bouts of depression.

Ron Kray, isolated as he was in the relative comfort of Broadmoor, had never seen the necessity of keeping fit, but his brother Reg had developed into an exercise freak. His daily workouts had kept him in tremendous condition and, shortly before his death in 2000, he looked like the aggressive and naturally gifted boxer he was back in the good old days of the Double R club. This strict routine had kept his brain active and his body lean and mean. No one would have wanted to cross Reg Kray, not even when he was well into his 60s.

So the question then was simple: when would he be released? Surely 30 years was enough for anyone. Most 'lifers' only serve a dozen years or so, so why should Reg have stayed in jail a moment longer, when his time was up, over, finished?

On 17 March 1995, at the age of 61, Ron Kray died of natural causes at Wexham Park Hospital, Slough, Berkshire. In Ron's case, 'natural causes' was 100 cigarettes a day for life.

He was rushed to Heatherwood Hospital near Ascot on Wednesday, 15 March, complaining of acute tiredness and suffering from anaemia. He had collapsed earlier in the day in the top-security ward at Broadmoor NHS Hospital that he shared with, amongst others, Peter Sutcliffe, the 'Yorkshire Ripper'.

The following day, 16 March, he was still fighting to get back to Broadmoor where he could resume his smoking habit, but in the end time ran out and by Friday he was only a ghost of his former self. Having suffered a series of heart attacks, Ron had not been in good health for a number of years and his incessant chain smoking did nothing to improve things.

He was eventually transferred to Wexham Park, Slough, but it was a trip too far for Ron. He died immediately on arrival at the hospital after another massive heart attack. A hospital pathologist, Dr Mufeed Ali, said: 'He must have died instantly, but he would have been in some pain.'

'After being locked up for 27 years, he's free at last,' said Reg on hearing the news. 'He beat the system, didn't he? He didn't die in Broadmoor as everyone expected him to.' Reg was playing the game and trying to keep up appearances, but inwardly he was appalled that the authorities had not let him see his brother prior to his death. In fact, he hadn't seen him for more than nine months, despite having seen him every six months throughout their prison sentences. There was even a possibility that they would not let him visit the chapel of rest but, in the end, permission was given and Reg was able to pay his last tribute to Ron personally, accompanied by his elder brother Charlie.

The hospital kept everything under wraps. Even the inquest was held in secret. This was carried out by retired Maidenhead solicitor Robert Wilson, at his Waltham St Lawrence home. It was a brief hearing by all accounts, with the 'natural causes' verdict being faxed to the coroner's office in Slough. Ron Kray had died from a massive heart attack; natural causes, indeed. The inquest was performed only 24 hours after his death; something of an irregularity.

There were numerous complaints about this procedure, with even the pressure group Inquest joining in the fray. Barrister June Tweedle, a co-director of the group, said that the inquest should have been held in public – sentiments echoed by both Reg and Charlie. 'Although the coroner does have a great deal of discretion,' she told journalists, 'he does have obligations to tell people who want to be informed. He really has gone beyond the pale.'

The Home Office didn't want to get involved, even though Broadmoor is a government institution. So there was controversy even after death.

Everyone had warned Ron about the cigarette problem. A Broadmoor source said: 'We have warned him time and time again that he is killing himself.' And the Heatherwood Hospital at Ascot made it known that: 'He is banned from smoking here and says he wants to leave to have a cigarette. But he is too weak to get out of bed.' The transfer to Wexham Park didn't help either. Ultimately Ron Kray killed himself. By the time of his death he was down to a mere shadow of himself and weighed only nine stone.

Reg and Charlie kept up their attack on the authorities in the hope of getting some answers as to why Ron wasn't taken to hospital sooner and, I am sure, in the knowledge of being front-page news in the media. The Krays had always played with a double-edged sword and they continued even after the death of Ron. Every Sunday newspaper in the country had a huge spread talking about the terror twins, the gangsters from the East End of London. They had lists of killings, of deals and of celebrity friends. Even in death Ron Kray was front-page news.

Reg was now the Kray in the limelight. He eagerly spoke with all the journalists, pouring out his soul and displaying the remorse expected of him.

'I didn't sleep much last night,' he told reporters on the Saturday, 'but I forced myself not to think back over all the years because it would have been too hurtful.'

It might seem a pity that he didn't think about the pain he and his brother had inflicted on others all those years ago. But those deeds were conveniently forgotten, for the time being at least.

'Reggie is obviously really upset,' remarked brother Charlie on leaving Maidstone Prison on the morning of 18 March 1995. 'But he is coping with it the best he can. He's trying his hardest to get his head round what has happened.' Prompted further, he added: 'When I first met him he was a bit emotional, but then he tried for my sake to pull himself together.'

There were no frills from Charlie. For once, he was telling the truth, the whole truth and nothing but the truth. 'The tragedy about this is that when you are an identical twin you must feel the loss even stronger, and I think half of Reggie has died with Ronnie.'

Sad words indeed. For an identical twin the sudden death of one half (and I mean that sincerely) must be a devastating thing. As an identical twin myself, I can commiserate with him completely as my brother died a few years ago and I feel the pain daily. Every time I look in the mirror I see my brother, and that must have been the same for Reg.

* * *

When the twins were arrested in May 1968 they were first sent, on remand, to Brixton Prison, together with brother Charlie and other members of the Firm. Even here they managed to have fights with their so-called friends who had shopped them to the police in return for their freedom or light sentences. But the twins still thought they could survive and asked the Firm to accept the killings in return for payments to their families and good jobs when they eventually got out. No one took them up on their offer and the twins were convicted of the killings. They tried to do a deal for Charlie, but since they would not own up to the killings then the authorities would not listen, so in the end he too went down for ten years. They wouldn't admit guilt at any cost – and it got them 30 years apiece.

The first 17 years must have been hell on earth for Reg, spent as they were as a 'Category A' prisoner in maximum security in Parkhurst Prison on the Isle of Wight. His only consolation was that his brother, Ron, was nearby. But he had no contact with others so he was left to his own devices with only time on his side. It would have killed many, but it made Reg even more determined to serve out his time and he decided there and then not to try to escape. He would take his penalty like a man, even though he was not used to being on the receiving end of punishment.

He spent his time painting and planning, writing and planning, keeping fit and planning. It was the only way he could keep his mind active, let alone the rest of him. It was a lonely world and the time passed slowly. He was moved around a few times, to other prisons, but the tour normally led back to Parkhurst and the extremes of solitary confinement. At one time, when he was at Long Larten Prison in 1982, he attempted to commit suicide, but that only got him sent back to Parkhurst, with a special note on his file – 'this prisoner is unstable'. But he pulled himself round, with the help of his mother, who visited her sons throughout these years, and slowly but surely he could see the sentence fading away. Another year missed was another year closer to getting out, or so he thought. It spurred him on then, and it continued to give him hope all the way through his life in prison.

Shortly before his final move from Parkhurst they sent him to Wandsworth Prison for a spell in 1986, and he realised that he would soon be downgraded and moved to a more leisurely prison. This happened in 1987, when he was moved to Gartree Prison in Leicestershire. Reg had passed the halfway point and he was on his way home, but there were a few years to overcome first and a few final hurdles to be negotiated. This is when his writing really took off and when he and his brother Ron made a cool £100,000 for their book *Our Story*. Since that day, Reg was always on the lookout for easy money and he never looked back. The film *The Krays* followed, and Reg was kept busy with moves to Nottingham, Blundeston, Maidstone and then Wayland Prison. But all the time he managed to get in a periodic six-month trip to see Ron, who in latter years had spent most of his time in Broadmoor, a mental hospital in Berkshire.

On 16 June 1991, the front page of *The People* told the story of how the Krays had managed to get rid of the body of Jack 'The Hat' McVitie, when their old pal Tony Lambrianou sold the serialisation rights to his book *Inside the Firm*. It did nothing to throw more light on the disappearance of the body, but it did bring the whole story of the Krays back into the limelight. In reality, the book told more about the loose arrangements within the Firm and the story of the Lambrianou brothers than revealing anything new about the twins, but that was the real purpose of the book anyway. It was no telltale study of the Krays, since Tony Lambrianou was one of the few members of the Firm who did not turn Queen's evidence. But Ron and Reg were back on page one, where they intended to stay.

The film was well publicised, as was another book by Reg, but the newspapers didn't really pick up on another Kray story until they ran an article about Reg and some of his paintings, which he had given away for auction so he could help a sick little boy, Paul Stapleton, aged only six at the time. The paintings were very child-like, but since he was trying to help a child to get equipment so he could better handle his muscular disorder, they were very apt and much appreciated by Paul's mother, Stephanie. They showed a simple touch in pencil and crayon and the ex-mobster was praised for his actions. He was apparently the only 'celebrity' who had responded to the appeal. He also sent a signed copy of his latest book, *Born Fighter*, along for good measure. No matter what the real intention of the gesture, Reg's good deed was something that got him to think about others and he started, from then on, a vast array of charitable events all over the country, purely for the benefit of those worse off than himself. For a man so long a 'Category A' prisoner in Parkhurst, that was indeed a charitable thing to do. When he died, however, we soon learned that much of the money raised went into his own pocket, for use after he got out of jail.

In December 1993 journalists could not agree on what made the best Kray story. The *Daily Mail* ran a story of a jail's Shakespeare company, featuring a guest actress – the 29-year-old Lady Alice Douglas, daughter of the Marquess of Queensberry. She was featured on page 23 with Reggie Kray, who somehow managed to get in the shot when Blundeston put on their play, *Macbeth. The Sun*, however, had Reg Kray talking a fellow inmate into giving himself up in a hold-up that went disastrously wrong. The fact that the hold-up occurred in Blundeston Prison showed the culprit to be a bit of an idiot, but it was indeed a brave thing to do since the madman had a knife at the inmate's throat. I am pleased to report that the man survived the ordeal. Reg Kray, prisoner no. 058111, enjoyed the play and played according to the 'Queensberry Rules', by holding his punches for later in the evening when he really had a chance to talk to journalists.

The early part of 1994 saw Reg move to Maidstone Prison in Kent, where he embarked on a gearing down for future release. This was a landmark move for the ex-gangland boss, and there was much speculation about an early parole, although nothing materialised. But Reg still managed to keep himself in the news by writing to *The People* and calling for Myra Hindley to be kept in jail for the rest of her life. Ron had agreed that Reg should write the letter about the 'Moors Murderer', in which he said that 95 per cent of all prisoners in the country wanted to see her stay in prison and never be released.

'Let her rot!' he told the newspaper, while agonising over her abuse and murder of children. Again, after his death, there were many stories about Ron and Reg Kray and boys. It seems that Reg had a change of mind while in jail but, back in the old days, he enjoyed the company of boys, children really, between the ages of

16 and 18. There have even been rumours of a paedophile ring that was run by Ron.

Reg was also moved from prison to prison quite often because of his association with young offenders. He was warned time and time again, but it must have been difficult for the most famous face in prison not to be grateful for the adulation of his young fans. He got very close to some of them, even adopting one of them as his 'son'. The governors didn't like it, and they separated him from the younger inmates as much as they could.

But Reg was now in full swing with his games inside prison and he always had a keen eye on the news, both in the press and on television. One day he would be asking the Home Office to make him a university lecturer so he could tour the country with his show and the next he would be organising a rave. Then it would be talk about a new house or two and then a series of billiard or snooker establishments spread all over the country. There was no end to his plans and his release from prison was looming ever closer.

But the world of Reg Kray took a turn for the worse in the spring of 1995 when his twin brother Ron died. He had lost one half of his persona, the crazy half. This monozygotic twin was now just an ordinary person, just like any other mere mortal. His world was about to change for ever.

Ron had spent the last 20 years of his life in Broadmoor, an NHS hospital for mentally disturbed patients. He escaped the high walls of Broadmoor on 17 March 1995 by dying as a result of his constant smoking. It was his joy and it was his downfall. No one killed Ron Kray, he killed himself; the bullet didn't get him, but the smoke did.

Ron was sent to Durham Prison in 1969, separating him from his twin brother Reg, who was allocated to Parkhurst. There is no good reason why they were split up, and soon the authorities had cause to regret their decision. Ron was a most unruly prisoner and caused the governor much concern. So much so that, in 1972, he was sent to Parkhurst to join his twin, who they thought could control him. They were wrong, since no one could control Ron without proper medical supervision.

More fights followed and Ron became a problem to the governor of Parkhurst. Eventually he was sent to the mental hospital Broadmoor, in Berkshire, where he could get the required medical and psychological treatment. It had taken the authorities seven years to admit that Ron Kray needed treatment for his schizophrenia, something that Long Grove Asylum knew back in June 1958. So why did they send a man suffering from chronic paranoid schizophrenia to an ordinary prison? The question has never been answered and it is impossible to access Ron's files at Broadmoor because of the extreme secrecy of the institution.

So Ron was now in a safe environment where he could be cared for and supplied with the necessary medication to give him a normal existence, even though it was still behind bars. But Ron, like Reg, had sworn never to escape. He had no problems with the sentence, other than that he thought it was too long and a waste of time, but he did have a problem with authority, as in the days of his military service. His early treatment at the hands of the prison service, therefore, must seem very harsh indeed, since the man was ill and in urgent need of the correct treatment, something that no prison could offer him. Broadmoor gave him the breathing space that he needed and he settled down quickly into the moderate regime of the establishment.

Ron, from this time on, thought almost entirely of his friends and of those he could help. This may be a little difficult to understand, but as he told me many times: 'I have everything I need in here. What do I need money for?' So he gave it all away and that is why, on 17 March 1995 when he passed away, he died penniless. His only luxuries were his designer clothes and his well-decorated room; nothing else was important to him, except maybe his cigarettes. But then a book or a press interview would cover that very nicely, thank you. He didn't believe in money for money's sake, only in the good it could do. Sure enough, if he was a free man then he would spend it and enjoy it, but he wasn't, so it could benefit others instead. Somewhat strange for an ex-gangland boss, once the most wanted man in Britain.

I went to see Ron in the early '90s, together with a journalist who had bought the rights to an interview. The young man was in for a torrid time, with Ron kicking him under the table and telling him constantly to 'Fuck off!' But the journalist kept most of his cool, although he stuttered more and more as the meeting progressed, and finally emerged into the daylight with something that he thought his editor would be pleased with. Ron told me afterwards how much he had enjoyed the day – playing up to his image was one of the few joys he had left. He treated it all as a crazy joke, but I am sure the young journalist was having nightmares. 'I didn't like his long hair,' he told me, 'so I decided to have some fun.'

Ron was, indeed, schizophrenic; good guy and bad guy all rolled into one. The problem was that this could be difficult to understand if you didn't know him reasonably well. Fortunately, being a twin myself, we had common ground and that made me acceptable – thank God!

In 1993 the Krays were again back in the headlines with an article in the *Sunday Times* about the Boothby scandal. Once more, Ron could see his name in the newspapers and have a little chuckle to himself. It was all really about Lord Boothby, but the stars were the Krays and Ron in particular. But he was used to all the attention and it didn't mean much any more. He was more interested in what other people were doing and listened intently to their tales. He was not a very good talker, but he excelled at listening.

So when the newspapers started to talk about Broadmoor being run by the inmates – literally the loonies taking over the asylum – at the end of 1993, he took it all with a pinch of salt.

'Where have they done that?' he asked.

'Here, Ron,' I told him.

'Why hasn't anyone told me?' he mocked.

I am sure he was completely unaware of the newspaper articles commenting on statements from MPs and union leaders alike, that the authorities had no control any more at Broadmoor. But it didn't matter, since he didn't really care. As long as they all left him alone, then he could get on with what was left of his life. Even when further political documents were made available in 1995 under the 30-year rule, Ron took it all in his stride. Boothby and Driberg were, once again, headline news and scandal filled the pages of the newspapers. But Ron tended to his garden at Broadmoor as if nothing was happening in the outside world. He wasn't bothered about politics, corruption and headlines any more; it was only the inside of Broadmoor and his medicine that kept him going.

He continued to smoke his 100 cigarettes a day and never thought about tomorrow. He joked that they couldn't make him pay tax because he was a madman, but his health was by now suffering from his smoking habit and he was taken to hospital more than once for suspected heart attacks. But the final blow came in March 1995. This time it was for real and Ron Kray suffered a massive heart attack and died shortly afterwards.

19

BUSINESS AS USUAL INSIDE 'NICK'

I've never seen the film. We only wanted the money,
but next time we want more!

Reg Kray

In the summer of 1992 I went to visit Reg when he was a guest of
Her Majesty in Nottingham Prison. We met in the usual
surroundings of the visitors' hall, where prisoners met their wives,
their lovers, their families and their children.

The talk among the brothers had recently been films and, in
particular, the making of another Kray film. The movie *The Krays*
had done well through Rank Film Distributors, not that the twins
had had much pleasure in the project. So this time around they
wanted full control and much, much more money.

'I want £2 million!' said Reg, impatiently, but then everything
Reg said was tarnished with impatience.

'That could be possible,' I replied. 'But surely you must have made
something like that from the first film?' I queried. It was a mistake.

'We got a miserly £255,000,' said Reg angrily, his eyes lighting
up like fireworks.

I didn't know what to say. Neither did anyone else. I had gone
there with an old friend, and someone else who just wanted to
meet Reg and enjoy the privilege of conversing with one of the
UK's all-time criminal greats. The other guy did the driving and
paid for the trip and he even gave Reg a well-deserved 'drink' by
smuggling in alcohol.

What was even more disturbing than the aggressive tone used by Reg was the feeling that he was, somehow, in another world. I put it down at first to his being in jail for so many years. But then it dawned on me – he was slowly but surely getting stoned out of his tiny mind on booze.

True, he had a glass of orange juice on the table in the meeting hall. But there were guards all around, so how could he get the alcohol?

The answer lay nearby, where a mother was attending to her baby, brought in that day to visit with his or her father, another inmate of Nottingham Prison. They had brought in the vodka in the baby's drinking bottle, right under the noses of the prison staff.

Reg was still angry, but the booze was beginning to get to him. 'I don't want Charlie involved this time,' he said. 'It was all his fault last time. We should have made over £1 million!'

Reg went on to explain that originally he had insisted on an initial upfront payment with a royalty, depending on the success of the film. This was a clever move, but then Reg had always been keen on money. Charlie, however, together with another of the negotiators, Wilf Pine, was in dire need of cash funds. These two conspired to re-negotiate the deal with a once-only upfront figure of £255,000. There would be no royalty, no further payments, no future millions.

Once again, I felt ill at ease. I didn't want to tell him that I knew all about the film negotiations and of the trouble that the twins had had with elder brother Charlie. It wasn't really my place to tell tales. I didn't want to tell him that his brother had been selling off the rights for chunks of money – £5,000 a shot. I also didn't want to tell him that I had also invested in Charlie's royalty, like so many others. And I certainly didn't want to be the one who told him of Charlie's constant and incessant debt.

As for the other negotiator, Wilf Pine, he had other things on his mind, too. He had been a bouncer and a bodyguard in his younger days, but success was something he was still searching for. Wilf was a true friend of both Ron and Reg, but he also wanted to help Charlie and would do anything Charlie asked him to do, so, in reality, the team doing the deal on the film were more interested in their own well-being than that of the twins. Even before they started their negotiations they were in a lose–lose situation.

'I'm fed up with being ripped off,' said Reg, slurping down another shot of vodka. 'We never get what we are owed.'

He was right, but it was in reality all his own fault. He never had business people around to do anything in a legitimate way and he could never put his trust in the right people. So he got the people he deserved – nothing more, nothing less.

I was beginning to wonder what Reg thought he was owed, but he once again intervened. He was unusually intense, probably due to being banged up for all those years, and later I found out that this was quite normal for him. For almost 30 years Reg Kray had been all dressed up with nowhere to go.

'And if I find out who has been ripping us off with those East Enders T-shirts, then I'll teach him a lesson or two!' He was fuming and it was not a pretty sight. Reg was getting very hot and I was becoming quite bothered.

Once again, I was beginning to feel the heat. Was it my duty to inform on his old pals? Should I tell him of the deals that were being done in the name of the Krays? Should I spill the beans? Or should I just be quiet and say nothing, shut up and not 'grass' on his old friends?

The meeting was soon over and I was relieved to be leaving Nottingham. It had been a long day. The session had gone reasonably well and the driver talked about Reg Kray all the way back to London. My friend and I, however, were a little thoughtful, so we let him talk and the time passed quickly.

I parted company with my two companions and set about trying to get the last train from Waterloo. These trips were a little tiring, but nevertheless they were necessary, especially when working on business deals and ideas where it is important to deal face to face. For that was what the trip was all about, ideas to make money and seeing people who could make things happen.

On the way back home I sat alone in the carriage. There was plenty of time to think about film deals, about merchandise and about books. Whatever was going to happen, I had made up my mind I would not be the one who had to tell Reg Kray that it was his brother, 'Champagne Charlie', who had done the deals on the

East Ender T-shirts. This had infuriated both twins. And I would certainly not be the one to tell him that I was the one who actually set up the deal for Charlie!

On 31 May 1989 a meeting took place at the offices of Gold Mann & Co in Fleet Street to determine, in contractual form, the proceedings regarding the development of a feature film, provisionally entitled *The Krays*. Those present were representatives of the company Parkfield Group plc, Wilf Pine and Nicky Treeby who were acting as agents for Reg and Ron Kray, Charlie Kray and a solicitor acting on behalf of Gold Mann & Co.

The main points were read aloud in the office, but all that really interested Charlie were the figures that appeared in clause three of the agreement, the one which spelt out the money that the three brothers would receive for the film rights. No one said that they couldn't get paid for these rights. No one mentioned the fact that Ron and Reg were convicted murderers, or the fact that Charlie had received a sentence of ten years for getting rid of a corpse. No one even doubted the fact that they were due payment under the law of the land. But then some would say that rewarding murderers is not what justice should really be all about.

The moment came and the solicitor read out the most important of all the clauses in the agreement. For the sake of clarity, and since I do not want to be sued for including the wrong information in this book, I will now show, word for word, the full details included in clause three, the one about the money. It reads as follows:

To the Kray Family:-

Within 7 days after the occurrence of the events set out in clause 4.1 the payments due to the Kray Family under clauses 4 (ii) and (iii) of the Kray Agreement (and in full and final satisfaction thereof) amounting to £110,000;

£25,000 within 30 days after the payment pursuant to clause 3.3.1 above;

£50,000 within 30 days after the payment pursuant to clause 3.3.2 above;

£50,000 within 30 days after the payment pursuant to clause 3.3.2 above;

£20,000 within 21 days after the expiry of six calendar months after the calendar month during which the Film is first theatrically released in the United Kingdom.

Charlie Kray's share would be one third of this total, amounting to some £85,000. Not bad for a villain. And his brothers would each receive the same amount. Naturally enough, they would be obliged to give some of this to their agents, Mr Pine and Mr Treeby, but that would still not be a bad day's work for a couple of crooks from the East End of London.

Naturally the Krays, together with their agents, had to sign, guaranteeing that they held the rights in the first place. But just how anyone can sign away the story rights to a couple of killings is beyond my own limited knowledge of the law. Don't the dead men have rights too, or their families? I wonder if they, too, were paid any vast sums of money?

Anyway, the solicitor continued to read out the agreement, clause by complicated clause, but for those present the main points had already been covered. It was the money they wanted and, of course, the publicity too. There was however, a minor complication about the payment. Ron and Reg wanted a smaller upfront payment and a fixed royalty rate from the takings. But Charlie was in such dire need of cash that he was willing to risk the wrath of the twins to get his hands on the filthy lucre. And remember, Ron and Reg were not exactly in any position to negotiate themselves. There are certain laws involved when doing deals from jail and the Krays were keen to bypass these normal proceedings to get hold of some cash that they could keep for themselves, away from anyone else's prying eyes.

Tales were told and stories invented to convince the twins that this was the best deal possible and they fell for it, deceived by their own brother. He wouldn't be getting the millions he was after, but Charlie would be getting himself out of a fix. In the event, it still wasn't enough to pay off his debts, since he had already sold these film rights for ready cash – cash that had already gone walkabout.

The real story of the film began back in 1982, when Roger Daltrey and a film company known as Boyd & Co Film Productions

Ltd managed to secure a written agreement from the twins for a film to be made about their lives. It was originally to be called 'The Kray Brothers', but things didn't really happen before Bejubop Ltd entered the fray and finally started developing a workable script. Roger Daltrey, the lead singer of The Who and a budding actor at the time, had made a good start, but Bejubop progressed with the script until Fugitive Films were ready to make the film themselves. But again, there was just one little snag that had to be overcome – that of finances. That was where Parkfield came into the picture. The agreement, as outlined above, gave Fugitive Films the money to work with and gave the Krays the assurances that they needed and, of course, let's not forget the money.

But even with the finances guaranteed, the company Fugitive Films ran into trouble. The first thing they did was to run back to Parkfield Entertainment and tell them that they needed more money or they couldn't finish the film. So Parkfield had to put their hands in their pockets once more and cough up another couple of million. In all, the film cost some £6 million, which was grossly over budget, but it did very well at the box office in the UK and even sold well throughout Europe. Miramax, the American company who took the film for the USA and paid about £2 million for the fun of it, took it off the circuit after only two weeks. But later the film did well when released on video in the USA and many television companies took it for late-night showing. So, all in all, it recouped its investment. Video rights here in the UK, however, were something else, since by that time Parkfield Group plc were in liquidation.

Cork Gully, who handled receivership of the company, were looking to sell the video rights to the highest bidder when I went to see them at their offices in Noble Street, in early 1991. I was shown all the receipts from the film, including details of sales through United Media, who handled the film here in the UK. They hadn't quite reached the £6 million mark at that time, but with the sale of the video rights success was assured, for the film at least. Parkfield, with their unexpected extra investment in the project, went bust.

To try to sort out the rights and the contracts I even went to see a pal of Charlie's at Pinewood Studios. But the man in charge was none other than that old Kray pal Joseph 'you can call me Joe' Pyle. Pal Joey showed me some more paperwork.

I was there simply because I had promised Charlie to look into matters for him. I had seen most of this paperwork before, although I was not initially involved in the original project, but some of it did surprise me and the letters were all headed 'confidential'. Everyone wanted to keep things quiet, and when that happens it normally means that someone wants to make money out of the situation. Whether it was the liquidator or the boss of Touchdown Entertainment, as Joe called his company, was not very clear. But I didn't get to see Joe Pyle again, as he was caught up in a cocaine bust and sentenced to five years' imprisonment. Just after he got out of jail he died, so he never had the opportunity to clarify the situation.

In any case, the video rights were sold and the film became profitable, but if Ron and Reg had had their way, they really would have become millionaires. This would have come in over a period of time, but every time the film is shown now around the world, it does absolutely nothing to fill the coffers of the Kray brothers, which is what it was intended to do right from day one.

'Why didn't you want to meet the Kemp brothers, who played you in the film?' I asked Ron once, when I met him in Broadmoor. He looked up and sighed as he reached over for his non-alcoholic beer and his cigarettes.

'Why would I want to meet a couple of wimps like them?' he asked, putting another cigarette in his mouth. A guard came over and lit the cigarette for him and Ron sat back and relaxed. After all, there wasn't much else to do in Broadmoor.

'But weren't you interested?' I asked, as curious as ever. Maybe this is a writer's lot, or possibly it was because of my own knowledge of Ron and his particular kind of vanity. Surely, I felt, he was interested in who would portray him on the silver screen.

'We got the money and that was all we wanted,' he said in reply as he continued to chain smoke the cigarettes I had brought in for him. That was it. Once again it was all about money. But Ron didn't care about the money, so why the big deal about getting as much as he could, I wondered? Kate Kray came up with the answer. She told me that Ron didn't care about what money could do for him, since he couldn't spend it in Broadmoor, but he did care about the people he could help, so he gave it all away. In his own inimitable way Ron Kray was a true philanthropist.

The demise of the distribution company was an event completely out of the hands of the Krays and unforeseen and unexpected by everyone, including Ron, Reg and Charlie. By accepting a one-off payment instead of royalties the Krays didn't get their nice pension every month, in the way of a royalty cheque, as planned. It was all down to the greed of two men who gave up the opportunity for riches in the future for something here and now, all determined by their own predicaments and outstanding debts. So Ron and Reg would not be millionaires because of the film; they would have to continue to wheel and deal in their own ways to make a buck and to keep the funds flowing in their direction.

As they say, you can choose your friends, but you can't choose your family.

The T-shirt deal was simplicity itself. Charlie Kray and I shared an office on the Mile End Road in the East End at the time, and he had seen all the T-shirts selling all over London, showing the sights, the Beefeaters, the Horse Guards and such. So he wanted to cash in on the popularity of his brothers and make a buck or two. He asked me if I knew anyone in the business who might be interested in manufacturing Kray T-shirts and so I made a few phone calls and quickly came up with a short list of companies. He told me that the twins would also be getting some of the royalties, but then, I would say that, wouldn't I? In the end he pocketed the money and kept the whole operation quiet. He thought it was a 'need to know' situation, and the twins didn't need to know.

My brother and I went for a stroll one day along Oxford Street, to check out the T-shirt business that was doing a roaring trade with all kinds of product, such as *EastEnders* T-shirts and other souvenirs. We could very easily see the possibilities for Kray T-shirts and asked a few of the storekeepers about their suppliers. They were very cagey about giving us any names, but when we mentioned the Krays attitudes changed as if I were talking about aliens. It was simply astounding that just a name could have that effect. So, with a little friendly persuasion, one of the traders met us in a pub and spilled the beans about the T-shirt trade. That was all we needed.

I talked to three companies about the proposed deal, but we couldn't agree on a percentage that sounded reasonable. So I turned my attentions to a small company run by an old friend from South Africa. He had a good business going and his company, Flash Merchandising, was doing well within the T-shirt sector, which is very competitive indeed. I spoke to Charlie about the kind of deal that I would be looking for in this type of arrangement and we sorted out some royalty rates that he felt the twins would be satisfied with. The rest was, for me, normal business and this kind of business is best handled on the river.

I met my friend, let us call him Gerry, and we sailed in his boat down the River Thames to a quite delightful pub, right on the river bank. After a few drinks we eventually got around to talking about the deal, but then we decided that it was too hot for business and we had a few more drinks. It was a sunny summer's day and the river was the best place to be. But everyone must eat, so we ordered some of the best food in the house and went outside to eat and to talk a little business. Actually, the deal was all arranged well before this meeting of minds, since it was all negotiated on the telephone and by fax. This jaunt on the river was simply to seal the arrangements and to pick up the contracts. Contracts secure in my briefcase, we sailed back to his moorings and parted company. The rest is history.

Charlie Kray, from that time on in 1986, was on a pension, as the Krays called it. He was in receipt of a regular income paid directly to him and he could do anything he liked with it. He was the one who chose not to give any of this money to his brothers and thereby put me in an embarrassing situation that time in 1992 when Reg was talking about the T-shirts. As I said, I couldn't volunteer the information then, but now, with the benefit of hindsight, maybe I should have told him that his brother was cheating him out of another fortune.

As for me, all I got out of the deal was a measly T-shirt, and that was for proof purposes only. It just goes to show that the old saying is quite right: 'Once a crook, always a crook.'

But the deals didn't stop there, they just continued. Charlie had tasted success and the trappings of success and I was, again, asked to perform a miracle when I was presented with a cassette tape. It was purportedly an old tape of Reg talking to some old pals over a few glasses of whisky, but there was a catch. It was instantly obvious to my trained ear (I was once a student at the Royal Academy of Music) that the tape was of recent origin, and not old at all. No, no, no, they all told me, it's the genuine article. But I knew different. I did nothing with the tape for a few weeks, waiting for someone to call asking about progress. When the call came, I laid it on the line.

'You can tell everyone else that it was made 20 years ago, but don't try to tell me that,' I told the man acting as agent for Reg, since this was Reg's deal and no one else, not even Ron or Charlie, was involved. This is how it was with the Krays. They tell you that they support each other, but in reality they are helping themselves. The guy on the other end of the phone line didn't know what to say. I had rumbled him and I had rumbled the plan. Finally he had to tell me the whole plot.

Someone had taken a hidden cassette recorder into the prison to record a bogus conversation in which Reg was telling stories about the old days. He talked of the Mafia, Judy Garland, George Raft, Joan Collins and many, many more – all crammed into 25 minutes of recording. In fact, it sounded very much as though he was reading from a script. They even had him asking for another scotch. This was all set up to make money out of the lucrative interview disc market, something that I was very good at back in the mid-1980s.

So the truth about the fake was out, but Charlie wanted me to play along with the hoax, and who was I to go against the wishes of the Krays? I designed the disc, edited the tape and put the whole production process into motion. It turned out to be a great picture disc, with one of Reg's favourite pictures of himself on the A-side and a picture of the twins on the back. There was no room for Charlie, however, but he didn't mind. When the product was finished, however, and ready to go to the distributor, no one could agree on the selling side, so for six months the records lay on the factory floor. It was just another operation where there were too many cooks (or should that be crooks?) spoiling the broth.

These deals were always there, be it posters or photographs, records or CDs, articles for inclusion in various magazines or books. The most lucrative of all their book deals was the first one, called *My Story*, written by Fred Dinenage in 1988. It is interesting to note here that the actual copyright in the book is held by Bejubop, one of the companies that tried to establish the film *The Krays*. This was possibly to get around the law at the time, which didn't like to see money going to convicted criminals for the sale of rights, be they book or film. But Ron and Reg Kray pocketed a £100,000 advance for their rights, and Fred Dinenage pocketed a sizeable sum for the writing. It did well in the bookshops, reaching the Top 10 in the paperback lists, and the critics say that it is well worth the reading. But it didn't shine any light on controversial issues such as whether or not they killed 'The Mad Axeman' Frank Mitchell. Now, of course, we know that they did give the orders for his immediate death and Frank Mitchell was dumped at sea off the coast of Kent. But it still makes interesting reading.

Fred Dinenage had previously worked on a television documentary about Broadmoor and it was here that he had first met Ron, one of the hospital's most illustrious patients. So when it came time to write the book, it was Ron who suggested the TVS man for the job.

Later on, in 1991, Ron was asked by the same publisher, Sidgwick and Jackson, to write another book. He took the money and set about writing some notes for inclusion, using a ghostwriter, but in the end he had to give up the idea. He couldn't think of anything to say! He couldn't write about Reg, because Reg wouldn't let him. He couldn't write about Charlie because that could put Charlie back in prison, and he couldn't write about his own past, since that could also result in the acceptance of guilt and Reg would not let him do that. Maybe with the right encouragement he could have complied with the wishes of the publishers and I, for one, would have been interested to read the book, but ultimately Reg stopped the book and forced his brother to return the money to the publisher. And believe me, that was not an easy task for Ron Kray.

Reg wrote a number of books and four of these have been published in the UK, but by far the best is *Born Fighter* in 1990. It is what you would expect from the title, and Reg doesn't let the reader down. In his latter years he tried to interest a publisher in his memoirs of prison life and eventually these were published by Macmillan. I had a preview of these memoirs some years before the final deal and they were really just a bunch of stories, ramblings, thoughts, but in the right hands I knew it would make good reading. In the end, however, the publishers were forced to remove much of the content and it turned out to be a bit tame, but still worth a read, nonetheless.

The book sagas rolled on and on, and newspapers in the late '90s were again carrying reports that another new book would soon be available written by none other than Reg's new wife, Roberta Jones, or should that be Kray? So she had now joined the rest of the family in trying her hand at publishing. But, in reality, it was just another nice little earner for the Krays. As far as this new extravaganza was concerned, I really don't think that Reg said anything that we didn't already know since it was too close to his possible parole, which could have come about any time after May 1998.

Reg, on the other hand, continued to give his newspaper interviews for around £1,500 a time and his man-to-man chats for about £200. Other little earners included Kray waistcoats and belt buckles – all adding to the Kray bank balance. He would even sign a photo or two, for a price.

In 1994 Ron and Reg even tried their hands at recording a CD. It used clips of interviews smuggled out of prison along with a jungle beat, popular at the time. Nigel Benn, the boxer, put it together with various main artists, but it didn't get the right publicity or distribution so the twins didn't have a hit on their hands. It is strange to think of such tough guys as rave artists, when the only time Ron ever talked about a hit list was when he was working out who to kill next.

The twins, in particular, used every trick to get publicity and one of the crazes, in the late '90s, was to get a Kray tattoo. Just why teenagers and youngsters should be interested in getting jabbed all over like this is a little bewildering – all those needles only to get a picture of Ron and Reg Kray plastered all over your body? And like the twins, you've got them for life. But it kept the profile of the

Krays right up there with all the other celebrities of the day and therefore it served its purpose. The Kray bandwagon rolled on.

Perhaps the most amazing story that never came to light during the early part of 1992, when it all happened, was the relationship between Ron and Reg Kray and two brothers from South Wales, known as Leighton and Lindsay Frayne. The newspapers of the time told the story of two bungling 'boyos' from the valleys who tried to emulate the Krays in both lifestyle and action. On 3 June 1992, the tabloids pictured the brothers on the front page after they had appeared in Newport Crown Court on charges of robbing a building society in Newbridge, Gwent, of £10,000. The offence had been committed, said Mr Patrick Harrington, the previous July when Lindsay Frayne and a friend, Stephen Cook, entered the building society wielding guns and asking for money.

'Lindsay Frayne held a gun while going backwards out of the door, just like in a TV film,' said Mr Harrington, who was prosecuting the case. He also spoke of sawn-off shotguns and other firearms, while condemning the brothers for their actions. Although only one of the brothers was accused of being involved in the robbery, the other brother, Leighton, was accused of masterminding the crime. Lindsay, then 25, and Leighton, then 31, were between a rock and a hard place.

They had appeared in *The People* the previous year, posing as the Krays in one of the famous David Bailey photographs, and were paid well for their time. This, unfortunately, fitted well into their plans, since they were working for Ron and Reg. It was part of an elaborate plan, one that the Krays had instigated as part of a plot to put them back as number one in the hierarchy of British crime. In the end the whole thing was covered up as a bungling attempt at robbery, but behind the headlines was the real truth about the deal between the Krays and Leighton and Lindsay Frayne.

The plan was nothing new in the realms of gangsterism: Ron and Reg would use the Fraynes as surrogate gangsters to control the underworld, waiting for their time of freedom. When released from jail, the Krays would once again take up the reins of leading UK villains and pay off the Fraynes for their work. The Krays would use their contacts to create the right image for the lads from Wales, and they would use their muscle and money too. It was simple and it almost worked. What they didn't know at the time was that the police had already started taking an interest in the Frayne boys when they were in Cardiff Prison, where they corresponded with the twins. The police knew the kinds of tricks that the Krays could play and they were there waiting for them at the pass, to cut off their retreat and to get their men.

It is by no means certain that Lindsay Frayne was involved in the robbery at the building society, but the police were looking for something to hang on the brothers, so this was a good opportunity. Since most of their private dealings were just that, very private, then it was a simple matter to frame the boys from the valley. The authorities were not bothered about getting them for one particular crime; they just wanted them at all costs. They could see the writing on the wall, and it had the name of Kray written all over it.

In many ways the boys played right into the hands of the Krays, giving them a good get-out clause in the whole deal. If they succeeded, then the twins would control the underworld, but if they failed they could call the youngsters a bunch of stupid hillbillies, which is exactly what they did. And Leighton and Lindsay Frayne gave them all the evidence they needed. They used to drive to London in an old Vauxhall Cavalier, well past its sell-by date, and they would be careful with the money too, eating small portions and keeping an eye on the budget. This was mainly done because the twins were covering the costs and the idea was to make money, not spend it.

The Fraynes also visited Violet's grave, paying their respects to their heroes' mother, and they met Tony Lambrianou, one of the old gang members and the man who did 15 years for his involvement in the killing of Jack 'The Hat' McVitie. They even visited The Blind Beggar, where Ron shot and killed George Cornell, and it all added spice to their lives, but the good life got the better of them. One day, when they were at The King's Oak in Epping Forest, they bragged about having money, supposedly from the robbery in Wales, and they partied the night away with a stripper and some pals. Unfortunately, one of these pals took some photographs of the lads, photos that are still classified as 'top secret' even today. It may be the pornographic content that has made them unsuitable for publication or there may have been an informer or two in the shots, but the police had had enough of their antics and the brothers were arrested.

By the middle of June 1993 the brothers from the valleys of South Wales were sentenced to eight years for their parts in the robbery in Newbridge. Their relationship with the Krays stopped abruptly with their arrest, and apart from a mugging or two to try to protect their image, they were finished, for the time being at least. The guns were real enough and the right intentions were there, but they just couldn't pull it off. The Krays had played their cards well and were never questioned by police over the incident, but the Fraynes were behind bars and of no further use to the twins. If they were ever going to take over London, then they would have to find another way.

My own investigations have revealed a plot by the Frayne brothers to kill Reg and to take over the underworld for themselves. The Fraynes, however, got too big for their boots and the arrest for the building society robbery stopped them in their tracks. We may never really know the real reason behind the capture of the Frayne brothers, but I think we all owe a debt of gratitude to the boys in blue from South Wales.

When it comes to charitable work, then Ron and Reg Kray did their fair share of fund-raising for good and honourable purposes. In the majority of cases, they used their contacts within the fight game to organise a boxing match, with all proceeds going to the chosen cause. Some time ago, back in the early '90s, I was myself privileged to be present at such a charitable event, where stars of boxing and television were present. So, too, were the usual suspects, including Charlie Kray, Tony Lambrianou and Leighton and Lindsay Frayne. Garry Bushell was there representing the press and there was the normal gathering of assorted hoods and cheap crooks.

There they were in their tuxedos, bulging at the necks and sweating like nobody's business. The auction was the highlight of the evening and most of the big London clubs had supplied footballs signed by the teams. There were some from Arsenal,

Tottenham, West Ham, and so on – they had all put themselves out for the charity and now it was the turn of the guests to make their bids. They put their hands in their pockets, all right, and the evening was a tremendous success, enabling the twins to send off a large sum of money to their cause.

This was typical of the Krays, but sometimes the organisers got a little greedy. Since the twins were never present then they had to leave the collections up to old pals, and these old pals were all crooks. No wonder they didn't always get what was pledged on the night. This has caused many problems through the years, culminating in an investigation into charities run and organised by Reg from inside prison. This concerned charity fraud, and central to the police enquiries was the use of telephones from inside the prison. Since the prisoners had access to these phones then it was possible for all kinds of crooked dealings to be planned and organised from inside the jail, simply by making a phone call.

The Krays had always used these events to further their own causes and to get them the publicity that they craved, but it has also been revealed, since their demise, that the Krays systematically ripped off the givers and kept a large proportion of the funds for themselves. Once again, their so-called friends didn't do the Krays any favours, since they kept records of the amounts paid to the twins and they were quick enough to lay the blame on them, even though they all profited from the scam. They lined their own pockets on the back of sincere desires to help other unfortunate people, especially children. Reg wanted to continue the practice, and I am sure that he wanted many to benefit from his philanthropic charity work, but in the end he took too much and gave too little.

In July 1985, some 17 years after the Krays were put away, officials at Broadmoor made an astonishing discovery. On searching Ron Kray's room they found a business card. But this was not from a lawyer, a journalist or a medical practitioner – it was his own business card for his own firm, known as Krayleigh Enterprises.

All three Kray brothers were listed on the card as directors – Ron, Reg and Charlie Kray. This was their lucrative bodyguard and protection business for Hollywood stars and it was run from behind bars, from wherever they were at the time. The prison authorities and those at Broadmoor were powerless to stop them.

This let the twins rake in the money and gave Charlie an extra opportunity to make a quick buck or two. Ron may have been schizophrenic but was he was not crazy; he knew where there was money to be made.

The twins even used to brag that they had never lost a client, and they listed their customers as 'Hollywood stars and Arab noblemen'. They laughed when they said that their services included bodyguards, security and house protection. But I don't think anyone from the old days, in the East End of London, would have been laughing; they knew what protection was all about, and with Ron and Reg that meant only one thing – extreme violence and mayhem.

When Frank Sinatra came to London in June 1985, to visit Wimbledon for the tennis, he took on 18 minders from Krayleigh Enterprises, just to be sure he was safe. He was charged £100 per bodyguard for the day at Centre Court. And remember, this was some 17 years after they were imprisoned. The Mafia never forget their pals.

There was even a memo sent to the Home Office, asking if running a business from Broadmoor was legal, but they were simply told that there was nothing in the Mental Health Act that prevented Ron from setting up companies. Whether or not the prison authorities took this further, with regard to Reg, is unknown but if they tried to stop it then they didn't succeed. The company continued to operate throughout the '80s from an office just off Mile End Road.

Charlie used to enjoy it there, spending most of his time in the coffee shop with his son Gary. While the others were doing the business he was talking to old pals and planning his next big move. When he wanted to make a private phone call he used to use another office, just down the corridor, so the others didn't know what he was doing. He did anything to make a little extra money, from handling stolen property to making deals on Kray merchandise and talking to publishers about possible book deals.

This was Charlie's life, and it was all down to Krayleigh Enterprises.

One memo from the authorities at Broadmoor at the time actually said: 'Clearly, however, I do not want the Krays to be seen to be using Broadmoor, and it may well be that if he is well enough to be a director of a company, he is too well to be in Broadmoor.' This was perfectly logical, but nothing was done about it, not then, not later.

This all came out into the public domain in early 2010 when the memos were released under the Freedom of Information Act. Someone, on one of the memos, wrote the words 'advice please', and it certainly looked as though they needed some advice, but they needed answers too.

The problems with holding Ron in custody started almost immediately. While he was in Parkhurst before being sent to Broadmoor, a progress report on him said: 'Ronald Kray remains an active and predatory homosexual and cares little who knows it.' He was, as they called it, a problem, and one that was very difficult to handle. Their answer, apparently, was to let Ron indulge himself in his sexual activities with other inmates – they called it a 'stabilising influence' on him.

When Ron was found in bed with another man, a fellow con, in Parkhurst, the authorities cautioned the other man and threatened him with solitary confinement. But, in the main, they turned a blind eye to his relationships just to keep him docile. Fortunately for them he was soon moved to Broadmoor, but he continued in his ways – taking on lovers, some young and some not so young.

Ron would fly off the handle, into fits of despair, when his passions were not satisfied and he became violent, throwing things around and smashing everything in sight. He didn't care what he did and he didn't care who knew about it. So letting him be part of a company was their way of letting him win, appealing to his ego, giving him something to think about besides boys.

So the business was a success and the money flowed. But if you look for the company Krayleigh Enterprises, then you will not find it anywhere. What happened to it? Where are the accounts? Where are the people who ran it for the Krays? As always with the

Krays, it is not easy to investigate these things. So who else was involved with the company? What did they do and when? How much money did they make? And why all the secrecy?

The last great scam was created when Reg was on his deathbed. He became involved with a film company, run by an old inmate pal, to make a film of his last days. Reg was used to this as he had written the books, he had had a film made about his life, there had been documentaries made about him and his brothers, and he had made a lot of money from it. So why shouldn't he get a good payout from the BBC?

The film company received £280,000 from the BBC and they promised to reveal all on television, as Reg Kray was about to take his final breath. But the BBC came under a lot of criticism at the time, with politicians from all sides getting involved.

Labour MP Steven Pound said: 'It really does show that crime does pay. The Kray victims will be sick to the stomach that a so-called public service broadcaster is glamorising villains and criminality.' The MP was no stranger to stories of the Krays. 'I remember the sheer brutality of these gangs,' he told friends, and then added, 'The Krays corrupted many police and youngsters.' I, for one, would like to know which policemen he is talking about here.

Just before his death a film crew went to the Norfolk and General Hospital and filmed the 67-year-old Reg Kray. He showed no remorse for killing McVitie, preferring to offer curious views of how the streets were so much safer when he and his brother were around. He didn't like the modern criminal, and complained about a lack of morality.

When finished the film was offered to all television stations and the BBC won the bidding. When the money was paid, the BBC were told that neither Reg nor Roberta would be getting any of it – neither of them would benefit. But it was Roberta who inherited his estate when Reg died – so don't tell me they didn't get some of the money, disguised in some way. But then, maybe I am wrong.

20

THE FUNERAL OF RON KRAY

Ron was the first to go, but it was the cigarettes that got
him in the end. Thank God he didn't get hung!

Charlie Kray

The Sun ran the story on their front pages on 18 March 1995, and
they even supplied Ron Kray's last words: 'Oh God, Mother, help
me!' *The Star* did the same, with all the usual suspects and all the
well-used photographs, and even the *Daily Mail* used a whole page
to cover the event. The usually indignant *Mail* offered sympathetic
words and even carried a quote from me. But the shock didn't sink
in straight away to a nation used to having the Kray twins around
and in the news. One of them was dead. Was it the mad one, or
the other one? How long had they been in prison? Were they
really that bad? The questions were endless, and many prominent
folk tried their best to answer them, but there are still so many
unanswered questions surrounding the Krays. Even the *Electronic
Telegraph* ran an obituary on the Internet, in which they tried to
summarise the life and times of the Krays in only three pages.
Impossible!

During the following days, when the true meaning of his death
became apparent, there were more stories about Ron and his gay
lovers at Broadmoor, about the heavy mob standing guard over
his coffin and about the inquest that was held in secret. But the
news that his brain had been removed shortly after death was kept
from the media. Even now, we have not had a reasonable

explanation for this surgical procedure, and the fact that it was so hush-hush makes me want to ask why.

Reg was put on medication when he heard the news of his brother's death. He had wanted to visit Ronnie in Broadmoor some days prior to his demise, but the authorities at Maidstone had refused, without giving any reasons for the decision. He was furious and so, too, was Charlie Kray. The brothers immediately set about making plans for the funeral, and part of the arrangements would be the attendance of Reg Kray at the graveyard in Chingford in Essex. The Krays, once again, contacted their pals in the media and laid on a funeral of funerals to mark the passing of one of the biggest and most notorious gangsters this country has ever seen.

Reg's main concern, apart from the actual funeral arrangements, was that he had given away his black suit to a friend only a few weeks before, so he had to get fitted up for a new one a bit sharpish. Reg was never keen on being fitted up!

Ron had had one last typical request, and that was to be carried to his grave in a coach pulled by six black horses decked out in plumes. It was outrageous and extravagant, but he was the big showman to the end. He wanted to go out in style, and Reg and Charlie made sure that they honoured this request. After all, they were honourable men.

Again, the newspapers were full of stories about Ron and his burial, some of them even mentioning the hatred between Ron and one particular inmate of Broadmoor, Peter Sutcliffe, the 'Yorkshire Ripper'. I was there once with Ron Kray when Peter Sutcliffe was sitting just behind me with a pretty woman who had come to see him on many occasions. Ron and he exchanged a few sordid words before Ron told me of his dislike of Sutcliffe, a man who had mistreated women in such a depraved and debauched way. Ron always treated women with respect and expected others to do likewise. Sutcliffe, shortly afterwards, tried to strangle Ron, thinking that he had given information to the press regarding his pretty blonde visitor. This was, of course, untrue. Someone else was present that day who sought to take photographs of the visitor. It was, in fact, one of Ron's visitors that day who protected the woman and got her away from the press. So Sutcliffe should have thanked Ron, instead of trying to kill him.

On 21 March 1995 Reggie hit the headlines with the news that he had been given permission to go to his brother's funeral. Stars John Altman, who played Nick Cotton in the soap opera *EastEnders*, and Page Three girl Debee Ashby were also at the prison to lend a supporting voice or two, to add to the theatrical occasion and to ask for the release of their pal. The funeral was all set for Wednesday, 29 March 1995, with the service to be held at St Matthew's Church, Bethnal Green, and the burial at Chingford Cemetery, alongside Mum and Dad and Reggie's first wife Frances.

There were something like 60,000 people lining the streets from the church to the cemetery, to see the procession led by the glass-sided hearse and the black plumed horses. Among the guests were the crazy gang led by 'Mad' Frankie Fraser and Freddie Foreman, who has only recently admitted to killing 'The Mad Axeman' Frank Mitchell. There were tributes from far and wide, including the regulars such as Barbara Windsor and Roger Daltrey, but the US Mob also sent a wreath to show their respects. The newspapers spread the news all over the following day's issues, with photos of jailbird Reggie with his brother Charlie. The *Daily Mail* had a photo depicting 'the grinning gangster', while others were again more sympathetic, with tributes from stars of show business and especially chosen ex-gangsters.

Reg said: 'Ron had a great humour, a vicious temper, was kind and generous. Above all, he was a man.' Strange words for a twin brother to say, but they were true enough.

The 30-vehicle cortège was ready, with only the funeral itself to be conducted prior to the trip to Chingford. Father Bedford led the way and the coffin was brought in by, amongst others, Charlie Kray, Johnny Nash and Freddie Foreman, while Frank Sinatra was played singing 'My Way' through the loudspeakers on the church walls. Charlie joined his brother and a few well-chosen friends around the coffin and poems were read out loud. Then the congregation sang the hymns 'Morning Has Broken' and 'Fight the Good Fight' – somewhat typical of Ron Kray. Whitney Houston's voice was heard singing 'I Will Always Love You' as the service came to a close.

Outside the church the photographers were waiting for their best opportunity and Father Christopher Bedford explained why he had conducted the service. 'It was my duty to commend Ron's soul to God,' he told them. 'I don't make judgements. God does, and thankfully he is far better at it than me.'

The pall-bearers carried out the coffin and the Rolls-Royces and Daimlers were ready for the slow drive over the Bow flyover and out to the cemetery, and all the way with a police escort to clear the road. The photographers got their chances and the bulbs flashed and hands shook in greetings. Well-wishers waved to Reg as he took his place in the first of the limousines together with Charlie. Reg waved back, giving rise to the *Mail* headline about the grinning gangster.

When Ron's oak coffin, complete with gold-plated handles, was laid in the ground, Reg was led away and straight back to Maidstone Prison, but not before he had had the chance to throw a red rose into the grave. Some of their old gangland pals stayed for a while at the graveside while others left to have a drink and a chat in a nearby pub. Reggie's wreath, which was left on display in the cemetery, said 'To the other half of me', and a painting of the twins was left on the grave as a reminder to everyone of the importance of the terrible twosome in the annals of British crime. Only some of the newspapers mentioned that the whole time, during the service and afterwards, Reg had been handcuffed to a guard from Maidstone, all part of the deal that Reg was forced to make with the authorities.

But the others, including 'Mad' Frankie Fraser, Johnny Nash, Freddie Foreman, Charlie Kray and the bodyguards, all thanked each other for being there. This was a part of their history and a day that will be remembered for a long time in the East End of London. The funeral was actually larger than that for Winston Churchill, which must say something, although it really only confirms that the Krays had many pals who were still willing to organise on their behalf. And the painting, so deliberately laid on the grave by Reg, was just as deliberately stolen during the night by souvenir hunters. They also took a floral boxing glove that was given by prisoners at Maidstone.

* * *

The analysis started shortly after the funeral, with all the experts giving their opinion on the Krays, and Ron Kray in particular. Even Kate, who had been divorced from Ron some time earlier, was asked for her opinion. No one was left out and indeed I was asked by many national newspapers to supply a remark or two for their latest editions. And this is where the problems begin, since it is extremely difficult to say for certain whether or not we, as a country, have learned anything from the experience of the Krays.

Was Ron really evil? Or was he misunderstood? Could his kind have come from anywhere else, other than the East End of London? Has nostalgia taken over, making us blind to the realities of the Kray empire? And had they been in jail long enough? These and many others were the topics of the day. Ron would have had a good laugh at it all. He always said he did what he had to do. He didn't think about it or analyse it. And I do not think that he expected others to do so. 'It's all a waste of time,' would be his reply, as he reached for a cigarette.

What Ron did leave behind was about £10,000 that he asked to be shared among his close friends at Broadmoor and his twin brother Reg. Kate got nothing; likewise Charlie. He had given his fortune away through the years at Broadmoor. In fact, he had made his millions and disposed of it as he saw fit. It was his way of sticking two fingers up at the taxman and saying 'get it if you can'. But he couldn't. And they say that Ron was mad!

Funnily enough, £10,000 was just about the same amount of money that was owed to the funeral companies to settle the debts for Ron's funeral. By August 1995 they were still unpaid, but this, I thought, was a simple matter to settle – surely it would all be sorted out in an amicable way. W. English & Son, part of the world's biggest funeral services company SCI, said that they would not be using strong-arm tactics to get their money. 'We are entirely comfortable with the situation,' said a company spokesman.

As for Reg, he was very busy back in the mid- to late '90s. An amateur football club had asked him to be their president and he had also been writing about his love of music. One piece, entitled 'East End Promise', was actually commissioned for the theatrical newspaper *The Stage* and due to go out through their nostalgia pages. He talked about the old days at La Scala in Milan, where he enjoyed opera with his wife Frances. He had also been busy remembering and honouring the name of his brother Ron. In March 1997 he actually organised a fly-past tribute to his brother, over Chingford Mount Cemetery, where a memorial service was to take place.

'Ron would be pleased that we are doing this for him. He would have done the same for me,' he told reporters.

Even now, many years after their deaths, the Krays can still be front-page news – so what is there still to come?

But the news he received during this time was not good for Reg Kray. Michael Howard, when he was head of the Home Office, disregarded pleas for Reg Kray to be released early. It was also apparent that his successor, Jack Straw, was also intent on Reg serving out his full 30 years in prison. Then came the news that the Home Office had announced an investigation into Reg Kray and charity fraud.

Back in the 1990s Reg was the best-known 'lifer' in the country. Those who care to remember all know what he did, but in this modern age a 30-year sentence is hard to defend. But Reg was still there behind bars at the start of the millennium, writing his books and his letters and waiting for the time when he would be free and an instant millionaire. It may be hard for some murderers and criminals to survive in the outside world once they are released, but for Reg Kray the media of the country were waiting in solemn silence for the date and the time of his freedom, when they could coax him to the South of France, put him up in an expensive villa and get the whole story of his imprisonment straight from the horse's mouth. Reg Kray wanted to be rich and to be free, but it never happened. He would have loved to be the richest 'lifer' in the country!

21

'GOTCHA': THE CAPTURE OF CHARLIE KRAY

> I only got people together, that's all I've ever done. I didn't mean any harm. Sure, it went too far, but I needed the money. It was my last chance.
>
> *Charlie Kray*

'Gotcha,' said the police officer as he arrested Charlie Kray. For Charlie it was all a case of déjà vu or, as he put it, a case of mistaken identity. But it was he who had mistaken the identity of the man with whom he had just made a 2 kg cocaine deal, with the promise of supplying 5 kg every two weeks for the foreseeable future. For the man, known as Jack, was really an undercover officer from the Metropolitan Police masquerading as a northern businessman who wanted a new supplier of drugs, his previous supplier having been killed.

The date was 31 July 1996, just another pleasant Wednesday, and a new Kray prosecution was imminent. Charlie had been settling down for the evening with his girlfriend Judy Stanley to watch television at her home near Croydon, South London. He was well aware of the fact that the drugs deal was going down, since he had played a major part in setting it up, but he had covered his tracks well, or so he thought, and he was not present when the cocaine changed hands. This was an old trick and it had helped Charlie out of many a hole. He was often there or thereabouts, but never caught with his pants down. This time, however, he had supplied his own evidence for his own downfall. For, unknown to him at the time, his incriminating conversations with Jack and his friends had been recorded on tape. He was soon to be his own irrefutable witness, his own worst nightmare.

Charlie was led away by jubilant police officers to Ilford Police Station, next door to the regional criminal operations unit, where he was questioned about the £80 million deal. Plain-clothes detectives, involved in the arrest, quizzed him about his part in the drugs syndicate and the subsequent supply of cocaine. He maintained his innocence throughout, even though he was informed of the capture of his two partners in crime, Ronald Field and Robert Gould. The case against Charlie looked convincing, but it all rested on police evidence, evidence that could stand up in a court of law. And Charlie had usually been able to wriggle out of trouble. The only real exception here was back in 1969, when he was found guilty of helping to get rid of the body of Jack 'The Hat' McVitie and subsequently sentenced to ten years in prison. On that occasion, however, his luck was not with him, since he had not taken part in the killing, neither before nor after, when other members of the Firm got rid of the body at sea. So what did he have to fear this time around?

Judy Stanley stopped to talk to the press as she left Ilford Police Station that night after vainly attempting to see her lover.

'Charlie has done nothing wrong,' she said tearfully. 'We are utterly amazed!' As a parting gesture she asked them: 'Can you imagine a 70-year-old man who has a hatred of drugs being involved in the distribution of them?'

No one answered. Later, back at her Sanderstead semi-detached house, she spoke again to the press. 'Someone has thrown his name into the hat because of what he is,' she said. 'He is no stranger to all this, but he's 70 now and doesn't need the hassle.'

The police issued a statement saying that it was 'one of the largest and most significant drugs raids this year'. Indeed, the Metropolitan Police had been very busy that evening, arresting 31 people in south-east London.

Charlie had much to think about as he sat in his cell that night. What kind of case did the police really have against him? Would the others talk and implicate him in the deal? How long would he spend behind bars if found guilty? When would he be permitted to see his lawyer, Ralph Haems, a close Kray family friend?

It reminded him of the days when he was behind bars in Canada. That time he was thrown out of the country for lack of evidence. His Mafia pals had played their cards right, unlike their English cousins who had had a traitor in their midst, a man who almost led them to life in the 'Tombs' in Montreal. But the Mob weren't around this time, so who could he rely on? Charlie began to think, to wonder why it had happened this way, to speculate on the outcome and to reflect on the events that had led to this most terrifying ordeal. The only question that concerned him was the reason why.

It had been a long night, a night without end. But the story had only just begun to unwind. It followed a devious path; no straight and narrow for Charlie Kray. But then this had always been the case. The only way to get rich was to outsmart the other guy – why do it legally if you can do it easily and reasonably safely by using the Kray name? This same Kray name that had caused so many complications in his life. He should have known better. His brothers, Ron and Reg, had always been able to control situations, to use the Kray name to make lots of dosh. But Charlie had never really been very successful at trading on the fear and violence that the name conjures up in the minds of good guys and bad guys alike. His nice little earners often turned to dismal tales of what might have been. The get-rich-quick schemes had always worked for others, but not for him. This was like 'Del-boy', out of his league, playing with the big boys, those who know all the tricks and always come out on top.

As Charlie slept his mind wandered back to the first time he had met Jack and to the meeting that was to seal his fate. This lonely character, down on his luck and 70 years old, was soon to be called simply a 'foolish old man'. So what had gone wrong? And why?

'Done, mate.'

That was all it took to secure the multi-million-pound drugs deal. Charlie was feeling fine. It was the deal of a lifetime, but he had to be careful.

'I put people together,' Charlie told Jack. 'But I won't go there when they do these things because I have too many eyes on me.' How right he was.

Jack had to be careful as well. He needed the right kind of proof of Charlie's complicity in the deal, so a hidden tape recorder was always at hand. It wouldn't do to tip anyone off accidentally. Since this was the hard-core drugs trade intruders were dealt with speedily and forever. There was no room for errors of any kind.

The idea of the sting came in May, when a phone tap revealed the name of Charlie Kray. The Metropolitan Police were aware of drugs deals being set up in and around London, and they had arranged for numerous phone taps to try to gain useful information concerning future trades. They felt sure that the known drugs barons would be involved somewhere along the line, but the Kray name must have been a real bonus. High profile, high status, a good career move in the making.

However, a recent cocaine bust involving Dave Courtney, a friend of Reg Kray's and the man in charge of security at Ron Kray's funeral, may also have played a part in calculations. He had been arrested at Heathrow Airport with £1 million worth of cocaine. Further back, there was the cocaine bust involving Pete Gillett, Reg Kray's adopted son, and then there was the bust involving Joe Pyle, ex-Kray Firm member and still a close pal of the twins. There was no end to cocaine connections in the Kray family.

An introduction was made through a go-between, establishing Jack (not his real name) as a northern businessman with connections in the underworld and in need of a supplier. Cocaine was his chosen vital ingredient and Jack did all he could to impress Charlie with his good humour, his money and lots of champagne. They didn't call Charlie 'Champagne Charlie' for no reason.

It worked well and soon Jack had been invited to attend a party, a benefit for Charlie's son Gary who had recently died of cancer. Jack and another plain-clothes man called Brian (again, not his real name) met with Charlie and the discussion inevitably came around to drugs. Ronald Field, a 49-year-old builder, and Robert Gould, a 39-year-old electrician, were introduced to Jack and Brian as a good supply source of cocaine.

Later, Charlie would be thankful that his son Gary was not alive to witness the depths of deprivation that had enticed his father to deal drugs, something that his brothers, even in their heyday, had never resorted to. But drugs were not then the scourge of society that they are now. If Reg and Ron Kray were starting on a life of crime today, then it would be difficult indeed not to be involved in one way or another in drugs.

Soon afterwards, Jack invited Charlie and his accomplice Ronald Field to visit with him in Newcastle. This was to seal the connection and to show good faith. Once again, throwing money around as though there was no tomorrow had apparently worked, and Jack became just another do-gooder in the long line of Kray benefactors. The two Londoners stayed at the Linden Hall Hotel at the expense of Jack and his friend Brian, although in reality every taxpayer in the UK was footing the bill. Jack had set things up very well. The scheming had paid off. Charlie and Ronald Field fell for the bait; they took it hook, line and sinker. Jack, on behalf of the Metropolitan Police and the country, and in order to trap Charlie Kray once and for all, agreed to pay £31,500 per kilogram, for an initial drop of 2 kg. The money was to be paid in cash at a time and a place to be determined later by mutual agreement. The arrangements included future supplies of 5 kg every two weeks for at least the following two years, a deal that would net Charlie and his pals a cool £80 million. And it was all recorded for posterity on a hidden tape recorder, to be used later in the trial of the Crown v. Charles Kray.

The deal was done and the men shook hands on a prosperous business venture. And that is what it was to Charlie, just another deal, another chance to make a fortune and to give Judy Stanley the good life he thought she deserved. This was to him a last chance, a chance to gain some kind of prestige and to live the rest of his petty life in some kind of grandeur.

But Charlie wasn't through playing his mind games. He was well aware of the fact that he was now playing very near the line, the barrier between good and evil; some would say that he had already crossed over to the other side. If Charlie could find a way of getting the money, and that was what this was really all about, without really going through with the deal, then he would jump at the chance. After all, it had often worked on previous occasions.

I do not want to bore readers with sordid details of other 'petty con tricks', suffice it to say that these are well documented at Scotland Yard and through other 'informed' sources. This time, however, the deal could not be termed petty. How could anyone call £80 million anything but a major scam?

There were numerous delays to the deal going through, as Charlie tried to evade the question of drugs and to get on to the question of the money. He even managed to borrow a small amount (about £500) from Jack, saying that he had recently lost £1 million on a deal that had gone wrong. Now that doesn't appear to be far-fetched, considering Charlie's proven track record, but anyway it did the trick for the time being. Something is better than nothing, had always been Charlie's motto. Again, the state stood the bill.

Eventually Jack and Brian managed to fix a meeting with Field and Gould at the Swallow Hotel in Waltham Abbey. The date was 31 May 1996. The drugs would be delivered and the money would change hands, £63,000 in cool cash. As arranged previously with Charlie, he would not be present at the exchange.

As planned, the cocaine was handed over in a brown paper bag to the undercover policemen known as Jack and Brian, in the early part of the evening at the chosen venue. The deal done, Field and Gould left the scene with their ready cash, also in brown paper bags. Jack and Brian inspected their delivery of the cocaine and phoned in to headquarters that the sting had gone off well and that 'Operation Crackdown' was a success.

When Ronald Field and Robert Gould stopped to refuel their car at the Lakeside Service Station on the M25 motorway at Thurrock police swooped to capture both men and the cash. Further drugs were also seized. Jack was right. 'Operation Crackdown' had been a complete success. At the same moment, officers were on their way to visit Charlie – his champagne days would soon be over for good.

On Friday, 2 August 1996, Charlie Kray appeared in Redbridge Court, East London, charged with plotting to supply and supplying drugs. The 30-minute hearing was a simple affair. Charlie smiled at Judy and Judy smiled back. Charlie even managed to blow her a kiss as he stood quite motionless in his smart navy blue suit, waiting for a decision. He and the other accused were given a further 28 days' remand, although this was later changed to 6 days since the magistrates had made a little mistake regarding their powers in such a case. But the major details remained the same – conspiring to and arranging to supply approximately £80 million of cocaine.

Judy took it well and vowed to continue her fight to save her Charlie, a man who, according to her, hated the mere mention of drugs.

The following days, weeks, months saw a routine of visits to court for all three accused. They were in deep trouble and the police were not about to release any of them so that they could conveniently leave the country or intimidate witnesses, or anything else for that matter. They would remain in jail until a date could be fixed for a trial.

They had a long wait. On Monday, 2 December 1996, Charlie stood in court at Woolwich, South London, and was duly remanded in custody for plotting an £80 million cocaine importation and supply deal. His pals, Ronald Field and Robert Gould, were in court with him, accused of the same crime, and therefore all three men could await the same fate.

Judy was there again, but there were no kisses this time.

The only good thing to come out of this period for Charlie was that he didn't have to feed himself, or to supply a roof over his own head. And his debtors couldn't get hold of him. The problems hadn't gone away, since he still owed money. But they had been shelved for a while and time, as they say, is a great healer. But it hadn't worked before, so why should it work this time? Sooner or later, Charlie would have to face up to his problems, his debts, his deals and his nightmares.

Charlie was soon standing in Woolwich Crown Court, accused of offering to supply cocaine supposedly to a value of £39 million. Why the figure had been reduced from £80 million is not quite clear. But it was still enough to put him away for a very long time indeed. It was now Wednesday, 14 May 1997, and Charlie had already spent almost a year in custody.

John Kelsey-Fry, for the prosecution, opened with a few general remarks addressed to the jury. First of all he told them that: 'Kray is an unusual name and you may have guessed that the defendant, now over 70 years old, is the brother of the Kray twins, the late Ronnie and Reggie Kray.' He continued: 'You will appreciate that no man is his brother's keeper, and whatever his brothers may or may not have done 30 years ago cannot adversely reflect on this defendant in the same vein.' He added: 'The brothers' past actions can in no way help you determine his guilt or innocence of these charges.'

Well, that was plain enough, and it must surely have helped to set the record straight. The seven women and five men of the jury were, I am quite certain, put at ease by these remarks. However, to put their minds completely at rest, they were told that they were being put under police surveillance throughout the expected six weeks of the trial, just as a security measure. That remark must surely have helped their concentration.

The Kray name was now established. It was time to continue.

'As the evidence unfolds it will become clear that Charlie Kray presents himself as an affable, slightly down-at-heel character much liked for his amusing tales of the old days and the twins,' said the learned prosecutor. But he added, just for good measure: 'But the Crown alleges that behind that affable and charitable image there was another side to Charlie Kray. He was a man prepared to be involved in the drugs trade.'

John Kelsey-Fry had made his point, and everyone in the court room knew it.

The prosecutor told the court that Charlie took care never to be present when the drugs were handed over. He also reminded the jury of the Kray name with all the associations and implications that go with it: 'But he was the kingpin, the link in the chain without whom the deal could not be done.'

Details of the cocaine itself were also outlined in the court room: it was 92 per cent pure, and lethal. A 5 kg delivery every other week would have had serious consequences. Then Kelsey-Fry delivered a telling blow by informing the jury that the other defendants in the case had admitted their involvement: Field from Raynes Park and Gould from Wimbledon had pleaded guilty prior to the trial. Charlie Kray was the last man standing.

Charlie had not helped his case by refusing to answer questions that night at Ilford Police Station, when he was first taken into custody. Mr Kelsey-Fry pressed home his advantage by repeating this fact several times, and added that they would be hearing tape recordings of Mr Kray setting up the deals. Also on the recordings, according to a somewhat jovial John Kelsey-Fry, they would be hearing Charlie talking about his old friends Rocky Marciano and Frank Sinatra, but the main facts to listen out for were those involving the proposed cocaine deal. These first tape recordings were made at Charlie Kray's 70th birthday party in Birmingham. It was here, according to the prosecution, that the first talk of supplying drugs took place. The jury would hear Mr Kray himself admitting to be able to supply cocaine. These were damaging remarks indeed, and the trial had only just begun.

The first witness in the case was our old friend Jack, the undercover policeman, and to protect his identity he was hidden behind a screen. Jack told his story of the sting and of the eventual handing over of the cocaine. He missed nothing out about 'Operation Crackdown', and even talked about his back-up story of being a northern businessman with criminal connections.

'I told Mr Kray that my dealer had been topped,' he told the jury. He continued to relate a tale of intrigue and guile. 'Kray said he had people who were sat on a ton [of cocaine] and he could put my name on it,' he told them. "That is a lot of puff," I told him.' Charlie was then reported to have said: 'I know it is not the place, we will talk in the morning.'

No mention was made of who it was who set up the initial meeting with Charlie and how his name had come up in the phone-tapping part of the investigation.

Still, the prosecution had a good case against Charlie and the jury heard a lot of incriminating evidence against him during the first week of the trial. It was just something that he had to get through, before he could have his own particular day in court. But a betting man wouldn't have given him very good odds during this first part of the trial.

The whole idea and presentation of the interrogation of witness Jack had all been a little bizarre. It had been staged to impress the jury and it had been very convincing, although it would have been more at home in an American TV trial. The press had been there in force; no one wanted to miss a historic Kray trial and it was well reported throughout the media. But it didn't look as though the force was with Charlie Kray this time around. It was soon to become even more peculiar and theatrical, acrimonious even. For it was now the turn of Jonathan Goldberg QC, for the defence.

On Thursday, 22 May 1997, Jonathan Goldberg QC was ready and eager to cross-examine Jack, the prosecution's main witness. Was this to be a revival of good fortunes for Charlie? Or was it just a last-ditch gamble, with all the cards stacked against him? At first it looked as though all he had were jokers in his hand.

'Did you tell a barmaid at a hotel in Essex that you and Brian, a colleague, were into security – guarding wealthy Arabs and jewels?' he asked a surprised Jack. Was this Mr Goldberg's trump card?

Jack replied that he couldn't remember.

It was now time to add a little spice into the trial of Charlie Kray. The defence QC continued to attack Jack on that point. Referring to an evening that Jack and Brian had spent with the girl group the Spice Girls at the Essex hotel where the drugs deal was supposed to be shortly concluded, he asked if Jack had said to the barmaid, 'Why don't we kidnap Victoria Adams [Posh Spice], then release her and put ourselves forward as bodyguards?' His intention was to imply that Jack and his colleague Brian had compromised themselves and the investigation by drinking and partying with the girls at the hotel. Four hours of such behaviour, remarked Mr Goldberg QC, was surely tantamount to misconduct.

Jack denied that he had said anything of the kind to the barmaid.

Jonathan Goldberg continued to talk about the 'Spice Girl' incident, something that seemed to have happened by chance after the girls had appeared on the TV chart show *Top of the Pops*.

Questioned about making phone calls that evening, Jack admitted phoning Michelle Hamdouchi, a hostess he had met at Charlie's 70th birthday party, to ask her over to the hotel. The undercover policeman was asked if he had said, 'Come and have some drinks with Posh Spice.'

Jack replied that it had all been a prank, but that she had

surprisingly arrived at the hotel. It was apparently a surprise to both Jack and his colleague.

But Jonathan Goldberg wasn't finished with his questioning yet.

'Isn't it true that Miss Hamdouchi and your colleague Brian went for a "quickie" in the bedroom?' he asked. The idea was that both Jack and Brian wanted their own bit of spice entering their lives, at the taxpayers' expense too.

'I don't think so, sir,' said Jack solemnly.

The aforementioned sleeping together had not apparently been reported to superior officers in subsequent reports, and Mr Goldberg suggested that the whole thing had been one huge cover-up to disguise their own misdemeanours as a genuine 'sting' operation, in which they were 'setting up' his client. 'You got caught trying to protect him [Brian] and both of you have ended up telling a tissue of lies.'

It had all been a case of 'give me what I want, what I really, really want' suggested Jonathan Goldberg QC. Brian had managed to get what he wanted, but it certainly looked as though the whole thing could have backfired on them and blown their cover. It was a sorry and sordid episode, if a bit of a joke, and Jack had difficulty in answering the many questions put to him that day. They had been a couple of cops whoopin' it up in the Swallow Hotel Saloon, but for the moment they appeared to have got away with it. That Thursday, for Jack and Brian, couldn't end quickly enough.

If these previous days had been a comedy of errors, then what awaited the jury on Monday, 2 June 1997 was a character assassination. The man doing the assassin's work was none other than Jonathan Goldberg, QC. And the man being crucified was his client, Charlie Kray.

First, Mr Goldberg had a few words to say about the treatment of his client. Outside Woolwich Crown Court armed police were on patrol. People going into the court were searched. His client had been kept at Belmarsh Prison, as a Category Triple A security inmate (the same as for IRA prisoners). 'The hype surrounding his case is the biggest obstacle I face in defending him,' he concluded.

Now the assassination could begin. 'Charlie Kray is no more

than a skint old man trying to charm cash out of his victims.' Now that was pretty bad, but worse was to come. 'He is a pathetic old has-been, cashing in on the family name and cadging drinks whenever he could.'

Charlie stood motionless, head down in the dock, while his life was torn to shreds. What a sight he made. He wore a smart suit, clean shirt and polished shoes. But behind the façade stood the real Charlie Kray, with fake watch, schooled smile and false reputation. In tears, he told of how he couldn't even bury his own son, who had died of cancer at the age of 44 the year before. His brother Reg, he told the jury, had paid all of Gary's funeral expenses. He spoke quietly and was subdued about living with his girlfriend Judy Stanley, a headmaster's daughter, at her semi in Sanderstead, and about how he shared the home with her three sons. It was a sad experience, for everyone there.

Mr Goldberg didn't let up, however. He said that police had lured a foolish old man into a carefully laid trap. 'This old fool thought he could string them along and con them.'

A pitiful Charlie Kray, his reputation in tatters, had to continue to hear his life pulled apart. It must have been a terrifying ordeal for a man who had lived his life with pride. For no matter what he had done, or had tried to do, Charlie Kray was indeed a man who had tried to live up to a certain code. It may not have been a recognised moral code, but it was, in the main, the style of a man with dignity. It may appear strange to an outsider, but Charlie Kray was not all bad – he had, however, difficulty in telling right from wrong, and this time he had gone just a little too far across that line between good and evil.

The jury were now witnessing a curious double act. First Jonathan Goldberg would say something quite detrimental about his client and then it would be Charlie's turn to do himself damage and to imply a simplicity of actions. The reason for these actions, as stated by both men, was to simply get money out of a punter. Charlie didn't care who the punter was, just how much money he could con out of him.

Charlie now told the jury that he had even had to borrow £50 on the night when he first went out to meet Jack and his pal. He said that he had always been broke, with no bank account, no credit cards, nothing. Now that is something of a little white lie, since I just happen to have a copy of a cheque from Charlie in my possession. Certainly, he didn't have the account for very long, but it did exist and it is not difficult to prove. However, the police were not interested in such minor details. They had a fish to catch and, bank account or no, they wanted their man.

Jonathan Goldberg continued the act. 'Charlie Kray is nothing, but he looks everything,' he told the court. He was quoting Lady Bracknell, from *The Importance of Being Earnest*, where Oscar Wilde is describing Algernon. 'He might seem suave, like a million dollars, but he is just an old trouper doing his best.' It might have been his best, but it wasn't working.

Something new was needed, and the defendant himself had, once more, to step into the breach. 'It was just a load of bull,' he told them. 'I swear on the grave of my son that it's just a load of rubbish.' He was clearly trying to establish the fact, alluded to earlier, that he was trying to con money out of Jack and his pals, not trying to supply drugs.

Mr Goldberg took up the argument once again by telling the jury how Charlie had 'frittered away the money from the Kray film'. Perhaps he forgot to tell them the amount involved. Maybe £99,000 would have made a different kind of impression on them. He may also have forgotten to tell them of the problems Charlie had had with his brothers about his handling of the deal. Instead of more than £1 million, they only received £297,000 between them. Charlie, as usual, needed the money fast and took a huge discount to get cash. Ron and Reg were furious with him at the time and didn't speak to him for almost a year. But that was of little interest to Mr Goldberg.

'Charlie Kray has been a victim of his surname throughout his life,' said the defence counsel. This may have been right, but it was also his 'cash cow' and he had milked it for all he could get. 'He is sociable, loveable, anti-crime, a wonderful father, anti-drugs and anti-violence,' he continued. And, for good measure, he added: 'He is a man with a heart of gold, naive and gullible.' Well, I may very well agree with some of that, but really, to call Charlie Kray anti-crime is like calling David Cameron anti-politics. Charlie had always been on the fringes of criminal activity, and how any man can say such garbage about the man who laundered stolen bearer bonds from the US Mafia is really quite beyond me.

But Jonathan Goldberg did hit the right note when he began to argue the case against the police, saying that the whole operation looked like 'an elaborate and devious sting'. To clarify matters, he added: 'No doubt it has been quite a feather in the cap of many officers to nick the last of the Kray brothers.' The police, he said, had acted like 'agent provocateurs'. There may have been some truth in this, but Charlie didn't have to do the business, to arrange for the supply of cocaine.

It was revealed in court that Charlie had been involved in various businesses. He had managed a failed pop band, gone bankrupt with a clothing company, existed as a celebrity doing talk shows and interviews, and so on. Again the talk came round to famous film stars such as Judy Garland and Frank Sinatra. The only other conviction that Charlie had against his name, apart from disposing of McVitie's body, was a £5 fine for theft in 1950.

To change tack a little, Mr Goldberg asked Charlie about his brothers. Ron was ill, he said, but he could be kind-hearted. Reg, he said, went crazy after Frances died, but they always treated normal people with respect. I, for one, would have liked to know what Charlie Kray called 'normal people'. He was probably talking about anyone who didn't get in their way.

The day was drawing to an end and it was time to make a point or two. To explain the way Charlie looked at people and money, Mr Goldberg said: 'Charlie Kray would offer to sell Scud missiles if he thought he could get some cash out of the deal. But only as a con.' This was indeed a dangerous ploy, for it showed a devious side to Charlie's character. Anything for money was not really the kind of thing to say to a jury and certainly not one trying a Kray. To balance things up the QC added that the police officers in the case had swilled champagne and encouraged Charlie to deal with them. But seeing that kind of money was too enticing, he had just explained that in open court. It was an apparent fact that Charlie was a crime waiting to happen!

To Jonathan Goldberg QC, Charlie Kray was 'a thoroughly washed-up figure whom the hype by the police and prosecution has made to appear something he is not.' The day was over for

Charlie, no more time for elaborate excuses. No more time for a cosy chat over a pint down the pub, only time to remember. It had been a gruelling day for everyone, and now Charlie Kray only had his thoughts for company.

If anyone had imagined that this trial would continue with a whimper, then they were very much mistaken. Wednesday, 4 June, started with a bang!

In a bid for sympathy Charlie began to describe the events following Ron's death. 'My brother found out before I did that they had removed Ronnie's brain after he was dead for experiments. Everyone was ringing up about it and was very upset about it and wondering, why?' Charlie was near to tears as he continued his grim tale. 'Finally they returned the brain in a casket and it was re-buried,' he told the court. Exactly how anyone had recognised the brain of the deceased murderer was not exactly made clear. But it probably had a label on it saying 'Ron Kray's brain'. The family had complained to the Home Office about it, but no one had had the decency to explain the need to remove the brain, or the need to keep it such a secret. So the complaint situation had not yet been resolved.

'They didn't admit it at the time,' said Charlie. 'We thought we were burying the full body.'

In fact, brain tissue was removed by Home Office pathologists and pickled in a jar, then found their way to Oxford for testing. A statement was issued at the time, but hidden away for only academics to find. A spokeswoman for Wexham Park said: 'Tissue is sent away to specialist centres if we don't have the right facilities.' She added: 'They can find out if there was any damage to the brain or any illness. It is not standard, but it happens in about one in three cases.'

Radcliffe Infirmary at Oxford had been in possession of the tissue for almost a year, while tests were carried out in order to establish whether Ron Kray had suffered any brain damage or illness prior to his death. However, officials denied that tests were linked to research into criminality. Still, the brain tissue had been removed without consent or the knowledge of Kate Kray, Ron's wife, when the post-mortem examination had taken place at Wexham Park, near Slough. It was confirmed by Radcliffe that researchers had not found any abnormalities in Ron Kray's brain cells. Well, that is good to know.

This was just one of many macabre interludes during the trial of Charlie Kray, but still more drama was to follow.

For the moment, however, Jonathan Goldberg QC was content to repeat his summing up. He said once more that the police had lured his client because of his name and that he was a 'foolish old man' who had been trapped by devious methods. Mr Goldberg had used all his aces. The only cards left were character witnesses, who were due to appear the following week. But could convicted villains like 'Mad' Frankie Fraser and actors such as Bill Murray from ITV's *The Bill* really get Charlie out of trouble? Only time would tell.

'Charles is a lovely, lovely man who would not know how to steal a penny,' said 'Mad' Frankie Fraser, replying to a question put to him by Jonathan Goldberg QC. 'He wouldn't say boo to a goose,' he continued as he poured praise on the man in the dock. The trial had moved on to Monday, 9 June 1997, and the former Richardson gang member (some would say executioner) was presented as a character witness in the case. It may appear puzzling that a villain such as Frankie Fraser was in court at all, especially when he was not being prosecuted himself. For during his seventy-three years he had been inside for forty-one of them, and had openly admitted to killing two people. This was the kind of man who was now acting as a character witness on behalf of Charlie Kray.

'To this day the Krays are quite rightly idolised,' he said, when questioned about his relationship with the brothers. As a Richardson enforcer he had spoken with Charlie and his brothers many times, mainly to sort out minor problems that had arisen between the gangs, he told the court. He even went on to talk about the time when Ron Kray shot and killed George Cornell, and when questioned further he said: 'Theory has it that he [Cornell] had called Ronnie a big fat poof!'

Asked by John Kelsey-Fry for the prosecution as to whether he thought Charlie could deal in drugs, 'Mad' Frankie replied: 'He could not do it, not for a single day. You are probably more into drugs than him.' This was gradually developing into the 'Mad' Frankie Fraser show, and it was not helping Charlie one bit. But then 'Mad' Frankie has always had a way of helping himself. As a final gesture to the jury he told them: 'This is the first time I have come out of court free.' He was free all right, but his so-called pal Charlie was beginning to pray for a miracle, for that was what he needed now.

Next in line as a character witness was Bill Murray, the actor who played Detective Sergeant Beech in *The Bill*. 'Charlie Kray was a gentleman,' he told them. He had even been helped by the Krays early on in his career.

Then came a procession of do-gooders such as Eileen Sheridan-Price, the first ever Miss UK, Robin McGibbon, who had written a book with Charlie some years earlier, and Michelle Hamdouchi, who had been mentioned earlier in the trial.

It was all very interesting, but not interesting enough. The tape recordings, previously played 'live' in court, where Charlie openly talked about supplying drugs, had done their trick for the prosecution. From then on in it had been downhill all the way.

Charlie had now spent a lot of time in the dock, behind the glass screen. His only companions had been two prison officers standing by his side. His only movement was a glance or two upwards, to see who was testifying. He was still the last man standing.

The five-week trial was over and the jury of four men and seven women (one man had been excused during the trial) had to bring in their verdict. Guilty or not guilty?

What would it be? Charlie knew he would soon find out.

On Friday, 20 June, the jury brought in their verdict. They had deliberated for three whole days. The verdict was delivered soberly and simply. Charlie Kray had been found guilty on all counts. He was guilty of offering to supply undercover police officers with a consignment of cocaine every fortnight for two years. He was guilty of supplying 2 kg of cocaine worth £63,000 the previous July. They could have added that he was also guilty of being a man named Kray.

Judy Stanley wept as she sat in Woolwich Crown Court, her hands covering her face. Other women in the packed public gallery started to cry, while men just shook their heads in amazement.

But all this time Charlie Kray sat in the dock without the slightest emotion. He knew it was all over bar the shouting and, when it came, it was something of a relief. Judge Carroll had already, earlier in the day, told him that he could expect a custodial sentence. He rose from the dock to shake hands with his barrister, Jonathan Goldberg QC. As he shook his hands he also found time to blow Judy a kiss, but he didn't smile on this occasion, although he did manage to receive one back. He knew he faced a possible life sentence.

Outside the court Judy Stanley was too upset to speak to the press, so friends said a few words on her behalf. Diana Buffini told them that there was evidence that the jury were not allowed to see. And Maureen Cox, a former Page Three girl, said: 'Our biggest fear is that he will not come out alive.' Later, Judy did speak to the media, but only to say, 'I am in a state of shock.' Their only hope now was a light sentence and everyone stressed Charlie's age, over 70 years old, and the problems of incarceration at that time of life. For Charlie Kray, any sentence could be life.

Judge Michael Carroll began proceedings on Monday, 23 June 1997 by launching a withering attack on Charlie, whom he called a 'veteran villain'.

'You show yourself to be ready, willing and able to lend yourself to any criminal enterprise,' he told him. 'But when caught you cried foul,' he continued. 'I'm pleased to see that this jury saw through that hollow cry.'

He sentenced Charlie to 12 years' imprisonment, part of which was to be as a Triple A prisoner. 'Throughout this case you have professed your abhorrence for drugs, but the jury's verdict has shown your oft-repeated protestations to be hypocrisy.'

Charlie showed no emotion as the sentence was passed. The game was up.

'Those who deal in class-A drugs can expect justice from the courts, but little mercy,' said Judge Carroll bitterly.

Judy Stanley waved goodbye to her ageing lover as she left the court.

It was left to Mr Goldberg QC, a man who had torn his own client to pieces, to say that he thought Charlie would have trouble in prison and be the target for thugs. 'Every young hoodlum will want to take a potshot at Charlie Kray. Public interest does not require a sentence that means he dies in prison,' he said. Perhaps Jonathan Goldberg had already said enough. Giving young offenders ideas of that nature is not a good thing to do. At the time, I thought he would survive, since he had been a survivor all his life. But it was not to be. As he had always feared, he died in prison. He was broke in more ways than one.

The irony of the case is that his accomplices, Ronald Field and Robert Gould, received nine years and five years, respectively. And these were the men who actually did the business. So what price justice?

Reg Kray immediately complained about the verdict and the sentence. He thought the whole case had been arranged and that it was a set-up to lengthen his own prison term of 30 years. Then he quietly set about trying to find the man who had fingered his brother. That was the kind of man Reg had become.

All the stories of stars, such as Jackie Collins, Muhammad Ali, Sonny Liston, Judy Garland and Frank Sinatra, hadn't helped. The stories of Posh Spice and the 'quickie' incident hadn't helped. The demeaning summing up by his own defence counsel hadn't helped. Nothing had helped.

As trials go it was an expensive and protracted series of outlandish events that would have been more at home on the cinema screen than in a crown court. It was a tale of iniquitous dealings and personalities, with a debilitating series of assaults on the personal character and credibility of the accused, Charlie Kray. The country had incurred all the costs and would, if Charlie had stayed alive, have continued to do so for the next 12 years or so.

'We will appeal,' said Judy Stanley, finding her voice at last. 'Twelve years is a long time, but Charlie will be fine.' She left to start proceedings for the appeal and to drown her sorrows. She began to cry again.

Further down the road, however, stood a happy and contented man. Detective Superintendent Gavin Robertson, the man who led the inquiry known as 'Operation Crackdown', was overjoyed. He wasn't amazed at the verdict or at the sentence. 'No sad old fool has the capacity to produce that amount of cocaine,' he said solemnly. He was sadly right.

Still Charlie protested his innocence, but then he had nothing else left to do. At 71 he was behind bars and facing an eternity in prison, with all the low-lifes he thought he was getting away from. I well remember, only a few years ago, when I was walking with Charlie along the Waterloo Road. He stopped, turned and pulled me over to the other side of the street. When I asked for a reason for this action his answer came rather unexpectedly.

'It's that Buster,' he said, referring to the Great Train Robber, Buster Edwards, who ran a flower stall just outside Waterloo Station. 'He's always trying to get me into trouble.' Charlie didn't want the aggro back then, but maybe he had changed just a little.

Meanwhile the old-timers turned out to raise money for their old pal. 'Mad' Frankie Fraser and Tony Lambrianou organised a fund-raiser at the Ridge Golf Club in Kent, where they asked guests for £100 – just for the privilege of being invited. Once inside, they were asked for further donations to boost Charlie's appeal fund. The young hoods came in by the back door, while the older villains were openly looking for publicity.

'Charlie has lots of friends, many of whom do not believe that he was involved with smuggling cocaine,' said Tony Lambrianou. That is quite right, even though it rather distorts the truth. He wasn't pronounced guilty of smuggling cocaine; he was found guilty of selling and supplying it. Maybe Mr Lambrianou should get his facts right.

The gangsters turned up to pay tribute to Charlie Kray and to wine and dine the night away, to the music of The Rockin' Berries. There were more than 200 of them in all, just a token number of assorted villains and rogues, all there for a reason. It was a time to talk of old times and to plan new ventures, with quiet talk in dark, dingy corners. Hand-shaking looked as though it had come back into fashion in a big way, or should that be in a Mr Big way?

So the team of old lags was back in business. Maybe Charlie would have the help he so desperately needed, or maybe the crooks were just going to get a little richer. One way or another, I knew that Judy Stanley would have a long wait.

22

THE KRAYS AND THEIR WOMEN

Judy Garland was lovely. She invited me to join her at her
home in Hawaii. I never went.

Reg Kray

The idea of gangsters and their molls goes back to the early days
of cinema and to Hollywood's impression of the reality of the '20s
and '30s in places such as Chicago and the Lower East Side, New
York. The bad guy would be the stiff-upper-lip type, always ready
to mow down the enemy with a machine gun or to slap a kiss on
the face of the best-looking broad in the house. Well, at least that
was how Cagney and Bogart used to do it.

The Krays were different, not least because Ronnie was a self-
confessed homosexual. But their lives and the image of their times
that they tried to display as being representative of those days shows
something else. They followed the Cagney path true enough, by
trying to visibly emulate the Chicago gangsters. They even dressed
like them and drove American cars. Outwardly, both men tried to
show themselves as good-looking, normal, everyday types,
constantly in the company of attractive and beautiful women. Ron
was photographed with Christine Keeler, around the time of the
Profumo affair, and Reg was photographed with Judy Garland, even
though he tried to hide the photo from his wife Frances. So they
tried to convey an image of normality, one that they thought would
do them the most good. Image, especially to Ron, was an important
part of being one of the most feared people in the country.

It was Ron's downfall that he could not let George Cornell get away with calling him a 'big fat poof', since this was said in public and it didn't tie in with Ron being the violent underworld boss that he so rightly was. In fact, no one is really sure if that was what Cornell said, but the intent was there sure enough.

So was the image created by Ron, to hide the fact that he was homosexual, or was it just a way to get his name in the history books? And was Reg really the timid, shy lad we are told about in the books or was there another reason for his behaviour?

Women have always been fascinated by the Krays. That is a verifiable fact and they have had enough correspondence with them to fill the Royal Albert Hall. It is as true today as it was back in their heyday of the '50s and '60s, so what is it that attracted them?

Or maybe it is all just media hype. Have we all been brainwashed into imagining that Ron, Reg and Charlie Kray were just a bunch of nice East End boys who had sex appeal in abundance?

I heard an opinion recently that the tabloid press helps to fill a void, a need for emotional sentimentality. In common journalistic jargon it is expressed as the commerce of feeling or the politics of emotion – the death of Diana, Princess of Wales, was a good example. But is this outburst of feeling by the media representative of the country, or does it just make sentimental idiots of us all?

The press try to sell newspapers, and no one can blame them for that. But the trend now is for the tabloids to break one of these heart-rending stories, only to be followed three days later or so by the broadsheet newspapers. So is there an actual void or do the press create the need for a void?

Whether this kind of sexiness is contagious or not is something that I feel needs further research, but the truth of the matter is that many women did find the Krays sexy. They were attracted to these men. They wanted to contact them. They wrote to them. Such men filled an apparent void for these women.

So is it power that women are after, or is it purely fantasy that attracts them? Surely both are contenders among the young. Possibly the older women and those from more puritan backgrounds simply wanted to entice the Krays onto the straight and narrow. Or maybe others just wanted to become natural born killers and live out their fantasies in ways that they could only dream about. Whatever it was that turned them on, it appeared to work for the Krays. And the Krays loved it.

To establish the psychological background for this chapter I have enlisted the assistance of family psychologist Audrey Sandbank, from TAMBA, the twin organisation, and Tim Trimble, who lectured some time ago in psychology at King Alfred's College, Winchester.

All three Kray brothers idolised their mother, Violet. She was such a strong and powerful influence in their lives that comparisons with other women would have been extremely difficult, if not impossible. Even when it came to young girls it was very difficult for the Kray brothers to form relationships because of the protective devotion of their mother. Theirs, it seems, was a male-dominated world in which men made all the decisions and played out all the deeds according to their own macho rules. The only place for women was on the sidelines, urging their mate on to further great achievements at the cost of all other men. It was the call of the wild and the Krays were the king apes who dominated the landscape of the East End of London.

It was not a good environment for so-called normal relationships to develop, and remember the boys didn't have a father figure to look up to. 'Old Man' Charlie was normally on the run from the law, as he was classified as a deserter throughout their early and most formative years. So the dominance of their mother became an important part of their appreciation of women in general and girlfriends in particular. No one could compare with Mum!

But within this mother-and-son relationship came the ever growing powerful surge of egoism that was to make Ron, the younger of the twins, challenge his brother's position and assert himself as the more dominant of the two, even though he was homosexual. This situation did not provide for the stability and balance that Reg needed when he was maturing into adulthood. It also provided many with the theory that Reg himself was a homosexual. Twins look the same, they behave the same, they have similar sexual preferences, or so it appeared to 'outsiders' at the time. But those who knew Reg portray him as a womaniser and, indeed, he had his fair share of paternity suits, all of which he successfully fought in court. So the question remains, did Reg have similar tendencies to his brother Ron? It is quite clear that Reg was present at parties at Cedra Court, where Ron ran his orgies and invited pals such as Tom Driberg MP and Lord Boothby. Reg took part in all of the activities, laid on by Ron, at these parties. He enjoyed it while, in the flat below, his wife Frances was crying her eyes out.

In later years, Reg had a weird way with women, one that has shone light on to his apparent inability to have relationships with the opposite sex. In 1993 Sandra Wrightson was so beguiled with Reg that she was divorced from her husband Peter, naming Reg Kray as the other man in her life. She had written Reg a large number of letters and kept all the replies hidden under her bed, but her husband found the letters and their pornographic content persuaded him to file for divorce, which was granted. Her sons Lee and Harvey disowned her and she lost everything that was dear to her, except for the memory of Reg. He wrote to her about kinky orgies with his cellmate, suggesting three in a bed, or maybe she would like to have sex with his pal while he watched? So she started visiting him in Blundeston Prison in Suffolk, and soon things got out of hand. Reg had his hands on her best assets, her breasts, and had tried to entice her into his underpants – and all of this in front of the prison guards in the visitors' room. Things went sour when Reg asked her to take care of a friend by letting him stay at her home near Northampton, but she couldn't handle it, like Frances, and many others before. Reg became belligerent and threatening. It was all over and they hadn't even had sex.

Sandra was not the last to be besotted with Reg. In May 1995 Sophie Williams was pictured in *The Sun*, on the way to a mailbox with a letter to Reg. The 19 year old had visited him at Maidstone Prison on a number of occasions, sitting with him in the visitors' room and drinking coffee.

'He is the most wonderful man I have ever met,' she said. 'It is so cruel to keep him locked away,' she added, as she drooled over the ex-king of gangland. In fact, she had first started writing to him when she was 16 – now does that ring a bell? Guess who was living in the past? It would appear that Reg liked them young. Some may say a little naive, too.

Perhaps the strangest on–off relationship, however, was that between Reg and the actress Patsy Kensit. Reg was godfather to her and her brother and an old friend of her father, Jimmy Kensit, although around the millennium Patsy had denied even knowing Reg Kray and his twin Ron. In the summer of 1988 she wrote to Reg, thanking him for his kindness when her father had died in 1987. Jimmy 'The Dip', as her father was known, used to run errands for the Krays and asked Reg to be godfather to both his son and to his daughter Patsy. As her career went into overdrive Patsy Kensit sought to distance herself from the Krays, but Reg took offence in February 1997 when he heard rumours that Patsy had denied ever having known the twins. He asked *The People* to publish her letter. Patsy was then married to Liam Gallagher of Oasis. I hoped, at the time, that she could reconcile herself to the fact that we all know the connection between the Kensits and the Krays. I am sure Reg, likewise, forgave Patsy for denouncing him.

The whole Kray saga took a new turn on 14 July 1997, when Reg married Roberta Jones, a 38-year-old university graduate, in Maidstone Prison. Ron was dead, Charlie in jail, but now the 'Double R' was back in business. Reg and Roberta, it had a nice ring to it, didn't it? I am sure that was the idea. The cynics among us said that it was all part of Reg's plan to get parole, early in 1998, by proving that he had a home to go to and someone to look after him. Money had never been a problem for the Krays, but supplying a satisfactory home life, or ready-made family, had always been a complex issue. Reg had tried earlier with his old cellmate from Parkhurst, Pete Gillett, whom he legally adopted while in jail, but their relationship didn't last for long.

So Reg Kray married Roberta Jones. Just how did that happen and what did the future hold for the lovebirds?

The first mention of a new woman in Reg's life was a headline in *The People* of 6 July 1997, where Roberta Jones made the front page.

'Reg Kray is my life,' she said, adding, 'everything I do, everything I am, is about Reg.'

She had even sacrificed her home, her business and her normal family life to live near Maidstone Prison. She must have been shocked when Reg was suddenly and unceremoniously moved to Suffolk.

But the front-page news had a familiar ring to it – she was announcing the release, in the next year, of her book, telling all about Reg and her love and devotion for him. Roberta, an honours graduate in English literature, had moved down to London from Stockport some 20 years before, and had been involved in the marketing and media fields. It was when she was standing in for a friend, who had made an appointment to see Reg in Maidstone Prison, that she first met the gangland boss. The idea was to talk about Ron, who had only recently died, but they ended up talking intimately about themselves. It all developed from there. She moved into a small, rented two-bedroom terraced house near the prison, just to be close to Reg, waiting for the day he would be released. Her only comforts were a few cardboard boxes for clothes and a mattress on the floor, but her thoughts of Reg kept her happy and gave her a sense of belonging.

'Regarding our love life, I have just switched myself off,' she told reporters. But then she added: 'We can touch and hold hands but we both look forward to the day we can lie beside each other.' Whether this celibate lifestyle would actually help her to come to terms with the fact that Reg was a gangland boss of world renown was never discussed.

The following Sunday, 13 July, *The People* had another exclusive, this time telling all about Reg and his keep-fit sessions in prison. 'The cold showers help to keep his potency,' the report stated, but it didn't say if it did him any good. Reflexology was also apparently a key element in his physical training and Reg talked openly about the physical side of his attraction towards Roberta. 'Reg believes he has found a soulmate in Roberta,' the newspaper continued, 'despite their 25-year age gap and their cultural and educational differences.'

The term 'soulmate' sounds just a little too much like cellmate, but then that is probably what Roberta meant to Reg. Having lived so many years in prison, he was obviously aware of the fact that he would have many years of adjustment before him in outside life, once he was released. Forensic psychotherapy could play its part in rehabilitation but, without doubt, the presence of Roberta in his life would play a major and dominant role in his future. With 30 years behind bars, he deserved all the good fortune he could get.

The news of 15 July 1997, in the *Daily Mail*, said it all. 'The bride was late. But Reggie Kray wasn't about to go anywhere.' The white wedding was held inside Maidstone Prison in Kent, with only a few close friends and officials present, under the ever-watchful eyes of the security cameras. Reg was then 63 years old, the exact age Roberta's father was when he died when she was only 12 years old. So was she replacing her father with a father figure, and if so, couldn't she have chosen someone else? But they both had their own particular reasons for getting married and, as long as they could live with their decisions then I, for one, could not see any reason for doubting their mutual desire for a long and loving life together.

To mark the day, Reg had planned for a laser show the night before the wedding. The following morning bouquets of flowers began to arrive for their Church of England service in the prison chapel. Charlie, who was himself in prison, couldn't attend the wedding, so he too sent some flowers. The best man was there, Reg's prison pal Bradley Allardyce, and so, too, was Brentford FC manager Dave Webb. It was all over in 20 minutes, with Reg only speaking once to say, 'I do.' 'Amazing Grace' was played to supply the required aura of majesty and bliss.

Roberta Jones had overcome the journey, made by four-wheel-drive jeep, the metal detectors, the security, the razzmatazz of a Kray wedding in an ankle-length ivory beaded dress, and had come out the other side as Mrs Roberta Rachel Kray. Mark Goldstein, Reg's solicitor, said after the wedding: 'Mr Kray and Miss Jones wish to thank their family and friends for their love and support and look forward to the time when Reggie is released and they can spend the rest of their lives together.' The non-alcoholic reception lasted some two hours, with other friends celebrating in the pub opposite the prison. But with Roberta rushing to beat a retreat from the prison, the jeep that she had arrived in actually hit one of the photographers who were waiting outside for a shot of the bride. Knowing the Krays, he is lucky he didn't get shot.

Roberta's father, who taught at the Birkdale School for Hearing Impaired Children, and his wife Gladys doted on their daughter, who did so well at school, eventually going on to university. But the death of her father of cancer was a blow that Roberta never really overcame, although she would not show any outward signs of confusion. This had all changed when she met Reg and all the old pain re-emerged. She could remember the agony of his death and told a journalist: 'When I lost my father, I lost my protector – the member of my family who looks after problems and sorts things out.' She had certainly chosen a suitable father figure in Reg, who surely knew all there was to know about protection. Roberta knew that people would talk about her father and she had resigned herself to the banter and backchat.

But Roberta Jones, now Kray, has a sense of humour and she was going to need that in the times to come. When Reg proposed on the telephone from Maidstone Prison she asked if he was on one knee. His cellmate confirmed that he was, and Roberta told Reg that she would think about it, but that was all she needed. She had found her surrogate father and her new husband all rolled into one, in the person of Reg Kray. And who were we to say that she couldn't live the rest of her life in happiness, safe in the knowledge that her man would always take care of her?

'I live in the present,' she told reporters after the wedding. Her future was still undecided, but most people in the country were still wishing her well in the hope that she could help Reg to survive the rigours of release and family life. People were beginning to think that maybe there was a Kray dynasty to come after all.

That all changed when Reg died. The party was over – all three Kray brothers were dead and buried. Life could start again for Roberta, and she has been writing books about her life and her poor, departed husband ever since. She hardly has to work, as she inherited the Kray money – but did she inherit the family business as well?

Elaine Mildener married Ron Kray in Broadmoor in 1985. Originally she had started writing to his brother Reg but swapped allegiance for some reason, probably because writing to Ron was easier than dealing with the complexities of his brother. This may seem peculiar, when Ron was the more obviously homosexual of the two and the so-called violent madman, but Reg had served all his time in prison, and most of that in maximum security, so his attitude to life was urgent and somewhat forceful. Ron, on the other hand, was sedated with drugs and had convinced himself that he would never be a free man, so he was the casual, elegant twin and Reg became the exasperated, touchy twin. I can confirm that visiting Ron was like a Christmas dinner, compared with the austerity of prisons and the impatience of his brother.

So Elaine Mildener was now Elaine Kray, and *The Sun* was there to record events for posterity, even taking a photographer along with them to plaster pictures of the happy couple all over their inner pages. It was a coup, and Ron greatly appreciated the photographs. And the new Mrs Kray greatly appreciated the money paid for the privilege. She returned home to her children a happy woman, ready to play the part of Mrs Kray to the full. But it didn't last; the visits became a routine and her children, Andrew and Debbie, suffered as a result.

Ron had always told her that sex was out of the question, since he had his real soulmates inside Broadmoor with him. His few close friends were all he needed for sexual pleasure, but he wanted something else, that something that only a woman can give: he wanted a family, or the semblance of one. He felt the need to be in a family once more and to project that image of an identity within a family group. He felt safe in that environment. It made him feel at ease, as though he was leading a normal life, even though he was confined in such a dismal place as Broadmoor. In a way, a part of him had escaped outside those bleak walls and was living freely with his wife.

Elaine kept the visits going for as long as she could, but when it began to be a burden, she decided that a divorce was inevitable. Ron agreed. After all, he may have been mad but he was no idiot. So, in June 1989, they were divorced and Ron was free to set about the task of finding a new wife. He didn't have long to wait.

Only two months after the divorce, Ron was married once more inside the walls of Broadmoor. This time it was to be kissogram girl Kate Howard, a divorcée from Headcorn in Kent, and again photographers were there to take their shots and record the event for public scrutiny. The story is similar to that of Elaine Mildener, in that Kate first visited Reg before seeing Ron in the top-security hospital. Again, Ron's charm was the clincher and she fell madly in love. The diminutive, effervescent blonde was to be gangland boss Ron Kray's second wife.

Kate Kray was still the bubbly girl she always had been and nothing much has changed, even to the present day. Apart from visiting Ron on a regular basis she also found time to write books and to do television work, and I have been fortunate to meet her on several occasions. She has sex appeal in abundance and it is easy to imagine how Ron fell for her charms. Indeed, they always seemed to be ideally suited to each other. Laughter and giggles were the order of the day when they were together, but Kate made one big mistake when she decided to go public about an arrangement that they had agreed on, involving sex with other men – and it isn't Ron's sexual relations we are talking about, but Kate's.

In September 1993 she was publicising a book that they had written together, called *Murder, Madness and Marriage*. She had told several journalists that she and Ron had an arrangement about sex and that he had allowed her to sleep with other men. Naturally, the newspapers the following day were full of the story. Kate had broken one of Ron's strict rules about their love life: she had revealed their secret agreement to the nation and he was furious.

The papers had a field day, with column after column of spurious debate and conjecture, but for Kate it was almost the end of her marriage. Ron felt that he had lost face, respect even, among his society within Broadmoor, and he also had to deal with his brother Reg, who was also livid with the ex-kissogram girl. Their anger was understandable when reading all of those articles – it must have shocked the criminal fraternity as well as the gay community, even the whole country.

'I told him how frustrated I was getting. So we agreed I could make love to other men until he gets out of prison,' she told reporters. She even went on to tell them of her affairs that she and Ron discussed in the visiting room of Broadmoor. But she also confirmed that Ron didn't want her to take men friends to places frequented by his pals and to keep their agreement secret, and that meant not telling his brother Reg, whom he feared would not understand the pact. Ron was still keen to maintain his image, and secrecy was the key.

Ron had, in fact, taken an AIDS test before they were married and he had even told Kate of his first sexual experience with a woman when he was only sweet 16. So Ron was more AC/DC than purely gay. These revelations were, however, mentioned in the book, which was strangely co-written by Ron and should therefore not have been any surprise to him. But the publicity did the trick and the book sold well.

But there was a darker side to Kate Kray, which was apparent when she told of an incident when she nearly killed a man by running over him with her car. It was at the end of an affair, while she was married to Ron. Her married lover had taken her on holiday to California, but on their return he broke off the relationship and Kate took drastic action. The police even had to pull her off the man. On another occasion, Kate went on a spending spree with forged credit cards, knowingly amassing a huge debt. When Ron heard about it he told her: 'If you can't do the time, then don't do the crime!' But she apologised and once again did the rounds of TV studios and sold a few more books. It really was a no-lose situation. Some may say that it was all pre-planned.

Kate had trodden that fine line between intrigue and enticement, and she had been lured over that line by pure fantasy. She had believed her own stories and, like Ron, thought she was invincible. It must have been a rude awakening when Ron, on his 60th birthday, filed for divorce. At the end of September he had suffered a heart attack and he felt that Kate had betrayed his trust, something that was of utmost importance to Ron. So she had to go. 'She's made me out to be flash, arrogant, rude and ignorant, and I'm none of those things,' he told the press.

In March 1994 Kate went to see Ron to try to patch things up between them, but it only ended with Ron being restrained from punching her. 'Ronnie suddenly raised his voice and they both started shouting at each other,' was the word on the street. 'His heart condition, obviously made worse by the heavy smoking, has made him tetchy,' said one of the nurses at Broadmoor. Ron was still adamant about the divorce on the grounds of 'unreasonable behaviour'.

Kate told me once of the many letters that Ron received from women all over the country. 'During one visit, Ron asked me if I wanted to see some snaps one girl had sent him,' she told me. 'The girl was a blonde of about 22. She was posing naked on a bed in the sort of open-leg shot you see in girlie magazines,' she continued. She was not the only one to send Ron photographs in nude or semi-nude positions – his collection must have been quite something to see.

Ron was a good patient at Broadmoor, with his designer suits and his well-decorated and furnished room – he was their star attraction. Kate visited him regularly and kept him in touch with things going on outside, the life he could not live. She was good for Ron Kray, even taking the place of his brother Charlie, whom Ron could not forgive for his part in the Kray film, where he let the scriptwriters show his mother, Violet, swearing. Ron vowed never to see Charlie again. It could not have been easy for the jovial blonde from Kent to act as go-between between the three Kray brothers. Her own relationship with Ron was hard to define and the relationships between the brothers confused the issue, but one day we may see a new book outlining her attraction to Ron, now that he is dead, and giving the reasons why she felt so trapped in their marriage. Maybe there is already a book out there, but I just haven't seen it.

With Ron no longer with us, there is surely a void for all of those women who felt inextricably drawn towards his charm and reputation. And there are men who feel the same way, men who can no longer live out their fantasies in the safety of their urban and banal environment now that their 'god' has gone the way of mere mortals. Just why so many have felt this attraction is still a puzzling paradigm of modern life but, whatever the reasons, Ron enjoyed it all.

If Reg and Ron, the terrible twins, had a powerful sexual appeal, then what of their elder brother Charlie? In latter years he made it into the *Daily Telegraph*, where someone suggested that he would be marrying Diana, Princess of Wales, although I am sure that no one dared approach Diana on the subject. Charlie would, I am sure, have laughed it off as media hype and a good old East End joke. But it does display another kind of sexual fantasy as portrayed in the press, where some journalists dare to suggest such associations with an intolerable air of flippancy. Perhaps the innuendoes and false assertions commonly included in tabloid newspapers actually serve to titillate the British public, and are therefore just a way of selling newspapers. But this can, of course, be dangerous, as some people can let their fantasies get the better of them.

Charlie is the one brother who was just there for the fun, and he exploited his position to the full. When it came to partying, then Charlie was your man. And he loved it. He got as many girls as he could while the going was good, and they almost stood in line waiting for their chance.

One such girl was Barbara Windsor, who had an affair with Charlie while he was still married to his first and only wife, Dorothy. Dolly, as he called her, had her own affairs and Charlie had a troubled time at home, so he took solace in the arms of the lovely Barbara. Their affair was passionate and predictable, but Barbara could not come to terms with his marriage, since she was looking for stability and a long-term relationship. This stability she found in the unlikely arms of Ronnie Knight, club owner and crook. Knight was brought back to this country from the south of Spain in the early '90s to serve a sentence for his part in a huge robbery of Security Express. Barbara's ex-husband now has nowhere to go, as his creditors have taken it all, including his home in Spain. Barbara was wise to get out while the going was still relatively good.

Charlie, however, returned to Dolly and his son Gary, whom he dearly loved, but things didn't improve at home and Dolly divorced him while he was serving a ten-year sentence for his part in the killing of Jack 'The Hat' McVitie. Charlie, I am sure, was innocent, but his time was up and the champagne days were over, for the time being anyway. Dolly's affair with petty crook George Ince had been the talk of the East End, since they didn't try to hide their feelings towards each other, and Charlie felt relieved when the marriage ended in 1973. His only concern throughout his life was for his son Gary, but Gary was to die in 1996 from cancer, leaving Charlie Kray a lonely and vulnerable man.

On release from prison after serving seven years, Charlie looked up an old acquaintance, Diana Ward, who used to be a waitress in one of the Krays' clubs in Leicester. They actually lived together in Upper Norwood, South London, for many years, and I was a regular visitor to their flat when I wrote my book on the Krays, *Doing the Business*, back in 1992. Diana was a charming person with a ready wit and was good looking too, so it was a surprise when I heard that she and Charlie weren't together any more. The one thing that had kept them together was the fact that Diana had worked abroad for long periods of time, all through their long association. This had now stopped and Charlie was finding living with someone else a little trying. After all, he couldn't bring his girlfriends home with Diana there, so he was forced to meet them at hotels and restaurants, something that was costing him money. And when he hadn't worked for 30 years, had refused, because of his ego, to receive benefits for all of this time and didn't even have a credit card, then he was in serious trouble. Diana knew about his misdemeanours, but she wasn't prepared to pay for them. When the phone was cut off again, it became the last straw and she threw him out.

Whenever I met Charlie he always had a different woman on his arm and in his bed. He was an irrepressible womaniser who had lived on the legend of his brothers and on his own ability to con anyone out of money, all so he could keep up appearances. He was a charming rogue, however, and the women in his life had a way of forgiving and forgetting his transgressions.

Charlie's last 'acquisition' was Judy Stanley. This may not be exactly fair to the young divorcée, but it represents the attitude of the Krays to their women. Like the gangster's moll, they are a part of the image that they have all tried to represent as being the truth. But, in reality, they were generally used for whatever the Krays want from them.

Judy Stanley is a mother of three who worked at the time for the company Nestlé, near Croydon. She had a good administrative position and had been able to keep Charlie in the manner that he was accustomed to – good living and good loving. Although she only lived in a small end-of-terrace house, she managed to project an air of self-confidence and righteousness – something that Charlie put to good use during his appeal in the late '90s.

Her father, Ieuan Evans, an ex-headmaster, had many concerns for his daughter. Being only three years older than his daughter's lover, he had little good to say about Charlie Kray. 'I don't know why she chose to live with him,' he told a newspaper journalist. 'But she is a mature woman, very independent and she knows her own mind,' he added. And, at 46 years old, Judy should have known her own mind. But again, we have the situation of a schoolmaster's daughter and a Kray, just as in the case of Roberta Jones and Reggie. It may be a case of schoolmasters everywhere – lock up your daughters. But I doubt that it would do any good, and, if experience has anything to say in such circumstances, then the daughters would rebel just as their predecessors have done throughout history.

Charlie seemed to have forgotten that famous phrase of Ron's: 'If you can't do the time, then don't do the crime.' He had been found guilty of supplying cocaine, was rightly being held in prison and his chances of getting out in the near future were bleak indeed. So, once again, there is a touch of tragedy surrounding the Kray women, who have fought for their men but have all ended up losing the battle.

23

THE DEATH OF CHARLIE KRAY

I lost a friend that day. I know what he did and I know it was wrong, but Charlie was such a likeable soul that I still think the world would have been a poorer place without him.

Colin Fry

After being in and out of court for several years Charlie was not feeling good. He had been held at Frankland Prison and the conditions were not very suitable for a man of over 70 years of age. He had been complaining of heart trouble and a possible stroke was diagnosed. Although he had been treated on several occasions while in prison, the situation had deteriorated and he knew that his time was short.

When he lost his final appeal he was sent to Parkhurst Prison on the Isle of Wight where he received better medical treatment – but the damage had already been done.

Charlie's trial in 1997 had delivered its final verdict on the eldest Kray brother – it would be death in prison. Just why he received such a long sentence is probably down to his name and his reputation and not his crime. Being a Kray had its drawbacks and its advantages. He had enjoyed most of the advantages throughout his life, but now it was time to endure the disadvantage of being named Kray.

Charlie's death occurred on 4 April 2000, just into the new millennium. He was 3 years into his 12-year sentence for his part in a £39 million deal that involved the smuggling of cocaine. Once again he made the headlines – the death of the older Kray brother. All the old stories filled the newspapers, and old gangland pals and associates were on television telling of how they had enjoyed the company of the now deceased gangster.

Charlie's condition had worsened very quickly when he arrived at Parkhurst. He had poor circulation in both his legs and his feet, and his hair was also beginning to fall out at an alarming rate – very annoying for an elderly man who had always prided himself on his appearance.

He had also been talking about the trial and his sentencing, regretting that he had ever got involved in the deal. For Charlie it was a deal too far – his biggest deal, his only ever drug deal, his final deal. He told friends that he was only ever interested in the money, but things just got carried away and he ended up agreeing to handle the cocaine. How he wished he could retrace his steps and not go through with the deal.

The thing that hurt most was why the police had to set up the sting operation in the first place. Why was he singled out for punishment, and why did the others get far lighter sentences than him? He always told me that he put people together and this is what he had done. All he did was make introductions and nothing else. He didn't see the drugs, he didn't in fact touch the drugs or transport them – all he wanted was his share for introducing the buyer to the seller.

When he collapsed in Parkhurst he was immediately rushed to St Mary's Hospital, where he was treated and kept under observation. His hair had gone, and he was frail, extremely weak and nothing like his former self. The stabbing pains were still there, however, and the doctors concluded that he had suffered a major heart attack.

His brother, Reg, was informed through the authorities on 18 March when he was in Wayland Prison, Norfolk. They told him simply that his brother Charlie was dying and that if he wanted to see him again before he was gone then he had to get there fast. Arrangements were quickly made, and he was ready to see his brother, whom he hadn't seen since 1995 at the funeral of his twin brother Ron.

The following day, Sunday, 19 March, Reg set off early from Wayland Prison. Dogs searched the van before they could leave and then Reg was ushered into the back, along with three big prison wardens. Reg was quiet as they drove through the big gates and out into the Norfolk countryside.

After a quick stop at Winchester Prison for dinner they headed for the coast and the ferry to the Isle of Wight. Soon they were at Parkhurst, a place that Reg knew very well indeed, since he had served the first 17 years of his sentence there.

At first he was shown into Charlie's cell, where they removed his handcuffs for the very first time since leaving Norfolk. He checked through the photos and the letters, but there wasn't much left of Charlie's life so it was all over very quickly. It was now time to see Charlie himself.

With the handcuffs back on he was taken the short distance to the hospital, where he went immediately to see Charlie. Fortunately for Reg he was awake, but that was not very fortunate for Charlie. Reg started the chat by telling Charlie of all his faults, everything he had done that Reg didn't like, all the trouble he had caused.

It was hard for Reg to even recognise Charlie – he had no hair on his head, his legs were black and he was so feeble. After telling Charlie off for not being a good brother, Reg started to cry. Tears ran down his face as he sat quietly and watched his brother dying.

Statements were given to the press about Charlie's condition and Parkhurst Prison authorities said that Reg could stay in Charlie's cell as long as he wished. Reg even got to meet the press briefly outside the hospital, but he had nothing to say.

Over the following week Reg stayed in his brother's cell. He ate at the prison, meeting a few old pals to ease the pain of the moment. He hated it. He was waiting for Charlie to die and that was that. He started thinking about his own position, his own health, his own death.

On 4 April Reg went to see Charlie and sat by his bed for the whole morning. He didn't rant and rave any more about how Charlie had handled, or should that be mishandled, the film and the paltry amount they had been paid. He didn't accuse Charlie of stealing from him when he set up the deal for T-shirts. In fact, he said very little. What can you say when your brother is dying?

It was Charlie who did most of the talking. He apologised for doing all these deals without Reg and said sorry for getting involved in the cocaine deal – one that had caused Reg serious trouble, since a parole hearing was coming soon and he didn't want anything to spoil his chances of being free. It was when Charlie started talking of their mother, Violet, and of Aunt Rose, his son Gary and all the family, long deceased, that Reg knew that there was little time left.

And there was no time left for Reg that morning. The doctors told him that the monitors were showing signs of further problems. He would have to leave and they would contact the prison when he could visit again. So Reg was, once again, still handcuffed, taken back to Parkhurst and to Charlie's cell.

Reg could not stop thinking about his brother, dying in the nearby hospital. He had seen how his breathing was becoming shallow and intermittent, and that afternoon the hospital issued a statement saying: 'He has heart problems and respiratory problems. His condition is giving cause for concern.'

All Reg Kray could do was wait. He had so much more to tell his brother, and there was so much more that he wanted to know. Later that evening he was rushed to Charlie's bedside, but it was all too late. Charlie was dead.

Reg sat with the lifeless body of Charlie for some time. He thought about the past – all the good times and all the bad times. And he thought about the future, alone in a world that he didn't know – one without his brothers.

Again the authorities put out a statement. This time it was very precise; it simply said that Charlie Kray had died peacefully in his sleep at 8.50 p.m.

Back in Charlie's cell Reg sat and thought. Once again he had to organise a funeral, and once again he would do it right. He did it for his wife Frances, he did it for his mother Violet, he did it for his brother Ron, he did it for his nephew Gary, and now it was time to do it for Charlie. It was going to be big and brash, and he would see that Charlie went out with a bang!

Reg, being the kind of person he was, saw a possibility of getting some publicity – he had to get something good from all those days back in Parkhurst. So he became available for the press and had interview after interview talking about the death of his brother and how big the funeral was going to be. Money rolled in as he talked about his brother and about his own possible parole. In one interview he said: 'I visited him twice a day, once in the morning and then in the afternoon.' He then continued: 'He looked terrible, just lying there on his back, sucking in air from an oxygen mask. He was breathing really heavily and he was out of it.'

Reg was right when he told one reporter: 'It has been so sad to lose Charlie. Prison was not the place for him, he was too old to endure it.' I totally agree, he shouldn't have been there. But Charlie Kray made many mistakes in his life and the last one cost him dearly. 'Champagne Charlie' was gone, but whatever he did he didn't deserve to go like that.

English's Funeral Parlour did their work well and professionally, just like they had when they buried Ron and then Gary. They laid Charlie in his coffin and let well-wishers come and pay their last respects. Bodyguards, supplied by Reg, were on hand to see that there was no trouble and that's the way it was. Flowers and wreaths were laid around the parlour and everyone wore a sad face in respect for one of the last of the Kray family, a local boy who had lived the high life and was now shortly to be lowered into the ground to his final resting place.

One wreath, from Reg, was shaped like a boxing ring, with red roses and carnations. Another said 'Grandad', and still another said simply 'From C Wing, Parkhurst'. Barbara Windsor, an old fling of Charlie's, sent lilies, and she even said publicly that it was a sad day.

The funeral that Reg organised for Charlie took place on 19 April at St Matthew's Church in Bethnal Green, home turf for the Krays, but first there was the procession from the funeral parlour to the church. Every villain from the East End was there, including Charlie Richardson, an old adversary of the Krays. It was time to pay respect and these ex-gangland members knew everything about respect.

Reg kept them all waiting and some of the larger gang members, with short-cropped hair and tight collars, were feeling the strain. Eventually Reg arrived in a big blue Mercedes, handcuffed to a pretty female officer, and the funeral could begin.

Charlie's coffin was brought out and covered with more flowers and then the heavies moved in and placed the coffin in the rear of the first of two hearses. The rest of the flowers and wreaths were placed in the second and they were now ready to get the show on the road. As they headed off towards the church, the crowd could see the wording in the flowers placed along the side of the first hearse: it said 'Gentleman'.

People threw flowers in the road as the hearses passed by. And then came the procession of limos, some 18 in all. It was a little overwhelming for many, and the police were there in force to control the crowds and to check on the identity of the well-wishers. They knew many of the faces in the crowd and there were helicopters overhead if there should be trouble.

A minister, wearing a long white robe, led the way, together with a mourner complete with black top hat. Soon they were in Vallance Road, the old stomping ground of the Krays. This is where they lived in their younger days, during the war, and this was where they called home. But Reg didn't recognise the place – it had all changed since he had walked these streets.

Reg waved to the crowd as the hearses neared the church. And soon he was there, standing in the sunshine, shaking people by the hand. He looked well in his pinstripe suit, but he was no longer the young man who roamed Bethnal Green in the '50s and '60s. He was old and frail, nothing like the vigorous young boxer that he was in bygone days. But this was what he wanted – the adulation of his fans and to be seen smiling in the sunshine, back in the East End of London.

To make sure that there was no trouble at the church Reg had hired the local Hell's Angels to oversee events. They even stood to attention as he passed them by. 'One of ours' they were saying to themselves. Reg shook more hands of mourners who were gathered there in some force before walking towards the church. As he stood there, greeting young and old, the music started playing on the church loudspeakers. They played one of Charlie's favourite songs, Céline Dion's 'Up Close and Personal'. Charlie would have loved it, but he would have been thinking, 'Why didn't they do this when I was alive?'

Bill Murray from *The Bill* was there to pay his respects and so too was Charlie's old drinking buddy George Sewell. They, and many others, talked of 'Champagne Charlie' and there was not a bad word said about him. I must agree with them – on that day I held a glass in my hand and paid my last respects as best as I could. It was a sad day indeed.

Once in the church the reverend, Father Ken Rimini, took over proceedings as they all broke into song. 'Morning Has Broken' was first on the hymn sheet, next came 'Fight The Good Fight' and then 'Abide With Me'. Reg sat next to his wife Roberta and, while she sang, he held his head in his hands, tears running down his face.

The good father continued by saying: 'Many things have been said about Charlie, some true and some very untrue and hurtful.' Well, he got that right. And then he said: 'I can't judge him. He now stands before a greater authority than this life.' He then continued by saying something about Charlie's son, Gary, who had died some years earlier. 'It affected Charlie in many ways and changed his outlook on life,' soberly mentioning how it had changed Charlie's attitude to religion. 'It broke his heart,' he said finally.

Then it was the chance for well-chosen guests to say something about Charlie and they all stood in line waiting to pay their tribute. Finally a recording was played, made by Reg some time earlier, since he was unable to speak himself. Some may say that this was planned to have the required effect. Others may think differently.

The recording said simply, 'I am not there, I did not die, I am a thousand winds that blow, I am diamond glints on snow.' Reg called it his tribute to his brother Charlie, but it was really just an excuse to prolong proceedings and get the last word.

As they left the church, Shirley Bassey, one of Charlie's friends from the old days, sang them out with 'As Long As He Needs Me'. Reg stood up, kissed the coffin and prepared to go out into the daylight.

People cheered as they came outside, and 'Mad' Frankie Fraser even managed to shout out, 'Three cheers for Reggie!' After waiting for almost an hour the crowd needed cheering up. Immediately cars pulled up and took people away and the coffin was taken, ready for the actual burial in Chingford.

The procession proceeded slowly and deliberately – no fuss, no bother.

Soon they reached Chingford Mount Cemetery and Reg even had time to wander over to the final resting place of his wife Frances, lying nearby in a special plot bought by Reg a long time ago. He stroked the headstone, taking time for the photographers to catch up to record the moment for posterity. It was then time to move on.

Reg had the policewoman on one side of him, still handcuffed, and Roberta on the other, as they laid Charlie to rest, in a plot that was originally meant for him. But since Charlie was broke and had no plot himself, Reg had decided that it was the right thing to do. He had already decided that he would be buried in his brother Ron's grave. When Reg bought the plot, he did not buy a place for Charlie – for everyone else, but not for him.

As the coffin disappeared Reg managed to find a red rose and throw it into the grave, as a final tribute. As suddenly as he had arrived, Reg Kray was gone, driven away in the blue Mercedes, leaving others to stand and stare at the grave. He had to get back to Wayland Prison in Norfolk, so he had to leave early – no snacks, no beer, no taste of freedom.

One of his minders had one last statement for the press: 'He wishes you all well and he hopes to be among you soon,' he told them. It was a good job he was talking to the press and not to the inhabitants of the graves, or maybe it was his message to the ghosts of the Kray family.

Reg did not have long to live and this journey back to his roots was his last while still alive. He knew he had cancer and he knew that the end was near, but he was an old pro and he was going to go out like one.

24

THE DEATH OF REG KRAY

If there were no bad people then there would be no good lawyers.

The Old Curiosity Shop (Charles Dickens)

It had to happen. It's the one thing that we all quickly get to know when we are born – we are all going to die some day. Now it was the turn of the 'Godfather of Crime', Reg Kray.

On 1 October 2000 Reg Kray died. It was the bladder cancer that got him in the end, brought on by the poor prison diet during his sentence – not a bullet, nor a knife, nor the hangman's rope. He quietly passed away in the morning after a peaceful night. His wife, Roberta, was by his side and so too were a handful of friends including that well-known murderer Freddie Foreman and someone by the name of Jerry Powell.

A statement was issued by his lawyer, Mark Goldstein, saying: 'He was an icon of the twentieth century.' This was a little misleading – do we really make icons of murderers? If he had said that Reg was the best-known murderer in the country, then I would probably have agreed.

Even 'Nipper' Read, the man who finally brought the Krays to justice, was asked for a quote. He said: 'He was known to be aggressive as a character – the sort of guy, if you said two wrong words to him, he would immediately attack you!'

Now, this was more like the Reg Kray I knew. But you can't compare Reg to his brother Ron. This remark was more like Ron

– Reg would first have to think about it and then he would hit you.

He died at the Town House, a hotel in Thorpe St Andrew, just a few miles from the Norwich and Norfolk Hospital where he had been treated on his release from prison. His final home was the honeymoon suite, which he chose for himself. He wanted his final days to be peaceful, full of birdsong and the sound of freedom, with no bars on the windows.

There had been a couple of honeymooners already installed in the room when Reg arrived a few days earlier, in a Rolls-Royce, but they were persuaded to vacate the room in favour of the old gangster. This is where Reg wanted to be, and no one would stop him. And it was here he died.

Back in the spring and summer of 2000 Reg was not a well man. The prisoners knew it, the warden knew it, everyone knew it. He had been incarcerated for more than 32 years and he wanted his last days to be spent in the comfort of friendly surroundings, with his wife, Roberta, and his old pals – living as a free man.

Questions were being asked in the press – why was the former public enemy number one being kept in jail, after the expiry of his 30-year term of imprisonment? He had never tried to escape, so why should they hold him in jail any longer? He was almost a free man, since he even held the key to his room at Wayland Prison, so why not let him go to die as he chose?

It was, however, this same source that was actually keeping him inside. There was the book by Freddie Foreman, in which he admitted to shooting and killing Frank Mitchell, 'The Mad Axeman', on the orders of Ron and Reg Kray. He even told of how he had dumped the body at sea, off the coast of Kent, saying, 'He is sleeping with the fishes!' The book was serialised and quoted in all the daily and Sunday newspapers, and even Reg was reading it in his room at Wayland Prison.

This was not what Reg wanted to hear – it was just keeping him behind bars even longer than required. The television was even reporting the killing as though it was something sensational and new. To Reg, this was all from the past, from a forgotten time. Reg just wanted to forget it all, but all it did was make him ill.

He was rushed to the medical wing of Wayland Prison in July after he had doubled up in his room complaining of intense stomach ache. After a course of antibiotics, to stop any chance of infection, he was given something to ease the pain. His liver was in a bad way, inflamed and not working properly – the prognosis was not looking good.

A statement was issued by the prison: 'There is no doubt about it – he's caused some serious damage with his drinking.' No one said how he got the drink and they didn't say whether or not he had been treated for this condition previously.

'I feel like I'm dying!' he shouted out in the ambulance on the way to the nearby Norwich Prison. They knew it was true, and even Reg must have known it was true. A few days later, the prison spokesman put out a statement: 'Reggie was found in pain, clutching his stomach. He is very ill and he's lost the will to live. No one knows what will happen.' He was thin, gaunt and living on liquid food and painkillers. For someone who had always prided himself on his fitness, this must have been intolerable.

He was hoping it couldn't get any worse, but it did. On 3 August Reg was rushed to the Norwich and Norfolk Hospital where he immediately underwent surgery for a suspected tumour. He had a number of operations over the coming days and the doctors were hopeful. They had removed a tumour from his small intestine and the operation had gone surprisingly well. Even Roberta was smiling when she issued her own statement, but she knew the severity of the situation and that things were far from satisfactory. She told the press: 'The obstruction is a secondary growth and we are awaiting further scans to determine the source.' Then she added that Reggie's lawyer was asking for his immediate release on compassionate grounds.

Over the following few weeks Reg was operated on time and time again. Every time he got weaker, more lethargic, more frail. Every time he hoped that the doctors could fix it, cure him of the cancer, give him those few extra years that he longed for. But there was no easy fix, no cure for what ailed him, nothing they could do. The hospital then put out another statement on 19 August. 'Reg has terminal cancer,' they told the press. 'There is nothing anyone can do for him.' Doctors had still not found the source of the cancer so there was more in there. It was terminal.

Reg was so ill that the prison had to postpone a parole hearing, but his lawyers were busy with their appeal and quietly confident. And there were more old celebrities, entertainers, actors and such who were all clamouring to say a word or two about the gangster they called a friend.

The kind words, from Barbara Windsor, Johnny Briggs, Mike Reid, Bill Murray and others, came after new photos of Reg were published, showing him to be almost lifeless, gaunt and pale, almost breathless. He was, indeed, a sorry sight and rightly people felt sorry for him. Roberta issued a statement in support of her husband: 'There is no greater punishment this government can inflict upon him now other than denying him his last, small taste of freedom.' She continued: 'We've written to Jack Straw on numerous occasions but never once had a reply from him, not directly.'

Trevor Linn, acting as lawyer for Reg Kray, now applied to the Home Secretary, saying that in his opinion and those of others there were now adequate grounds for release on compassionate grounds.

The press were still in attendance at the hospital and they waited patiently for news. Roberta spoke to the press many times over these last days of the elderly gangster, one time saying, 'I'm virtually living here at the hospital and stay in a private room overnight. It's been hellish, but the one good thing is we've been able to spend time together since he's been here.'

The accolades, expressions of support and encouragement continued. Actor Johnny Briggs said: 'Reggie has been in prison a long time and has paid his debt to society. It's time to let him go home.' Barbara Windsor added: 'I have always said it is time to let Reggie out. In the light of this latest sad news about his cancer, it's only right to let him come home with Roberta.' Even Glen Murphy, from the TV drama *London's Burning*, said: 'Reggie should be allowed home. He can't harm anyone now. He should be freed to spend time with his family.'

Finally, on 26 August, Reg Kray was officially set free. Jack Straw, Home Secretary at the time, allowed him to go home to die. The lawyers had done their work well and he was freed on compassionate grounds. He was free at last, to do what he liked – to go on holiday, spend the money he had earned from his books, his interviews, his scams. But the old-time gangster could hardly walk, let alone do anything or go anywhere.

On television that evening they said: 'In the early part of August Reg had been rushed to the Norwich and Norfolk Hospital from Wayland Prison, complaining of severe stomach pains. The trouble that had started back in the summer of '96 has once again reared its ugly head – he has stomach cancer.'

The prison service also told of the operations and procedures that Reg Kray underwent at the time. 'The operation to remove a tumour went well, but the cancer has spread. Most of his internal organs are infected; especially damaged are the bladder and bowel regions. It is clear to everyone concerned that Reg Kray doesn't have long to live.'

If Reg Kray had blown up aircraft over Scotland then he would probably still be alive today, but he didn't and he isn't.

Reg was now a free man but he was not free to leave hospital. The handcuffs had been removed, but it didn't matter. He couldn't go anywhere, not even to the bathroom. He was simply free to stay there, to waste away, to speak a few words.

The old friends sent flowers, together with words of encouragement, but even they knew it was almost over. Barbara Windsor sent flowers again and a few words to cheer him up and, once again, Mike Reid and Bill Murray spoke to the press, wishing him well and hoping against hope for a full recovery. The usual suspects, the old pals from the good old days, were all pleased that he was free. At 65 years old, and now a pensioner, Reg Kray was again free to walk the streets of the East End, but he couldn't walk, he couldn't eat, he couldn't really remember.

The acting chief executive of the Norwich and Norfolk Hospital said later the same day that she could confirm that Reg Kray was currently too ill to leave hospital, even though he had been freed and had his handcuffs removed. Even after being held for more than 30 years he was still not free to leave.

The Home Office also issued a statement saying that they were satisfied that there was no risk of him committing further offences. That was just about right, since the only offence he could be blamed for would be of taking up a bed – one that could be used to save another person, another patient, maybe even a simple pensioner. Did they seriously consider him a risk after all this time?

Trevor Linn issued a statement saying: 'I'm hoping Reggie will confound the experts. He's as tough as old boots!' But Reg was not tough enough, and his old boots could not help him. It was a couple of weeks or maybe a month or two, that was all that was left to him.

After being set free, however, he perked up a bit. He asked for a hairdresser and one came to the hospital to give him a real haircut, not like those he had had in prison for the past 32 years. The hairdressers did it for free as long as they could keep the hair. In years to come we may even see this on eBay, so keep a lookout for it in the usual places.

By this time Reg had had enough of listening to everyone else – he wanted to get in on the act and make a little money, of course. Old habits never die, so he quickly contacted the press to see who could make the highest bid on one of his very last interviews. Ultimately he decided to get them all there, for maximum publicity, and gave a press conference.

'I've been cooped up for 32 years,' he told them, choking slightly as he spoke. 'I want to be able to sit out and smell the fresh air then I'll really feel free.' But he wasn't finished there, oh no, not our Reg. 'I'd like to sit down by a swimming pool and have a nice gin and tonic,' he told them as they all took his photograph.

He had decided to get them all there in his hospital bedroom as he didn't want his final whereabouts known. He had rented a house nearby and there had been photos in the newspapers, but Reg wanted its location kept secret. This was his way of giving them what they wanted, in exchange for privacy later.

He was on good form that day, talking freely and covering a wide range of topics. He enjoyed the limelight and it did him good. At last he was free to say what he wanted and no one would stop him now.

It was a tiring time for Reg and soon the hospital staff moved in and started his medication again. He was still getting treatment for pain, but there was not much else they could do in the circumstances. According to records at the time the trouble had started back in 1996 – if it had been caught at that time then there would have been a chance, but not now. When Mark Goldstein, Reg Kray's lawyer, heard this he threatened to sue the prison authorities for neglect. But he didn't have the time.

Things, however, did improve for a few days and Reg was able to go into the gardens at the hospital, being pushed around in a wheelchair by Roberta, who was still staying at the hospital. He enjoyed this immensely. It reminded him of the time he arranged for his brother Ron's escape from Long Grove Asylum, many years earlier. He even managed a smile when he thought of his brother. Roberta found time to go to Wayland Prison, to get the official document declaring Reg a free man. They enjoyed looking at it in his room – there it was, he was officially free.

Interviews with the press continued and on one occasion he said: 'I heard about my release on the radio. I never wanted to be a criminal, but that's where the circumstances took us!'

He also complained to the press about not being able to get used to the fact that his letters weren't intercepted and scrutinised by the authorities – getting an unopened letter was something new for him. In all, he took it well and, in return for his cooperation, he was rewarded time and time again. But in the end all the money couldn't give him a few more days, a week's holiday, a couple of months in which to live. He died.

Once again there was a burial at Chingford Mount Cemetery, and this time it was Reg Kray, the last of the Kray brothers, that was being buried. His own plot was now taken up by his brother, Charlie, so he was due to be buried on top of his twin brother, Ron. He was gently lowered down to join Ron and, once again, the Kray twins were together, only this time in the afterlife.

His mum and dad lay nearby and so, too, did his wife Frances and Charlie's son Gary, who were buried in the same plot. Charlie was already there and now Reg had joined Ron. The family was back together again.

Reg had made his plans carefully, but now that he was dead Roberta changed the funeral arrangements. She didn't want the old gang there or anyone from his past, so she went through the list made by Reg of his pall-bearers and changed everything. It may have been that the old lags just couldn't carry a coffin any more, but then that idea probably never came into the equation. She wanted to end things in a different way – she wanted it new, with no one connected to crime in the newspapers the following day.

Ultimately she decided to include Tony Mortimer, who used to be with pop group East 17, Mark Goldstein, Reggie's lawyer, Alex Myhill, a young boxer, and Bradley Allardyce, one of Reg Kray's lovers from his time in prison.

This was her choice and not that of her husband. This made old pal Freddie Foreman furious. He hated being left out and he hated being told what he could or couldn't do by a woman.

But she complied with the vast majority of Reg's wishes – she even contacted a local Spitfire squadron to arrange a fly-past. They agreed to do this, but on condition that the weather was suitable. After all, they didn't want the newspaper headline 'Reg Kray shoots down Spitfire!'

Just why such a fly-past was seen as necessary is a little difficult to understand. Reg hated his time in the army and was court-martialled, along with his brother Ron. His father was a deserter and he hated authority of any kind, so why should there be such a tribute? The answer is, of course, in the Kray psyche. Reg was a showman and he wanted to put on a show. He wanted it big and he wanted the memory of his funeral to live forever in the minds of the people of the East End of London.

Frank Sinatra's voice rang out as the coffin left St Matthew's Church in Bethnal Green. The tune 'My Way' had been chosen by Reg as another way of sticking two fingers up at the law, society in general, the public at large. People applauded as the coffin was loaded into the hearse. It was all handled with dignity and the crowd loved it.

It was once again W. English & Son who handled the funeral proceedings, giving Reg a great send-off with a hearse pulled by six black horses, all adorned with plumes. They were bridled with black leather and silver harnesses and it was a sight to see – a regal funeral for the 'King of Crime'. And, as befitting royalty, there were crowds of people following the hearse, all well-dressed, all patiently strolling along behind, all hoping to get to see well-known pals of the Krays. Would the celebrities be there? Would the gangsters be there? And would the television cameras be there?

The procession was calm and somewhat sedate, but being for Reg Kray it was, above all, a show of force. Reg had planned for the hearse, the flowers, the audience, and he had planned for the cameras. The only thing missing was a member of the Kray family, apart, that is, from Roberta.

Those who were not allowed at the funeral were allowed to send wreaths and flowers for the ceremony. I suppose this added to the magnitude of proceedings and made it larger than life. That was, after all, the plan. Freddie Foreman had his wreath on display, although he was not there. One said 'Reg Beloved', and another displayed the simple words 'Free at Last'. I could fill page after page with details of the wreaths but they all had one purpose – to praise the old 'Godfather of Crime', Reg Kray.

There were boxing gloves, there were words such as 'Respect' and simply 'Reg', there was a football and there was a wreath saying 'With Love' from Barbara Windsor.

Apart from sending flowers some of Reggie's old pals were allowed to attend the funeral in person. Bill Murray, from *The Bill*, was there along with 'Mad' Frankie Fraser and the actor Steven Berkoff, who had played the part of George Cornell in the film *The Krays*. But Ron was not there, neither were Charlie nor a living Reg, so it didn't have the impact of the other funerals.

The procession continued, along the almost ten miles from the church to Chingford Mount Cemetery, with minders guarding the coffin all the way. Some people walked all the way, some took a car to be there at the end of the journey. Wannabe gangsters shook hands and paraded their shaven heads, ready to be caught on camera, and others, including the police who were there in force, simply minded themselves, took their time and hoped that it would soon be over.

In fact, the police presence that day was huge and it must have cost the taxpayers of London a fortune. The Metropolitan Police had an unbelievable number of its force on parade – this included 8 inspectors, 26 sergeants and 170 officers. They were all there on the streets of East London to ensure public safety.

Alongside them were the minders, or private security guards, as they liked to be known, brought in to help the police in the performance of their duties. There were more than 400 of them, all burly and sinister looking, and all wearing RKF (Reg Kray Funeral) lapel badges.

It was soon over. The fly-past had to be cancelled because of the weather and there was a final sense of disappointment. Was this it? Was there no more? Was there to be no fanfare or giant get-together on this auspicious occasion? The answer was no. The grey day simply faded away with no more ceremonies and no more praise for Reg Kray.

The final ceremony had almost been over before it had begun. Roberta threw in a red rose and so did a few of the other mourners. This was a very private part of proceedings and by 3 p.m. it was over.

The man his lawyer called an icon was now dead and very much buried. How ironic that this word should be used in connection with Reg Kray. Is he an icon to be admired? Should we call him 'Reggie', as many did that day? What will history tell us about the Krays, and will the truth ever really be known? With so many questions and no answers there is still much to be revealed about the Krays and their violent ways, their empire of crime, their loves and their hates. Icon? No, I just can't see it.

The Victims of Crime Trust said: 'Reggie Kray was no hero or celebrity and should be remembered as neither. He was a career criminal and a convicted murderer and anyone who believes differently will have forgotten that he held part of the East End of London to ransom. To believe otherwise is to be detached from reality.'

Well said, Mr Norman Brennan, I thoroughly agree, but we all know the Kray name, we all know something about what they did, we all remember the funerals. So I would prefer the word 'infamous' instead of iconic.

Reg Kray told friends that he believed that he and his brother were destined for fame but he wasn't sure of how they would establish themselves in a prominent place in the history books. 'I believe that Ron and I were predestined to become known either by fame or infamy,' he told them. Well, he certainly did that!

Yet still celebrities, actors and the like praise Reg Kray – why? Barbara Windsor continues to say that Reg was charming and polite. She told reporters: 'Over the years I just kept in touch with him. We would often have a chat. He usually wanted me to do something for charity for him.' And I bet he planned for a nice little earner for himself at the same time.

Dave Courtney, another pal, said: 'Reggie is a prime example of how you should teach your children not to behave.' Well, he got that one right. And for Roberta he only had kind words. 'She's an absolute diamond. Most people think someone who marries a prisoner must have something wrong with them, but there's nothing wrong with her!'

Well, I think a lot of people doubt the validity of this, but I, too, am willing to give her the benefit of the doubt. She found a fatal attraction in Reg and now she has to live the rest of her life in the knowledge that everyone in the country knows what she did. Marrying such a man as Reg Kray was not an easy thing to do, but it was her choice and that must be respected by us all.

The name of Kray is still with us – they even have parodies of the Kray twins on the television, in gangland stories of the modern age. They are still killers, they are nasty people who epitomise the word gangster, yet apparently we can't get enough of them. They are there now and they will be there forever. The name Kray is synonymous with extreme violence, death and mayhem, so is that their real legacy?

Kate Kray, Ron's wife, said that it was Reg Kray's second death. The first time, she said, was when they buried Ron. Now he is back where he belongs, with his twin brother. Some would say that we are all a lot safer with them all underground, but many will disagree.

When the police release all their files on the Krays, some time in the future, then maybe we will see what made them special and why the authorities felt forced to keep their secrets. The Krays are all dead, that is for sure, but are they forgotten? No, not by a long, long way!

25

STORIES FROM THE GRAVE:
PAEDOPHILIA

I just didn't know what to say when Ron told me he liked
boys. But I was really knocked out when he told me that
he thought Reg did too. My brothers, a couple of queers
– I could never get over it.

Charlie Kray

Today, if I was writing a piece in a major newspaper, then I would
call the Krays and their pals Tom Driberg and Lord Robert Boothby
criminals of the highest order. Not because of the already
publicised crimes that the Krays committed or the lies and deceit
of Driberg and Boothby, but because of their association with,
and abuse of, young boys on an organised and huge scale, back in
the 1950s and 1960s, that was nothing other than paedophilia.

They all loved young boys, the younger the better. And Ron
groomed the boys to do anything he wanted and that meant
satisfying the needs of people in high places, people in positions
of power, people at the heart of the Establishment. Was this the
real reason for the suppression of information on the Krays
throughout their time in jail and beyond? Even now, the authorities
have decided that their voluminous files on the Krays should not
be made public, not for many years, not until certain people are
dead, buried and no longer of interest to the general public. It
cannot be the Krays they are protecting since they are all dead and
it cannot be the people they killed or their families, so who is it?

The decision preventing these records from becoming public, despite the Freedom of Information Act, comes from the highest echelons of the land. The people – you, me, everyone in the country – have a right to be told the truth, but the powers that be still hide the facts about the Krays and their 'friends', and give poor or misleading reasons for doing so. The question is why?

What other names appear in those documents and what was their true connection to the Krays? And how did they influence the police in their attempts to catch the Krays? Remember, it was always said that they had friends in high places.

Ron admitted to friends that he was gay when he was in his mid-teens. He did try it with a woman once, but he didn't like it, so he stuck with boys. Even when he got older he still liked them young, much to the annoyance of his father.

'Old Man' Charlie, Ron's dad, never did understand and neither did the twins' brother Charlie, but mother Violet didn't seem to worry about it. The only real problem was that Ron tried to influence his brother, Reg, who appeared to be bisexual. He was always urging Reg to try boys. 'They are so much better,' he would tell him. He also made fun of his sexual preferences when he joked with his brother Charlie, saying that Reg also liked boys.

Even Reg played games with the family, especially Charlie.

'Don't you think boys are nice, Charlie?' he would ask. 'I think I could fancy a few, just like Ron.'

So the twins played their games and they enjoyed the company of their 'boys'.

Ron had a number of male lovers, both when he was younger and inside prison, and in Broadmoor Hospital when he was older and incarcerated. One of the most memorable youngsters who took his fancy was an Arab lad he met when he and Reg were on holiday in Tangiers, visiting their old pal Billy Hill at his villa.

The twins enjoyed their time in Tangiers, which was then famous as the gay capital of the world. It was a favourite destination for many an author, including William Burroughs, Joe Orton, Kenneth Halliwell and, of course, Tennessee Williams. Kenneth Williams was also known to holiday there, and I am sure it wasn't the beach, its café life and the streets of the Medina that caught his fancy – it was the boys.

You can still see men, young and old, holding hands on every street corner of Tangiers. It has been a way of life there for centuries and it will not change overnight. Back in the '60s Orton called it the 'Costa del Sodomy', and he was right. While there have been hundreds of Europeans jailed for drug offences, there are few imprisoned for being gay. It just doesn't happen in Tangiers, despite the fact that homosexuality is illegal. In the 1960s, Tangiers was a paradise, particularly for those interested in paedophilia.

At this time almost half of the city's population were ex-pats, mainly from Britain or the USA, and a large proportion of these were there for one particular reason – paedophilia. Sure enough, there were 'straight' brothels and clubs, such as Churchill's, where Billy Hill would take Ron and Reg for a special night out, but the loose morals of Tangiers have always drawn this one particular type of visitor.

Nowadays, during daylight hours, the cafés and the bars still thrive through the patronage of the mainly French and Spanish ex-pat community and holidaymakers, but at night the clubs still capture the passing stranger, lured in by the touts and often taken to the cleaners by the club owners and their friends.

I can still remember the names of some of the clubs when I was there, just passing through, back in the '60s. It was the time of the hippies, and my wife and I were taking a brief holiday from working on films, down in Almería, in the south of Spain. The main club I remember was called The Dancing Boy. I always thought that the ex-pats went there for the drugs, but maybe some went there to see the dancing boy. Who knows?

The age of consent in Britain at that time was 16 for heterosexual sex but homosexuality was illegal until 1967, when it was decriminalised and the age of consent set at 21. In Morocco, the age of consent for heterosexual sex was also 16, but, whereas homosexuality was decriminalised in Britain, it was actually criminalised in Morocco in 1962. But this appears to have been a 'cosmetic law', and European visitors, like Ron and Reg, continued to do, and get away with, whatever they liked.

The Krays were not always welcome in Tangiers, however. They went there a few times, but their reputation followed them and the local police decided to do something about it. Reg told the story like this:

> When we went to Tangiers and got kicked out by the police, we were escorted by a young police detective. He was a gentleman, he was very different to the English police, and said that there was nothing personal, but that we had to go back to London. We enjoyed it in Tangiers. We used to go to Gypsy's club, who was the wife of Billy Hill, and Gypsy and Billy Hill made us very welcome. The club was called Churchill's and we would spend nearly every night in this particular club. It was very nice there – there used to be a lot of rich Arabs there and Gypsy had her two big poodles, massive they were. It was a nice club.

Both Ron and Reg enjoyed Tangiers for what they could get out of it – and that meant indulging their taste for young boys. Both men participated; both men pursued their sexual passions.

Ron, in later life, talking about his relationship with his brother Reg, said that they enjoyed each other's company in more ways than one. He didn't, however, want to go into details. But, apparently, he did talk to someone shortly before his death and admitted that, at one time, they were so concerned about revealing their sexuality that, for a while, they only had sex with each other.

One of Reg's cellmates, in later years, admitted publicly that he was Reg's lover. He wasn't the first and most likely not the last, but Bradley Allardyce should know.

The most telling of all of the Krays' relationships, however, was that with Lord Robert Boothby, closely followed by that with Tom Driberg MP. The stories are many, and sometimes horrendous. They show exactly how Ron Kray supplied boys for his friends, especially ones who could do him favours in return. If you want to know, then read on, but if not, then turn the page and read the next chapter. I promise not to be too explicit. I am not enjoying writing about this, but it has to be done to put the record straight.

Back in 1964 the British newspapers didn't want, or were unable legally, to report what Lord Boothby and Ron Kray were up to. But the German press, led by *Stern* magazine, had no such problems. They said it straight, which is more than Boothby did. They said that Boothby's relationship with Ron Kray was sinister and that the gangster had provided the lord with young boys, some young boxers – just youngsters who wanted to join the Firm. *Stern* did not go into details but the fact is that, in many cases, Ron terrorised them into compliance.

Boothby had been fond of boys long before he ever met Ron, but he quickly found out that Ron was a good supplier for his outrageous sexual practices. Boothby quite often had a live-in lover, but when he had the chance he would attend Ron's orgies, party all night long and indulge his passion for sex with underage boys. In fact, with Boothby, it was the younger the better.

In 1959 there was an incident when a 17-year-old Scottish lad got himself into trouble with the law while working for Boothby, cleaning and doing odd jobs at his flat in Eaton Square. He was arrested one evening when he was seen in the street outside Boothby's home with a champagne bottle in his hand and wearing one of Boothby's watches. The watch was easily identifiable as it had Boothby's name engraved on it.

When he appeared in court, facing charges of theft, the trial was ended prematurely, with Boothby bending the magistrate's ear. The case was forgotten and the lad was put on a train to Scotland. Being a lord does have its advantages.

In 1990, Sir John Junor, at the time of this incident a Fleet Street editor, wrote about it in his memoirs. He had decided to trace the boy, to see what had happened to him afterwards and to check the events leading up to the so-called theft.

It appeared that it was Boothby who had brought the lad down to London from his constituency, East Aberdeen. Boothby took him around London, something out of the ordinary for a working-class boy from Scotland, and they dined out at various places, drinking wine in abundance. When they eventually got back to Boothby's flat they continued to party, with the result that Boothby gave the lad the watch and a bottle of champagne, apparently for services rendered. When the lad left Boothby's flat he was reportedly boisterous and bragging about his outrageous evening.

The police soon put an end to that, the result being that he was quickly shifted off home to Scotland.

Shortly after this event, another lad was also caught with something in his hand – this time it was a cheque book that he told the police he had found. It was Boothby's cheque book and the police quickly put together a scenario for the theft. They were beginning to understand Boothby and his lifestyle, and they realised that the boy had been with Boothby at his flat and had taken the cheque book in lieu of payment. Needless to say, charges were dropped.

Lord Robert Boothby was very casual about his 'relationships' with his friends. He would often talk of his exploits and would, at times, introduce his latest lover. He even boasted to friends that his sometime lover, cat burglar Leslie Holt, who was a good friend of Ron Kray's and a regular member of the Firm, used to only rob people Boothby didn't like. He would draw up a list and tell Holt to go and have some fun.

Ron Kray was a regular at No. 1 Eaton Square. He was usually ushered in by Gordon Goodfellow, Boothby's butler of many years, and he usually had a boy with him, for the amusement of the peer. What struck many a guest was the casual way that Boothby behaved, kissing the boys fully on the lips and generally undressing them with his eyes, in front of everyone there, especially after a few drinks.

One journalist tells of the time he was with Boothby when Ron came around for tea. Ron was very well dressed, but he was wearing a shoulder holster and gun and, as usual, he had a boy with him. He told the boy to do whatever Boothby told him to do – this was a bit of a joke between the two men.

Leslie Holt was sharing Boothby's flat at the time, but he didn't mind the competition. Anyway, Ron was his boss, so he had to comply. The 'Guv'nor', as they called Ron in Broadmoor, was ready for a good time, but the boy had obviously had a hard day. His lip was split and he looked a bit battered and bruised, but this was normal practice. If they didn't want to come quietly, then it would have to be done the Kray way.

When Ron discovered that the man with Boothby was a journalist he asked if they would all like to go out to eat, and perhaps visit his casino and meet his brother Reg. They dined at The Society in Jermyn Street first and then later visited Esmeralda's Barn in Wilton Place, Knightsbridge.

The evening started well and they all enjoyed the meal and the drink. The journalist was beginning to think that Ron was a good host, just an ordinary guy from the East End, and then, unknowingly, he let his guard down. It happened when Reg arrived and joined the party. Reg was easier to talk to; not so frightening, not so overpowering. That was the journalist's mistake.

Ron didn't like the way he was with his twin, getting very friendly with him. It was as though Ron was not there and he hated it. Quickly they were all on their way to Esmeralda's Barn. Ron gave the order and that was that.

Once there, things got worse. Ron was looking at the journalist as if he fancied him, and he did. Soon the journalist realised what was going on and was ready to make a quick getaway, but not before Reg approached him and told him that he, Reg, was available if he didn't fancy Ron. He was between a rock and a hard place, and not wanting to get involved with either man.

He escaped that evening, only to be caught some days later. He ended up with 22 stitches in his forehead, a bloodied and broken nose, a cracked cheekbone and severe bruising. When the attacker left him lying on the pavement in Marylebone he told him, 'That will teach you to show some fucking respect to Ronnie!' The journalist never did that again, but what a story to tell. He was lucky – others received a different kind of reminder of who was the 'King of Crime' in London and they are all dead.

Boothby continued his association with the Krays and even argued their case in the House of Lords. He attended Ron's orgies when Ron had the flat in Cedra Court, where he indulged his pleasures alongside many prominent people, including his old friend Tom Driberg MP. The police have many files covering these get-togethers but we are simply not allowed to see them. The truth will be hidden for many years to come, with only small teasers being released from time to time to whet the appetite of journalists and writers alike.

* * *

Thomas Edward Neil Driberg was born on 22 May 1905 at Crowborough, Sussex. His mother was Amy Mary Bell and his father was John James Street Driberg, who worked for the Indian Civil Service, first as Chief of Police and then as Inspector of Jails for the province of Assam.

He and his brothers, Jack and James, enjoyed their middle-class lifestyle, with the young Tom attending first a local school and then Lancing College where he met Evelyn Waugh. Later he attended Christ Church, Oxford, where he studied classics. He first got into trouble for making 'unwelcome advances', as they were called, towards other boys at Lancing and was forced to leave earlier than expected. He joined the Communist Party at the age of 15.

In 1935 he stood trial for indecent assault after he invited two unemployed miners to share his bed. During the night his hands started to wander, here, there and everywhere, ending with the miners making a formal complaint to the police. He was acquitted due to a misunderstanding, as it was described, and his employer at the time, Lord Beaverbrook, made sure that the story never made it to the press. Tom Driberg was beginning to realise the power of the Establishment.

In 1941, he was expelled from the Communist Party when Anthony Blunt, later proven to be a KGB spy, named him as an informer. In fact, this was correct, since Driberg had been recruited by MI5 to spy on his fellow Labour MPs and also to spy, on their behalf, on the Communist Party. It was the start of the information age and knowledge was power.

He first became a member of parliament for Maldon, in a by-election in 1942, standing as an independent. But in 1945 he joined the Labour Party and held the seat until the 1955 General Election. Later, in 1959, he was to become the member of parliament for Barking, Essex, a seat he held until 1974.

During the Second World War he was again in trouble with the law when he was caught 'cottaging' with a Norwegian sailor. And then, in the '50s, he propositioned a man at Jockey Fields public lavatories, near Gray's Inn Gardens in London. Unfortunately for Driberg this man turned out to be a policeman. Despite this, he managed to get away with it on both occasions, again using his allies in the Establishment to get him off.

He felt so safe that he was able to visit friends who had found themselves in jail for committing similar offences but who weren't as fortunate, or connected, as Driberg and had to do time.

But Driberg had time on his hands, as he was no longer in Parliament, and this was when he took a commission to write a book about one of his old pals, Guy Burgess, the KGB spy who had escaped to the Soviet Union some years earlier. In 1956, he went to Moscow to interview Burgess, but he also found time for visiting one particular haunt, the men's public urinals behind the Metropole Hotel. Again, he was in trouble, as the man he tried to pick up was a member of the KGB. It was a honey trap and they had caught their man. From that day on, Tom Driberg was a spy for the KGB, reporting directly back to Moscow, and even worked closely with his old enemy, Anthony Blunt.

He had no problem with the regime as he had always supported Stalin and the Communist Party so actually getting paid for it was a bonus. He assumed the code name of Lepage and was activated immediately.

When he returned to the UK he found out that other members of the Labour Party had also been recruited to the KGB. One such man was Raymond Fletcher, who represented Ilkeston, Derbyshire, in Parliament. So Tom Driberg was not alone.

In June 1964, however, Driberg was in trouble with his party. Two Conservative backbenchers had seen Driberg and his friend Boothby importuning boys at a greyhound event in London. But, once again, nothing was done about it. Like Boothby, Driberg was leading a charmed life.

Driberg was an ex-chairman of the Labour Party and was still a senior figure in the party in 1966 when he wrote letters to the Home Office on behalf of Frank 'The Mad Axeman' Mitchell. Ron got him involved, as he had helped the twins before by writing to the authorities when Firm members had been imprisoned many miles away from their homes in the East End of London. He had had some success and prisoners had been moved nearer to the East End so their families could visit them on a more regular basis.

Ron wanted him to perform a similar trick with Mitchell, but he couldn't. He tried, but to no avail. Ron's solution was to have Mitchell killed and dumped at sea: no body, no crime.

Driberg was a regular visitor at the Kray clubs, where he associated with young criminals, especially thieves and burglars. He played the same games as Lord Boothby, giving details of houses where the owners were wealthy and the times when they would be away. It was a game with these people; it kept their boyfriends happy and it helped to supply untraceable funds for their various nefarious needs.

Ron encouraged Driberg, together with Boothby, to attend his orgies at Cedra Court and, needless to say, Driberg had the same desires as his host and the noble lord – young boys. Ron used similar tactics as he did with Boothby. The boys were told to behave 'or else'. And they knew what 'or else' meant.

Tom Driberg married some years later and he became Baron Bradwell shortly before his death in August 1976. So the writer of some renown eventually claimed the title that had evaded him all his life. He had the mansion, he had the wife, he had an outrageous lifestyle and, eventually, he joined the ranks of his old pal Lord Boothby.

Have no doubts about it, these two men, Lord Robert Boothby and Tom Driberg, were at the centre of what we would call today the Krays' paedophile ring. Although it may be the case that the 'boys' who were their victims were not as young as those we, sadly, all too frequently, read about being the victims of paedophiles today, they were below the age of consent as the law stated at the time and some were much, much younger.

What is astounding is that prominent people knew what Driberg was like, his peccadilloes, his gangster friends, his tastes in human flesh. Winston Churchill, who died in 1965, once said: 'Tom Driberg is the sort of person who gives sodomy a bad name!', and Peter Cook made fun of Driberg in 1977 when he said 'Lord Driberg, or Lord Bradwell I think he is called', and then added something about 'fine fishnet stockings and a chicken.' And, in Parliament, they knew where he would be when it was time to attend a vote – the police were told to drive over and escort him back from the public toilets on the Albert Embankment.

But, after he died, more astonishing news reached the

newspapers when it was discovered that Tom Driberg had also been spying for Czechoslovakia. MI5 had been tracking several Labour politicians and deserters from the Eastern Bloc had given up Driberg's name under interrogation. It was all there in their files and kept hidden away until a suitable time. The file on Driberg was getting bigger by the day.

There have been unsubstantiated rumours circulating recently that Ron Kray organised boys for hire from his Suffolk home, shortly before his arrest in 1968, and there have also been, again unsubstantiated, rumours of his involvement in a paedophile ring and the filming of so-called snuff films and other films for paedophiles. If there is any truth at all in these rumours then there is a scandal waiting to be told, but for the moment the authorities, whoever they may be, do not want this information in the public domain. One day it will be out there, everything out in the open and I hope I am around to write about it.

Why exactly did Lord Robert Boothby and Tom Driberg, or Lord Bradwell as he became, manage to survive all their lives without these facts becoming public knowledge? Who was protecting them and why? The answers, when they are revealed, will be shocking and scandalous; they are going to be almost unbelievable, the stuff of Hollywood films. If you want to hear more about Boothby and Driberg then keep reading.

26

STORIES FROM THE GRAVE: ASHES TO ASHES

I wanted my son Gary buried in the spare grave at the plot in Chingford, but Reg wanted him buried with Frances. I couldn't understand it then and I still don't – but he must have had a very good reason.

Charlie Kray

Capital punishment was abolished in Great Britain in 1965 and the Home Office let it be known that they would treat with sympathy any requests from the families of executed prisoners for the remains of their loved ones to be exhumed from their graves within prison grounds for reburial in a proper place of rest. Permission was granted on several occasions and bodies were moved, including the remains of convicted murderers James Hanratty, Derek Bentley and Timothy Evans.

You would think therefore that obtaining permission for the exhumation and re-interment of the innocent wife of a convicted killer, where the wife was buried in a public cemetery, would be a simple formality.

This is what Elsie Shea, Reg Kray's mother-in-law, thought when she applied in 1969 to the Home Secretary, James Callaghan, for permission to remove her daughter's body from the Kray family plot to rebury it elsewhere. Reg was a convicted murderer, so surely she should be granted her wish to have her daughter removed from her showpiece grave and buried again, with dignity, in her family's own plot under her maiden name of Shea.

It didn't turn out that way, as recently released documents from the Home Office show. Although Elsie was told at the time that they were viewing the case with some sympathy, her request was refused. Now, from these documents, we can see why and exactly what their problem was. They wrote: 'She [Elsie] is concerned to carry out the last wishes of her daughter, that she should be buried in the maiden name which she had re-assumed and to mitigate the family humiliation of being associated with a notorious criminal.' Civil servants from the Home Office invited Elsie to attend for discussions, and she told them the true story of her daughter's relationship with the notorious gangster.

Elsie told them that her son, Frank, was an old friend of Ronnie and Reggie Kray and it was through him that her daughter, Frances, had first met Reg when she was 16. Reg had written to her frequently while he was in Wandsworth Prison and the courtship had begun, but, knowing that her family would not give their permission, it was not until she was 21, in 1965, that they were married. Less than a year later Frances was back home with her family and had changed her name back to Shea. She was also trying to get the marriage annulled on the grounds that it was never consummated.

The documents include a statement made by Elsie Shea. 'The marriage was never much of a reality. After a week's honeymoon in Athens, Reginald Kray sent her to live with his mother. For the rest of her married life she stayed variously with her own family, alone in hotels and in flats provided for her by Kray, in hospital wards and occasionally with women friends of the Krays on trips abroad but never, apparently, together with Kray.'

This was strong stuff and the kind of talk that Reg did not want anyone to hear.

Elsie went on to tell of the times that Reg tried to delay the annulment proceedings and that her daughter was ready to go to court. Unfortunately, Frances died before the annulment proceedings could begin.

Even when Frances died and her brother, Frank, had already started the funeral arrangements, Reg had to take control, Elsie told the Home Office. He turned up at their house demanding to reschedule the burial, and he even brought a priest with him to help talk the family round.

Reg took over the funeral arrangements and made sure that everything was in the name of 'Frances Elsie Kray' and not the Shea name that she had retaken as her official name. Elsie and her family were even snubbed by Reg at the funeral and, shortly after the ceremony, their names were removed from the wreaths and flowers that they had sent.

The final indignation, however, was the headstone. It said: 'In loving memory of my darling wife, Frances Kray'. The headstone had cost Reg some £500 and was his way of saying that Frances was a Kray, not a Shea. Elsie told the Home Office that she felt that the words were hypocritical and offensive. Her final remarks, however, were somewhat confusing as she told them that she and her husband were very upset that they had to endure seeing their daughter settled in a grave that linked them with a murderer.

If anyone cares to look through the Shea family tree then you will see why I call it confusing. With so many thieves and criminals throughout their past it is hard to see why another murderer or two should make any difference to them or any other part of their family.

The Home Office people didn't know what to do, but the rules were straightforward: they had to contact Reg to see what he had to say about it. As the owner of the plot he had to give his permission, otherwise nothing could be done. Reg had just started a thirty-year sentence for murder, in Brixton Prison, London, so he was nearby and available, twenty-four hours a day, seven days a week. But what would his reaction be?

The Home Office knew all about Reg Kray – his trial had been the trial of the decade, if not the century. They also knew that they had a problem. He was noted by the prison service as 'extremely sensitive about any matter concerning his former wife', and they went on to say that his violent nature was something that they had to contend with on a daily basis. They knew that they had to contact him – after all, this was the law – and they contemplated suitable arrangements, letters and ways of doing this.

The civil servants at the Home Office, however, had another

plan. This was to pass the buck over to the governor of Brixton Prison, and they even wrote a memo to this effect, saying: 'He is an impulsive man who is prone to outbursts, so it would be best conducted by the governor.'

The governor of Brixton was shocked – he thought it a very bad idea and wanted nothing to do with it. He had already written in his records that there was great enmity between Reg Kray and Mrs Elsie Shea. He continued: 'Kray has said that the question of his wife's grave is of more interest to him at the moment than his appeal and that this is a subject over which he could not be held responsible for his actions.'

They were scared to death of him. Even in prison, Reg was still a powerful and dangerous man and he had already begun to run the prison in his own way, in his own style and as if it was his own private and privileged world.

Others joined the governor in commenting on Reg. 'If we can help it we should avoid anything likely to make the control problem worse. It would appear that the matter of the grave is a very delicate subject,' said the prison department.

So the buck was passed once more, this time to Sampson & Co, the lawyers who were representing Reg. The response from Reg, through his lawyers, was exactly what they had expected. The lawyers said that their client, Reginald Kray, 'makes the very strongest possible objection that the remains of his late wife be removed from her grave, or that any alteration be made to her memorial'. They continued: 'He is aware that during a period of separation resulting from a matrimonial dispute his wife purported to change her name, but they were afterwards reconciled.'

Reg knew that they couldn't hang him for the crimes that he had committed. All they could do was keep him in jail, but they would have to keep him right or there would be trouble.

The Home Office had their answer: 'No!' So they did nothing. They told Elsie Shea that their daughter's suicide was not enough for them to overrule the demand by Reg Kray that the body of Frances Kray should not be moved. An official told her: 'It is a great pity, but I cannot see any other decision is possible.' His final remark, however, was rather comical. 'The fact that a person has been sentenced for so serious an offence as murder does not make him a sort of outlaw deprived of all other rights.'

Well, if he hadn't been talking about Reg Kray, killer, gangland boss and one of the most dangerous and violent criminals in the history of the country, then maybe, just maybe, I would have agreed with him. But he wouldn't even call Reg Kray an outlaw. Why?

The answer is actually in the definition of the word 'outlaw', which means 'a person excluded from normal legal protection and rights' and not, as most people believe, a person who operates outside of, or breaks, the law. So, although Reg was a convicted criminal serving 30 years in prison, he was still able to benefit from the law of the land.

But, of course, there must have been more to it than just the Home Office agreeing with Reg's objection, which could easily have been overruled by them based on the compelling argument and evidence provided by Frances's family.

Why did the authorities treat Reg with kid gloves, why did they pander to his every need and why were so many people in both the Home Office and the prison service afraid of upsetting him? Maybe it was his friends in high places, such as Lord Boothby and Tom Driberg, or maybe it was the secrets that he took with him to prison. What did he know, and who was involved back in the days when he and his brother were the 'Kings of Crime'?

The prison authorities made one last remark, shown in the records of the time, which demonstrates that they were forced to make such a decision. Someone wrote the following, in summing up their problems: 'I fear we must run the risk of it being suggested that we are taking Reginald Kray's side. We have no ground at all for hoping that Kray will mellow in a year's time, or any number of years' time.'

And that is just the way it was. Elsie Shea tried on numerous occasions to move her daughter without success. Reg Kray never did change his mind, and he even went to additional lengths to ensure that Frances's body would never be exhumed, even after his death. The question here again is why?

On 8 March 1996, Reg made an interesting decision and a curious one too. He decided to bury Charlie's son, Gary, who had just died at the age of 44, in the same grave as his wife Frances, even though there was an empty grave space available in the same large family plot. Why do this when there was a vacant space where Charlie could eventually be buried with his only son, reuniting father and son again in death? This was hardly the action of a man who was devoted to his wife's memory. So why did he do it?

The answer isn't difficult to figure out – he did it to make it doubly difficult for anyone in the future to remove the coffin containing his late wife. As Elsie Shea had discovered, Reg, as owner of the plot, had to give his permission for Frances's coffin to be exhumed and this he had refused to do while he was alive. After his death, though, it is highly possible that the Home Office would have granted Elsie's wish despite any protest from Reg's heirs. But, in order to exhume Frances, they would have to exhume Gary first, and that makes it a far more complicated, if not impossible, process. This was a belt-and-braces job if ever I saw one. But the question is still why?

Whether or not the Sheas were notified, or asked for their permission, at the time of Gary's burial is not recorded anywhere. It appears that Reg made the decision and that was that. There were now two bodies in the grave and he could feel safe that they would remain there. I am sure that he left instructions with Roberta not to allow the grave to be disturbed and I am sure she will comply with his wishes, whatever the real reason for them.

Charlie said at the time of his son's death that he was penniless, broke and close to bankruptcy. He had to turn to Reg in order to bury his son and he was forced to accept the help that Reg was prepared to give. Charlie had nothing to say except thanks. But why did he agree to Gary being buried with Frances when there was an empty space that could take both Gary and himself?

When Reg died in 2000 he left clear instructions to Roberta that he should be buried together with his twin brother Ron in Chingford Mount Cemetery. So now we have mum Violet and dad Charlie together in the same grave; we have Ron and Reg together in the same grave; we have Charlie alone in his grave; and we have the peculiar situation of Reggie's first love, Frances, buried in the same grave as Charlie's son Gary.

Even stranger is the fact that when Bradley Allardyce, Reggie's cellmate and 'best friend' in prison, decided to get married, Reg gave him the engagement ring that he gave to Frances when they became engaged to use as a wedding ring. Again, is this the action of a man who was so devoted to and besotted with his wife, as Reg always claimed he was?

So why would Reg go to the lengths he did in order to stop the exhumation of his wife's coffin? Maybe it really was the fact that he was besotted with her and wanted her close by him in death, but, if this was the case, why bury Gary with her instead of burying him in the plot waiting for Charlie? Why, also, would he give her engagement ring to his, alleged, gay lover?

Maybe it is simply the case that he didn't like the Sheas because of the way they interfered in his marriage and this was his way of getting revenge. Or is it that there is something else in the coffin that Reg did not ever want made public knowledge?

I am sure many of you will come up with your own theories to explain the mystery of Frances's grave – that the Krays took advantage of Frances's death to do one of their 'double-up jobs' and there is another body under her coffin; that there is perhaps evidence that she was, as claimed by Allardyce, murdered by Ron. But, unless the Sheas are eventually granted their wish and poor Frances is eventually exhumed for reburial elsewhere, we will never know the real reason behind Reg's actions.

There are still many unanswered questions surrounding the Kray family plot in Chingford Mount Cemetery, to the east of London. But for the moment the graves are quiet. It is a place only frequented by ghosts, and they are not talking. We are getting nearer and nearer to the truth, but for the moment it lies buried along with the entire Kray family. The line has ended, the Krays are no more. But the legend lives on.

27

STORIES FROM THE GRAVE: SPIES, LIES AND NAKED THIGHS

I mean it's been a misery for me, living with Christine Keeler. Even a criminal has the right to a new life, but they made sure I never did that. They just didn't stop calling me a prostitute for ever and ever and ever and ever. How can anyone live like that?

Christine Keeler (The Observer, February 2001)

To fully understand the implications of this chapter, we have to take a brief look at a man who became the centre of media attention in the early 1960s when it was proved that he had lied to Parliament. The man was John Dennis Profumo, 5th Baron Profumo OBE (Mil), CBE, who, at the time, was the Secretary of State for War in the Macmillan government. We should also take a look at the woman who also became notorious worldwide because of the scandal that was to follow: Christine Keeler.

John Dennis Profumo, or Baron Profumo as he was officially entitled to call himself, was born in January 1915. His name actually originated in Sardinia, since his father was of Italian origin, but not many people knew that. After being educated at Harrow, one of the UK's best-known public schools, he went on to Brasenose College, Oxford.

Profumo served in the British army during the Second World War, with particular distinction in North Africa and during the D-Day landings in Normandy. He was first elected to Parliament in

1940 while he was still serving in the army, eventually leaving with the rank of brigadier in 1950 for a full-time career in politics.

He gradually advanced within the Conservative Party until, in 1960, he was made Secretary of State for War by Harold Macmillan, the prime minister of the day. He was married at the time to Valerie Hobson, a well-known actress of stage and screen, and she remained by his side during his most difficult days, which were just around the corner.

The girl at the centre of the scandal was Christine Keeler. She was born in Uxbridge, to the west of London, in 1942, and did not do particularly well at school. But what she lacked in academic achievement she was to make up for in her new profession as a nightclub hostess, high-class call-girl or just plain femme fatale.

It was when she was working at Murray's Cabaret Club in Soho that the affair, or should that be affairs, started. Keeler herself said of the club: 'There was a pervasive atmosphere of sex, with beautiful young girls all over the place, but customers would always say, if asked, that they only came along for the floor show and the food and drink.' She then added: 'When we weren't onstage, we were allowed to sit out with the audience for a hostess fee of £5.' A lot of money in those days when you think of the number of potential clients during an evening. One of those clients was John Profumo, Secretary of State for War.

It was soon after she started working there that she met Stephen Ward, a well-known osteopath with clients from the elite of London society, including Colin Coote, the then editor of the *Daily Telegraph*, Sir Roger Hollis, the head of MI5, Great Britain's espionage and counter-espionage organisation, Anthony Blunt, Surveyor of the Queen's Pictures and an old friend of Tom Driberg MP, who knew the Krays particularly well, and Geoffrey Nicholson, Conservative MP.

Already we begin to see the shape of what was to come: Blunt was KGB, Driberg was KGB and Christine Keeler, within a few short months, would be having an affair with Eugene Ivanov, a naval attaché with the Soviet Embassy in London, also rumoured to be KGB. And, all the time, MI5 was keeping a watchful eye on them all.

Ward was also a successful artist, having painted such people as Prince Philip, the Duke of Edinburgh and Madame Furtseva, the Soviet Minister of Culture. 'Philip's a snob,' he told Christine, 'not like the man he used to be. I used to know him before he was married to Elizabeth.'

Apart from her new friend Stephen Ward, Christine also met another girl who was also to become notorious because of the scandal. She was Mandy Rice-Davies, who worked with other girls such as Suzy Chang and Mariella Novotny throwing sex parties for London's elite. Christine also met Ron and Reg Kray, who were very good listeners when they had to be. In fact, she had dinner with the Krays many times and, on one such occasion, Ron brought along one of his friends, Leslie Holt, the well-known cat burglar and live-in lover of Lord Robert Boothby.

The scandal started on 21 January 1961 when Colin Coote, editor of the *Daily Telegraph*, invited Stephen Ward to have lunch with him and Eugene Ivanov, the naval attaché with the Soviet Embassy. They enjoyed each other's company so they decided to meet again.

A few months later, Ward moved out of his old flat and into a more luxurious version in Marylebone and Christine Keeler moved with him. Sir Roger Hollis, of MI5, was known by Ward, so Hollis asked an associate to go and check out Ward on his behalf, and to discuss the meeting with Ivanov which had been witnessed by the organisation. This meeting led to an agreement with Ward for him to spy on behalf of MI5. But also interested in Ivanov was another regular visitor to the Ward home, Anthony Blunt.

On 8 July 1961 Christine Keeler met John Profumo again at a house party thrown by Stephen Ward at Cliveden, the Buckinghamshire home of Lord Astor, where Ward used a cottage to entertain selected guests. It appears that he met her quite suddenly when he saw her standing in front of him wearing only a towel for a dress. Keeler was already at that time sleeping with both Ivanov and a drug dealer by the name of Johnny Edgecombe, but that didn't prevent a liaison between the two of them.

When Hollis of MI5 got to hear about this from Stephen Ward he set about trapping the KGB man. He asked Ward to get information through Keeler about the movement of nuclear warheads to Germany. This was to be done in the way of 'pillow talk' between Keeler, Profumo and Ivanov. So the spying game had begun, but who was spying on whom? Hollis also had a word with the government's Cabinet Secretary, Sir Norman Brook, who in turn spoke to Profumo. It was decided that Profumo should write to Keeler, breaking off the affair and stating, quite strongly, that they should never meet again.

By the following December Keeler was a regular at the parties thrown by Mandy Rice-Davies, who later described some of the events of one particular party held by her pal Mariella Novotny.

> The door was opened by Stephen, naked except for his socks. All the men were naked, the women naked except for wisps of clothing like suspender belts and stockings. I recognised our host and hostess, Mariella Novotny and her husband Horace Dibbins, and unfortunately I recognised too a fair number of the other faces as belonging to people so famous you could not fail to recognise them: a Harley Street gynaecologist, several politicians including a cabinet minister of the day who Stephen told us with great glee had served dinner of roast peacock wearing nothing but a mask and a bow tie, instead of a fig leaf.

When Keeler and Mandy Rice-Davies visited the USA on 11 July 1962 they discovered that their movements were being followed by none other than the FBI. So the news was out about Keeler and her affairs with the KGB man and the Secretary of State for War, and she was being watched on both sides of the Atlantic, possibly because she had information that could be of use to someone.

Later, Keeler told friends that Stephen Ward had once told her, after the Cuban Missile Crisis, that he believed that John F. Kennedy would be assassinated. 'A man like John Kennedy will not be allowed to stay in such an important position of power in the world, I assure you of that.' Also present on the day Ward made this comment, however, was Eugene Ivanov, who later fled the UK bound for Moscow. It wasn't just Keeler who was in danger; Ward was in trouble too, but he didn't know it.

When two of Keeler's lovers decided to shoot guns at each other, in the building where Stephen Ward's flat was located, the whole affair became front-page news. And it broke with a bang!

Keeler was contacted by the *Daily Mirror* and asked for her story. 'We know everything,' she was told. Soon everybody would know. The FBI already knew, MI5 already knew, Macmillan already knew, Harold Wilson, soon to be prime minister, already knew – in fact, everyone in a position of power already knew, but the people of Great Britain knew nothing.

It was Keeler's loose talk that brought the whole sordid business to the notice of the House of Commons. She had met John Lewis MP, during the Christmas of 1962, and had told him quite casually about what had been going on. 'I told him about Stephen asking me to get details about the bomb. I told him about John Profumo.' Lewis, in turn, told George Wigg, a Labour MP who was a close friend of Harold Wilson.

On 21 March 1963 George Wigg stood up in Parliament and asked the question: was there any truth in the rumours about John Profumo and Christine Keeler? He was joined by others, who were actually paying attention that day.

Profumo told them that it was all untrue. He lied in the House of Commons, a cardinal sin for a politician, and, by 5 June of the same year, he was forced to resign as War Minister. The scandal was all over the newspapers and almost brought the government to its knees. The prime minister, Harold Macmillan, was forced to resign, reportedly because of ill health.

Suddenly all the girls involved in the scandal were selling their stories to the press. It all made for great reading. What was Robert Mitchum doing at the parties? Was Lord Hailsham a regular? And how about George Peppard and Warren Beatty? It was like Christmas for the journalists and they couldn't get enough. The country couldn't get enough, either.

Ward was due to stand trial, even though he had done everything asked of him by MI5, but he shot and killed himself shortly before the trial could begin. It was all too much for him; his reputation was in tatters, his life was over. Ward was the one and only true victim of the scandal. Others, such as Keeler, had to spend a few months in jail, but Ward never had the opportunity to explain in court about his relationship with MI5 and Sir Roger Hollis.

Recently, an FBI classified memo was revealed. Dated 20 June 1963, it stated concerns held at the time by Robert McNamara about the Profumo affair: 'Mr McNamara referred to a memorandum from the FBI dated 14 June 1963, advising that Air Force personnel may have had a relationship with Christine Keeler.' Later on, it says: 'McNamara said he felt like he was sitting on a bomb in this matter as he could not tell what would come out of it and he wanted to be sure that every effort was being made to get information from the British, particularly as it affected US personnel.'

This was a scandal big enough to bring down the British government, and it very nearly did. It concerned people who were engaged in the spy game and the Krays were right in the middle of it all. Eugene Ivanov was KGB. So, too, were Tom Driberg MP, Anthony Blunt and Raymond Fletcher MP.

The Krays knew Christine Keeler, who was sleeping with the enemy, they knew Tom Driberg MP, who was also working for MI5 as well as the KGB and Czech intelligence, they knew Lord Robert Boothby, who was a danger to them all, and they knew the New York Mafia, who had been used by the CIA in the Bay of Pigs invasion of Cuba in 1961, and who many suspect played a role in the assassination of President John F. Kennedy. Then there is the memo regarding Keeler's involvement with US personnel. There were a lot of very important people involved in this affair, famous faces with famous names from the very heart of government on both sides of the Atlantic and beyond. The FBI, MI5, CIA and KGB were all involved to a greater or lesser extent.

The full truth about this affair and the level of the Krays' involvement will, as with the Boothby affair, not be known until the British government allows the release of the still-classified documents relating to both cases.

What we do know, however, is that the police and the FBI were watching the Krays and MI5 was watching the police and Driberg, Ward, Keeler and Blunt. Were they looking for a connection between the Krays and the KGB because of their relationships with Driberg and Keeler? Or was it just a case of gathering knowledge for its own sake? One thing is for certain, the Krays were planning their own version of the Mafia's Murder Inc., and they were definitely looking at, and developing relationships with, political figures, both in the UK and abroad.

What cannot be denied is the fact that, following the near fall of the Macmillan government over the Profumo affair in 1962, the British Establishment could not risk the same thing happening to the Harold Wilson government barely four years later when the Boothby affair reared its ugly head. Not only did both cases involve members of the government lying in Parliament, sexual deviation and depravity, and KGB agents and sympathisers, but they also featured some common central characters, most notably Tom Driberg, Harold Macmillan and his wife Dorothy, Harold Wilson, Lord Boothby and, of course, the Krays.

Boothby, therefore, had to win his case against the *Mirror*, because there was simply so much at stake. If the full story had come out at the time, then who knows what skeletons would have fallen out of the many locked government cupboards. What is certain is that, following so closely after the Profumo affair, the British public would not, even with the meagre information available to us now, have tolerated another scandalised Parliament and the Wilson government would, in all likelihood, have fallen.

In order to save the government of the day, Boothby was allowed to get away with lying in Parliament, the so-called free press was gagged and the Krays were allowed to continue their reign as London's crime lords for a few more years.

Until the government's secret papers relating to both affairs are released, if they ever are, we will not be finished with the story of the Krays and how they, unintentionally, came so close to changing the political history of Great Britain.

28

THE END OF THE LINE

The winners write history, be it true or false. Tellers of
history work under the old adage that you can't let the
truth get in the way of a good story!

Colin Fry

Above all, the Krays have taught the authorities to be more secretive
and the crooks to be better and more ingenious. No one was
prepared for the Krays, and they were quick to seize the opportunity
to create havoc in the East and West End of London alike. But have
there been any lasting lessons to be learned and will the Krays
have their place in history?

It seems that the police have now realised that they are ill
equipped to combat gang crime, as a report showed in February
1996, when crime researchers established that there were more
than 300 street gangs nationwide with a total force of more than
10,000 members. They deal in drugs and are a greater menace
than the Yardies, the Mafia and the Triads combined. The family
gang, represented by the Krays and the Richardsons, are on the
way out and the new gang bosses are taking over.

'These people are leaders because, when push comes to shove,
they will walk into a pub and shoot someone,' said one top London
police officer, reminding me of Ron Kray when he killed Cornell.
Maybe they have learned something after all, this new breed of
British gangster.

Manchester CID chief Colin Philips, who ran an internal

research team, said: 'These gangs even have their own network, and the common currency is drugs.' Usually numbering from some 15 members up to around 20, they are well organised and are quick to take revenge and retribution. He continued to outline the modern trends by saying: 'In the '50s and '60s it was vice, prostitution and pornography. In the '80s it was car crime and then fraud. Well into the new millennium the drug trade is worth millions.' Perhaps he should have mentioned protection, gambling, long-firm frauds and other racketeering, but the idea of change was brought across to the general public and to the police alike.

The conclusion of the report was that the police are ill prepared to cope with the new crisis. It goes on to blame poor cooperation between forces and inadequate intelligence. I, personally, would also say that secrecy is to blame. Because of this lack of cooperation in intelligence gathering, gangs and gang members are getting away with murder.

Recently, some politically sensitive material has been made available, giving more facts on the Lord Boothby case. Since it had been previously covered by the 30-year rule, this was a classified secret. But now we can see and research this case by sifting through the papers and documents released through government sources. Scotland Yard, however, have still refused to disclose their knowledge on the case, and when I enquired about the files on Lord Boothby and the Krays held at the Yard they slapped the 75-year rule on me and told me to come back in the year 2042. How's that for secrecy!

Until we have a more open society, events will be exploited by people like the Krays. In this matter the police have not yet learned that vital lesson – that it is better to let people make up their own minds by presenting the facts as they are and not hiding them away in a vault, thinking that inquisitive folk like myself will just go away. We will not!

Just who they are trying to protect is a very interesting question. Could it be officers high up in the hierarchy of Scotland Yard itself, who are afraid of not getting their pension? Could it be others, involved in homosexuality with Ron Kray and his friends Lord Boothby and Tom Driberg? Could it be further details about the Mafia and their involvement in crime in this country, a fact that the police are keen to deny? Or is it the total lack of proper organisation at Scotland Yard itself that they want to hide? Whatever it is, I can see no reason for withholding the truth from the British people.

In our present information age this lack of access to information surrounding the Krays does nothing to endear to us, the public, politicians and others in authority who use such rules or Acts of Parliament to suppress the truth. It is the 'Sir Humphrey' syndrome, made popular by the television series *Yes, Minister*, where we are only told enough to satisfy us, and the real reasons for their actions are hidden away from scrutiny. Not telling us what is happening and why is a downright disgrace. But such is the extent of secrecy in this country, this conspiracy of silence, that we, the general public, must urge the government to do more than just talk about a Freedom of Information Act; they must also improve it as quickly as possible.

When the present government is talking so much about this act, brought in not many years ago now, then I find it surprising that Scotland Yard are shielding themselves from investigation, by imposing a 75-year rule, one that is normally only used for national security. But maybe the Krays also have something to do with national security itself, since Ron was often photographed with Christine Keeler, the girl in the Profumo scandal. I have already discussed this in some detail but the mind still boggles.

Sir Paul Condon, previously Commissioner of the Metropolitan Police, went on television, some time ago, in front of a house select committee to say that in his opinion, there were about 0.5–1.0 per cent of police officers in the Metropolitan Police who were corrupt. This then means that these corrupt officers, some of whom must, by definition, work at Scotland Yard, have access to information that we, the public, are not allowed to see. Again, I must ask, why? Indeed, what kind of corruption are we addressing? If it is purely criminal in content, then what about the boys helping the boys – those in high office who want their misdemeanours kept quiet so that they can continue in their positions unhindered? There are too many possibilities for pure speculation – it's a minefield.

We have been informed about a new sense of awareness. Change is in the air. But with the same people in authority, surely they will just choose a rule that suits them if they really want to suppress information. Sir Humphrey will always be there in Whitehall, doing what he has to do to maintain his position of power. This will be for his own benefit, however, and not in the interest of the country.

When researching this book I was denied access to files at Broadmoor, I was denied access to information held by the prison authorities, I was denied information about the Krays held at Scotland Yard and I was denied information from the Police Federation. Even the officer in charge of the Charlie Kray case, many years ago now, didn't want to talk to me because he thought he would get into trouble with his bosses at the Yard. This conspiracy, which finally invoked the 75-year rule, has gone on long enough. What are they afraid of?

One of the good pieces of news that came out of my investigations is the fact that scientists have now found a way of repairing brain cells by injecting specially cultivated cells into the damaged area. This is apparently a genuine cure for, among other illnesses, Alzheimer's disease, although the method will not be available for some years to come. I can only hope that research into the brain of Ron Kray, that chronic paranoid schizophrenic, will also have helped in the field of medicine, and that one day his friends at Broadmoor will benefit from the findings.

One of the most curious findings of my own research has been that the Krays were never tried for anything other than murder. They were not accused of running protection rackets, or of doing deals with the Mafia, or of using long-firm frauds to amass a fortune, or of homosexuality. The police deliberately only charged them with one murder each. They didn't even look for all the missing gang members, most of whom were presumed dead. Why?

Why didn't the police press their case against the Krays when they had them under lock and key and the witnesses were ready, willing and available? Maybe that is the real reason for the long sentences but, for the time being, most of the media have conveniently forgotten about the truth. Instead, they follow the myth. After all, it sells more newspapers and gets more viewers.

EPILOGUE

I come to bury Caesar, not to praise him.
The evil that men do lives after them,
The good is oft interred with their bones;
So let it be with Caesar.

Julius Caesar (Act III, scene ii)

These words from Mark Anthony, written by Shakespeare in the sixteenth century, appear to ring true for Ron Kray, some 400 years later. The greatest danger is to believe the hype and the myth that the Krays have tried to project and evoke. The truth is out there and history must interpret these events in an unbiased and logical way; emotion can play no part in our judgements. The truth must be told time, time and time again, lest we forget.

Reg Kray, a prisoner for more than 30 years, left £210,000 in his will, although much more had already been passed on. And they say that crime does not pay. His wife, Roberta, 41 when Reg died back in 2000, inherited most of it, around 80 per cent, but some of his old cellmates and lovers also took their share of the pile. Bradley Allardyce and Paul Henry both received money, mainly for their 'friendship' behind bars, and they were told not to tell about their 'experiences' with Reg in prison, otherwise all the money would go back to Roberta. So there were no strings attached there.

But Roberta didn't only receive money – she inherited his books, his film rights and his merchandising contracts, together with some gold jewellery and other personal effects. And she

331

inherited his contacts, for whatever they are worth. So she can expect a good income for some years to come. Even now, in 2011, she is still writing Kray books, not telling all, but telling enough to keep the Kray name alive.

Both Ron and Reg made a lot of money behind bars from everything from books to T-shirts, from films to interviews, and from any firm that wanted the name of Kray on its letterhead. And, of course, there was the old business of extortion, blackmail, long-firm frauds, money laundering, paedophilia and such.

Some years ago, Ron's wife, Kate, said that companies used to queue up to get them involved in their scams, their protection rackets, their many and varied ways of conning people out of their well-earned money. The Krays were never out of business; they were in it up to their necks.

Even on his deathbed Reg was admitting to other killings. Whether it was him alone or whether he did it with his brother Ron or whether Ron did it all by himself, the fact remains that their old pal 'Mad' Teddy Smith went missing just prior to their arrest back in 1968. But this was possibly not whom Reg was talking about, although he did have a good story about their old friend.

> That was funny in the Cambridge Rooms. There was Lord Effingham [director of Esmeralda's Barn along with the Krays] and his wife sitting at a table with Ron and I and Teddy Smith was there. Teddy Smith had done about five years in Broadmoor Asylum and he was quite crackers really. Lord Effingham was sitting there with his wife and his wife says to him, 'Mowbray', she says, 'don't you think Teddy's quite charming and intelligent?' So Lord Effingham replied and says to her, 'Intelligent, he's spent half of his bloody life in prison, how can he be intelligent!' Teddy Smith was sick!

Shortly before his death, on 1 October 2000, Reg Kray was the subject of a TV documentary in which he confessed to a previously unknown murder. The documentary was screened by the BBC on 29 March 2001.

The press all ran stories of Reg's deathbed confession – all with the same assumption, that the victim was 'Mad' Teddy Smith, who disappeared, supposedly following an argument with Ron, in 1967. Leonard 'Nipper' Read, who was responsible for putting the twins behind bars, confirmed that he believed the unknown victim was 'Mad' Teddy.

There was, however, one dissenting voice. On the day the documentary was screened, 'Mad' Frankie Fraser posted a blog on his website claiming that the victim could not be 'Mad' Teddy – because 'Mad' Teddy Smith was still alive. Fraser claimed that, although Ron and 'Mad' Teddy did argue, these were regular occurrences and were always short-lived. Fraser said:

> However, arguments do cause stress, and it finally became too much for Teddy, who was more highly strung than most, and one day he just packed his bags and headed for the sunshine, and peace and quiet. He is still living in the sunshine, where he is hale and hearty.
>
> How do I know that he is now alive and well? From two reliable sources.
>
> One of the sources is a long-time friend who actually bought the air ticket for Teddy to travel as a going away present. Members of his family recently spent some time with Teddy, and for a 'dead' man he is very active.
>
> By now, everyone should know that you shouldn't believe all that you read in newspapers, and a policeman's guess is no more reliable than the guess of any other person.

Pete Gillett, a prison 'friend' of Reg's, claimed that Reg had confessed to the murder whilst they were in prison. Gillett refused to reveal the identity of the victim and told the television programme:

'Sixteen years ago Reg burdened me with the secret of this other murder he did. It was not a villain, not a policeman, but a young boy, a young gay boy . . . he was disgusted with himself for realising that he enjoyed that sort of thing, knowing he was gay or bisexual, and he shot the kid.'

Gillett's description of the victim does not fit 'Mad' Teddy, who was a known villain and could not be described as a 'young boy'.

So, if the victim was not 'Mad' Teddy, who was it?

In January 1967, the record producer Joe Meek shot and killed his landlady then himself. Meek was, at the time, involved in a battle with the Krays, who wanted to take over the management of one of his groups, The Tornados. Ron Kray had told Dave Watts of the band that he would 'take care of' Joe Meek.

But this was not Meek's only worry.

Earlier that January, a farm worker discovered two suitcases on a farm track next to a lay-by in the Suffolk village of Tattingstone. Inside were the dismembered remains of a young man who was later identified as 17-year-old Bernard Oliver. He had been homosexually assaulted, strangled and then cut into eight pieces.

Oliver was a rent boy from Highgate in North London who was well known on the London gay scene that was frequented by both Joe Meek and the Krays. Meek knew Oliver and was terrified that he was about to be questioned by the police about the killing. It is highly unlikely that Meek was directly responsible for the murder, but he may well have known more about it than he let on.

According to reports at the time, Oliver had been abducted from London and taken to Suffolk where he was held for up to a week in a cottage that, it was rumoured, hosted all-male orgies.

Throughout the 1960s Ron and Reg Kray were regular visitors to Suffolk, frequently staying at their friend Geoff Allen's cottage in the village of Lavenham. The twins had developed their love of Suffolk during the war when they had been evacuated from London to the village of Hadleigh, nine miles from Lavenham, and, prior to his arrest in 1968, Ron bought a Victorian manor house in nearby Bildeston.

Lavenham, Hadleigh and Bildeston are all less than 20 miles from Tattingstone, where Oliver's body was found. The night before his body was discovered, two witnesses, who were sleeping in their car in the lay-by near where the suitcase containing Oliver was found, saw two men pull up in a Jaguar and bundle something out of the boot – the two men spotted the witnesses and drove their car at them. The witnesses drove off and the Jag chased them all the way to Ipswich before they were able to lose them.

Whether the occupants of the Jag were Oliver's murderers has never been proved, and whether the police followed up this lead at the time is not known. Jaguars at that time were relatively expensive cars and reasonably exclusive. If the police had traced Jaguars belonging to regular visitors to the area they would have discovered that both Ron and Reg, along with their brother Charlie, owned Jaguars at the time of the murder.

Whether Bernard Oliver was Reg's unnamed victim will never be known, but there is more than enough circumstantial evidence to suggest that he should be considered seriously. Oliver certainly matches Pete Gillett's description (although Gillett claims Reg shot the boy, whereas Oliver was strangled), and the Krays were known to host homosexual orgies in the area where his body was found, knew the area well and drove cars similar to that which may have been used to dispose of his body.

The police, however, seem convinced that the murderers were two homosexual doctors from Highgate, with no connection to Suffolk, who fled the country shortly after Oliver's murder and are both now dead – so we will probably never know.

As a further footnote, however, Ron Kray spent a lot of his time in prison painting and, since his death, several of his pictures have been sold at auction. One scene that Ron painted repeatedly was that of a cottage surrounded by a moat.

The cottage in the picture is widely believed to be Geoff Allen's in Lavenham. Both Ron and Reg said how much they enjoyed their times there, and Ron painted many scenes of the area, including one showing himself and Reg fishing. If Ron loved the cottage so much, why is it that he always painted it in such a way that it looked dark and menacing? In one picture Ron painted a dark moat around the cottage on which two black swans are swimming, which are believed to portray him and Reg. Black swans, through history, have been used to represent the occult, traitors and the devil.

Another coincidence – or was Ron obsessed with the cottage at Lavenham for much darker reasons?

Confessing to other murders was a tame gesture, but the press enjoyed it and it was only done for the money. Reg could have listed many petty crooks that they had killed on their way to the top of the criminal tree, but he just told them about the one. If he had lived a little longer, then he would have doubtless told them of more for even more money. Is this what they call contract killing?

As stated earlier, the Krays were at the top of the criminal tree. When the Krays were sent down the police had simply cut off some of the branches – but the tree was still allowed to grow. The Krays, the Sheas and even the Adams family, the biggest crime family in London today, all grow from the same roots, the same prejudices, the same intolerance of the law.

The Krays are all dead – in fact, they have been dead and buried for more than ten years now. They were Kray-z people who did Kray-z things, and now they are all just plain Kray-zzzzzzz, sleeping with the fishes along with most of their old pals.

But please don't confuse Charlie Kray with his brothers, Ron and Reg. Charlie did not use knives or guns. He was a charmer with the gift of the gab. He always liked to think that he could get out of trouble as quickly as his brothers had got him into it by talking his way out. Charlie was not a bad person, he just got into trouble. If it wasn't Reg, then it was Ron; if it wasn't Ron, then it was Reg. But there was always someone who was trying to get him into trouble. That's just the way it was.

The Kray name spelt trouble for everyone, from politicians to the police, from MI5 to the KGB, from one sordid gangster to another. But it was Ron and Reg who stood for the violence, who didn't care what they had to do to get their way, who protected no one but themselves, and they didn't even help their brother Charlie when he was arrested for something he didn't do. Even when they were arrested they tried to get other members of the Firm to take the blame. They could do the crime, but they wanted others to do the time.

So, what now? Well, if you want to research the Krays then it may well be worth a trip across the pond to America. There they have been getting used to what we call 'freedom of information', and the results, at times, have been staggering. You will not get the information here, for one reason or another, but in the USA you may be able to connect the dots and get somewhere near the truth. In the UK we still revere members of the House of Lords, we still respect the police, we believe what we are told by the authorities. But should we? Now, that is a completely different question.